The Basics of
Interpersonal Communication

D1552979

The Basics of
Interpersonal Communication

Scott McLean
Arizona Western College

Boston   New York   San Francisco
Mexico City   Montreal   Toronto   London   Madrid   Munich   Paris
Hong Kong   Singapore   Tokyo   Cape Town   Sydney

Executive Editor: *Karon Bowers*
Senior Editor: *Brian Wheel*
Series Editorial Assistant: *Jennifer Trebby*
Senior Editorial-Production Administrator: *Beth Houston*
Editorial-Production Service: *Walsh & Associates, Inc.*
Senior Marketing Manager: *Mandee Eckersley*
Composition and Prepress Buyer: *Linda Cox*
Manufacturing Buyer: *JoAnne Sweeney*
Cover Administrator: *Joel Gendron*
Electronic Composition: *Cabot Computer Services*

For related titles and support materials, visit our online catalog at www.ablongman.com.

To obtain permission(s) to use material from this work, please submit a written request
to Allyn and Bacon, Permissions Department, 75 Arlington Street, Boston, MA 02116
or fax your request to 617-848-7320.

Between the time Website information is gathered and then published, it is not unusual
for some sites to have closed. Also, the transcription of URLs can result in typographical
errors. The publisher would appreciate notification where these occur so that they may be
corrected in subsequent editions.

Library of Congress Cataloging-in-Publication Data

McLean, Scott.
　　The basics of interpersonal communication / Scott McLean.
　　　p. cm.
　　Includes bibliographical references and index.
　　ISBN 0-205-40198-8
　　　1. Interpersonal communication—Textbooks. I. Title.
　　BF637.C45M26 2005
　　153.6—dc22　　　　　　　　　　　　　　　　　　　　　　2004044662

Printed in the United States of America

10 9 8 7 6 5 4　　　　　　　08 07 06

Photo Credits: pp. 79, 89, 96, 118, 138, 186, 228, 232, Pete Self; p. 161, Delia Garay.

For Lisa, my wife, and our children,
Mackenzie, John, and Katherine

Contents

2 *Perception and Listening*   21

3 *Verbal Communication*   46

Preface

This book introduces the practices and principles of interpersonal communication in a clear, concise, and engaging way. It is designed clearly with the student taking his or her first communication course in mind and assumes no prior academic preparation in the field. It does not, however, underestimate the vast knowledge and experience base that each student brings with him or her into the classroom setting. With this combination of prior knowledge and active instruction, students should be able to demonstrate interpersonal communication skills, apply basic principles to relationships, and manage conflict in effective ways.

This text:

1. Focuses on key concepts, class-tested to improve clarity.
2. Provides clear chapter objectives at the beginning of each chapter.
3. Features exercises and class activities to introduce concepts and spark curiosity.
4. Provides a view of communication from the student's perspective, with clear connections between abstract concepts and real-world examples.
5. Focuses on knowledge, skills, and active application.

Education has long been recognized as key to a democratic society. To facilitate learning, in a day and age when work, children, and responsibilities demand significant time and attention, is a challenge. Education is key to a civil society, and effective communication is essential to education. The degree to which we can understand its basic principles and effect positive changes in our lives, from performing more effectively in a job interview setting to forming and maintaining positive relationships, has an impact beyond ourselves. This textbook was specifically designed to offer a solid, affordable foundation in interpersonal communication for the instructor and student alike. Taking a communication course is an excellent first step to effective communication.

Organization

This text is organized in a straightforward, practical, and workable approach to teaching and learning the fundamentals of interpersonal communication. The first four chapters lay the foundation for understanding in key areas of communication, and the remaining chapters build on this foundation to explore interpersonal communication.

Each chapter features learning objectives and introductory exercises. The learning objectives communicate clearly what is to be learned in each chapter, and the exercises stimulate curiosity while providing a common reference for analysis.

In addition, each chapter includes boxed features to reinforce, highlight, and expand on information in the text. Case Study features go into more depth on a point, example, or theory. Intercultural Communication features provide examples of culture, language, race, and ethnicity as part of the communication process. Computer-Mediated Communication features, drawn from real-world experiences, provide examples of communication in this context.

Each chapter concludes with notes about additional information for further research and features four types of questions to use in class or for student-driven learning. Factual questions underline specific concepts or terms, while interpretative questions require more application and critical-thinking skills. Evaluative questions encourage students and instructors to go beyond the text, and application questions reinforce key concepts.

Note to the Student

This text was designed with your success in mind. It should prove itself to be accessible to read and locate information you need to understand and implement key concepts and skills. You are asked to reflect, take notes, and complete exercises on your own or in groups throughout the text. Like many things in life, you get out of something what you put into it. Read this text with an open mind, and draw on your years of making sense of your world, your relationships with yourself and others, and your own talent and skills as a communicator. You have been doing it all your life, and now this text and this class will help you understand this dynamic and interactive process better.

In addition, please note the cost of this text is low for a reason. Communication is an important part of all our lives, and the degree to which we can understand its basic principles and effect positive changes in our lives has an impact beyond ourselves. Taking a communication course is an excellent first step, and being able to afford the text is important.

Note to the Instructor

This text was also designed with your success in mind. Students juggle work, relationships, and other courses outside of our classrooms. The text can serve as a stand-alone, low-cost, "nuts and bolts" survey text of communication, providing the student the opportunity to prepare for classroom discussion by completing reading and note-taking assignments, and providing a solid foundation for the instructor to build upon, adapt, and/or complement with additional material depending on individual instruction methods, goals, or objectives. Please feel free to arrange the material presented in the order that works for you.

In addition, this text can be significantly complemented with the instructor's manual, with "zero-preparation" exercises, clear connections between interactive activities and concepts, assessment forms, and answer keys.

Acknowledgments

I would like to extend my thanks to all my friends and colleagues at Arizona Western College (AWC) for their encouragement and support. Karon Bowers at Allyn and Bacon suggested we extend the *Basics* approach to this new text and deserves many thanks for her continued support.

To my students I owe a debt of gratitude because you have taught me how to be more creative in the instruction of this knowledge, and your constructive feedback has contributed to the production of the text you now hold in your hands. Student models include Thomas Amarisca, Yukika Amma, Marcela Arceo, Scot Beebe, Jonathon Castillo, Alfredo Chavez, Kathy Molina, Emmanuella Nibigira, Cinthia Piva, Erika Salcedo, Miguel Sandoval, Brenda Soto, Charles Thompson, and Calvin Welch. Child models include Mackenzie, John, and Katherine McLean. All photos were taken by Pete Self, Professor of Philosophy and Photography at AWC, unless otherwise noted. Dalia Garay, a student photographer, has one photo featured in this book.

To Phi Theta Kappa (www.ptk.org), the International Honor Society for the Two Year College, thank you for the opportunity to participate in leadership and professional development opportunities, including the national Mosal Award, that lead to insights featured in this text.

To my reviewers in the field, I appreciate all the specific feedback that led to significant improvements in the text: Shirley Crum, Coastal Carolina Community College; Diane Ferrero-Paluzzi, Iona College; and Anneliese Harper, Scottsdale Community College.

Finally, I would like to acknowledge the significant contributions made to the text by my partner and wife, Lisa. Her complete emphasis on keeping the text clear and concise while editing challenged me to improve the text for everyone.

Foundations of Communication

Chapter Objectives _____

After completing this chapter, you should be able to:

1. Understand the importance of communication.
2. Define communication.
3. Describe communication as a process.
4. Identify and describe four models of communication.
5. Identify and describe eight essential components of communication.
6. Identify and describe five types of communication contexts.
7. Describe five key principles of communication.

Introductory Exercise 1 _____

Please list five terms to describe yourself. Consider completing the sentence:

I am:

1. _____.
2. _____.
3. _____.
4. _____.
5. _____.

Introductory Exercise 2 _____

It is also important to recognize what you consider to be important. Look back at the first exercise and consider your responses. Please create a priority list of what is important to you from your responses.

1. _____.
2. _____.

3. _____.
4. _____.
5. _____.

A Brief Introduction to Communication

> *The relationship is the communication bridge between people.*
> —Alfred Kadushin

We often think that common sense provides us with all we need to know about managing our interactions and relationships. We might hold the view that people have communicated with one another for ages and, while there have been problems, if we try hard enough, we can get our point across. Other times we may think that the way we communicate is a part of who we are that seemingly cannot be changed, and if we could only adapt to the setting or person with whom we want to communicate, then effective communication would be within our grasp. Surely, if we only communicated more clearly, accurately, creatively, assertively, or competently then we would be able to communicate effectively. In our discussion throughout this book we will explore interpersonal communication and the myths associated with effective communication, focusing on clear ideas and methods to improve communication between ourselves and others.

The goal of this book is to reveal how complex our interpersonal communication is, and through this discussion, to provide the tools to make conscious choices about one's self and one's relationships with others. The ability to articulate your ideas clearly is key to effective communication, but mastering this one aspect does not assure effective communication. Neither does accuracy, creativity, assertiveness, or competence in and of itself offer any guarantee. There is promise, however, that a better understanding of the basic concepts of communication and the mastering of skills associated with those concepts can improve interpersonal communication.

The format of this book combines a clear and concise discussion with real-world examples to cover the roles interpersonal communication plays in defining ourselves. Our discussion builds on this foundation with an analysis of how we use interpersonal communication to form impressions of others and to create, maintain, and end close relationships. The goal is to enhance your ability to perceive communication patterns, become articulate in your discussion of these patterns, and then use your observations and judgment to make active choices about your own communication and relationships.

The Basics of Interpersonal Communication is part of a series entitled *The Basic Series in Communication*. This series focuses on providing you with clear, concise, and engaging texts that combine theory and skill in a way that contributes effectively to your understanding of the field of communication. Each book focuses on the basic principles, functions, and characteristics of the dynamic process of communication across cultures, computers, and modern case studies in distinct areas of communication. Each book also presents this discussion in a similar way, with common definitions, scenarios, and overall format to increase your familiarity across the series. In each case, you should notice that you can easily find the information you need the first time, improving your reading and comprehension of the material.

In the first exercise, you prepared a list of words that may indicate your personal strengths, goals, plans, and interests. On many levels the way you describe yourself will underline your reasons for going to work, school, or even why you are taking this class. It may also begin to answer the question "Who am I?" To understand communication with others also requires self-knowledge. Your understanding of yourself in many ways is formed through communication from your earliest moments, and like a mirror, you tend to reflect the communication you have seen and heard. While we are all born with inherent traits, you communicate every day, with yourself as well as others, and this dynamic process of communication contributes to who you are and how you see yourself.

In the second introductory exercise, you created a priority list of what is important to you. Look back at the list and see if you find how many of your priorities are connected to relationships, formed through communication. In many respects, your world is formed through communication. Your attitudes, beliefs, and values do not just come from you but can also seen in people you interact with, like family members, friends, and acquaintances. One way to consider this point is to think about what you chose to wear today. Your might have chosen a comfortable shirt, or a favorite color, but where did you learn what is considered comfortable or preferred? You learned through interaction with others. You can look around and see this idea extend to your preference in music, friends, and even who to date. Many of our ideas about what is important in our lives have been formed through interpersonal communication.

Communication skills are learned through interactions throughout our lifetime and have a direct impact on our lives. If what you value most in life or want for your future, from your family to your partner, co-workers, or career involves communication, wouldn't you want to be good at it? Our ability to understand that dynamic process can further our ability to communicate effectively. This book is designed to do exactly that: give you the understanding of key concepts in communication with exercises and thought-provoking examples that can translate to an improvement of your communication skills.

A natural question might be "How do I improve my communication skills?" Let's first consider the school of "hard knocks." What happens when you go out there on your own, without advice or guidance? Sometimes you may get it right the first time, but many times you'll get hurt, make mistakes, and hopefully learn as you go along. This book and your class offer a second alternative: the research and experience of others. Consider the information provided in this chapter and the rest of the book as years of trial and error compiled for your benefit. Perhaps you will see information that applies to a relationship you have with someone you care about. If you want to improve that relationship, and the researchers offer helpful guidance, then you may improve both your understanding of relationships and the relationship itself. Keep an open mind and draw upon your years of experience communicating with others.

Exercise _____

Ask someone not in your class:
1. When was the last time he or she had miscommunication with someone.
2. Describe what happened.

Compare your notes with other students in the next class session.

Can you recall the last time you had a miscommunication with someone? Perhaps you signed up for the wrong class or bought the wrong book based on a misunderstanding. People miscommunicate everyday with a wide range of results. A simple misunderstanding might result in your waiting in one place while someone who has planned to pick you up waits in a different location. A serious misunderstanding may send an ambulance to the wrong address, losing valuable time needed to save a life. Regardless of the degree or severity of miscommunication, the negative consequences impact our lives in many ways. Consider a miscommunication on the job. What may be some possible consequences? The loss of an important client or credibility with co-workers may negatively impact your career.

The National Association of Colleges and Employers (http://www.naceweb.org) indicated in a 2003 survey of over 1,900 employer organizations, including the Fortune 500, that the top ten qualities employers seek are, in order of priority:

1. Communication skills (verbal and written)
2. Honesty/integrity
3. Teamwork skills
4. Interpersonal skills
5. Strong work ethic
6. Motiviation/initiative
7. Flexibility/adaptability
8. Analytical skills
9. Computer skills
10. Organizational skills

Please note that while all priorities listed are related to communication, three of the top four are explicitly communication. Interpersonal skills are ranked fourth according to employers nationwide, but there is no doubt that in terms of your own life and your relationships, they will rank even higher. Also consider that this survey mirrors similar surveys across the United States, and the results have only changed slightly over time. Finally, consider that this survey, like many current employer surveys, indicates that the job market is increasingly competitive and your ability to articulate your ideas clearly and maintain healthy relationships will help you stand out and get noticed by potential employers. Regardless of your chosen degree program or profession, the ability to communicate effectively is an essential skill.

In this book you will learn communication skills that can improve your life and the lives of those around you. By learning the basics of communication, you will be able to feel more confident in your abilities as a communicator. People use their communication skills every day to try to share their needs and wants, hopes and dreams. This book will help prepare you to be a better communicator.

Definition of Communication

The Latin word *communicare* is the root of the word *communication. Communicare* means to share, or to make common (Weekley, 1967, p. 338). The idea that we share is central to the process of communication. **Communication** is defined as "the process of understanding and sharing meaning" (Pearson & Nelson, 2000, p. 6). This definition serves us in many ways. It is short and to the point, but it also offers significant understanding of the depth of this process. By focusing on the key words in this definition we will examine this dynamic process and gain a greater understanding of its complexity.

A **process** is a natural continuing, dynamic activity or function that is hard to describe because it constantly changes. You may be in a conversation with someone, trying to listen to each other while thinking about your own responses, when a third person enters the conversation, changing the nature and direction of that conversation. As you and they adapt to this change, the communication process changes. This essential nature of communication is repeated and transformed throughout the day, and this constantly changing process can be challenging to examine from a detached point of view.

The second key word is **understanding.** To understand is to perceive, to interpret, and to relate our perception and interpretation to what we already know. In the previous conversation you may have been discussing a class that you have in common with the other person. When the third person, who is not taking this class, enters the conversation, that person's understanding will be different from yours. If you use words from the subject of the class that he or she is not familiar with, that person's interpretation of the conversation will be distinct from that of your classmate. Your common frame of reference enables you to have a closer understanding of what your classmate is saying, but if the conversation turns to a class that the other two speakers have in common, you may now be the one at a loss.

Next comes the word **sharing,** or the process by which we use, experience, give, or enjoy with others a sense of meaning or common understanding. You and your classmate may share your understanding of the lecture, your interpretation of a class assignment, or provide ideas for one another on common issues that spark discussion and clarify differences in your understanding. Through this sharing, you may come to understand that you missed a key point or thought you understood a concept when, in fact, you did not. See Computer-Mediated Communication 1.1 for an example of this aspect of communication.

Finally, **meaning** is to have in mind a purpose or covey an idea that we share through interaction. You have a collection of experiences and ways of making sense of your world that you have learned over time through interaction with others. Your previous experience enables you to relate new information, provided in class in this example, to what you know, providing context and helping you make sense of the new ideas. Your classmates also share this experience, but from entirely different perspectives and sets of experiences. Their understanding of the new ideas may

COMPUTER-MEDIATED COMMUNICATION 1.1 • *Computer-Mediated Communication in the Classroom*

If you take enough college courses, you'll eventually find yourself one of two or three hundred students in the same class. From a student's perspective, this can be a frustrating experience. The professor may seem like an actor on a stage and inaccessible. Teachers' assistants may not have the depth of understanding or may have a large number of students assigned to them, decreasing your ability to get to them to clarify your understanding of the material or to simply ask a question. From an instructor's perspective, this format may also be frustrating. It can be difficult to know if everyone "got it" the first time. If there is little feedback, there are few ways to know except for tests or quizzes. Email changed this situation to a certain extent, but there are new and surprising ways computer-mediated communication in the classroom is increasing feedback and hopefully improving education.

At Rice University, Dr. Nathan Harshman's physics students have "zapper days," where they are issued small, handheld devices that resemble a remote control. As part of a new program called the Personal Response System (PRS), each handheld device has numbered buttons, and Harshman has a series of questions that he can project onto a screen at any time during his lecture. If he has just covered a challenging concept, he can flash a multiple-choice question on the screen and students then respond, choosing the answer they understand to be correct. Harshman can control the voting time and display the results, showing both himself and the students the relative comprehension level. The process is anonymous, but students can quickly see if they got it right. If most students get it right but some don't, the students can talk with classmates or the teacher's assistant to clarify the concept and arrive at the right response.

Variations on this model are being tried nationwide. At Indiana University Just-In-Time Teaching (JITT) gives students warm-up questions and quizzes shortly before class. Professors have the results before class to better enable them to focus on important concepts. At Erskine College, cell phone technology and modified personal digital assistants use a format similar to Harshman's interactive questions during lecture. In each case, computer-mediated communication helps facilitate feedback and prepares professors, teachers' assistants, and students to engage in meaningful interpersonal communication as a result.

Source: Karnovsky & Warner (2002).

differ from yours, but the common context of class and the use of similar terms can help you understand each other. By looking at the context the word is used in, such as class, and by asking questions, we can discover the shared meaning of the word and understand the message.

Definition: Communication is the *process of understanding and sharing meaning.*

Exercise

Draw what you think communication looks like. Share with another student.

Models of Communication

In a modern economy where computers are not only on our desktops, but in our coffeemakers and cars, it may be hard for some to think of a time when computers were still a dream. Claude Shannon and Warren Weaver (1949) were two research-ers who studied the complexity of messages and the capabilities of circuits to trans-mit them, wanting to know how to control communication in order to communicate effectively and efficiently transmit the maximum amount of information. Claude Shannon stated the idea that all communication is essentially digital. *Digital,* in the measurement and transmission sense of the word, means that information can be represented with numbers. This idea, upon which all modern computers are based, enables a word, song, or even a movie to be stored and reproduced by the correct interpretation of the numbers. This idea also reduces communication to a scientific process that can be defined and repeated, losing some of the inherently dynamic qualities of human interaction.

In order to communicate this idea with others, Shannon and Weaver needed a model to express the concept clearly. One way they did this was to draw a picture of what they thought communication looked like, adapting their model from an earlier one (Laswell, 1948). This model is called the *linear model of communication* (Fig-ure 1.1). The source sends the message to the receiver (Shannon & Weaver, 1949). This model is elegant in its simplicity, but as we have discussed previously, commu-nication is a dynamic process full of complexity.

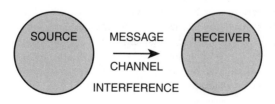

FIGURE 1.1 *Linear Model of Communication*

Subsequent researchers developed their model to better represent this complexity, giving more attention was focused on the interactive nature of communication. The source sends a message to a receiver, who in turn replies, continuing the conversation. This shift in emphasis changes how we perceive the source in an active role and the receiver in a passive one to a view of interactivity, adaptation, and shared roles called the *interactive view of communication* (Figure 1.2).

What happens when the source and receiver both try to play the role of the source, trying to talk to one another at the same time? There is overlap, but there is also the loss of clear roles. Who is the source and who is the receiver? Both. This observation leads us to the *transactional view of communication* (Figure 1.3). Rather than perceiving communication as being linear or one way, as if one person is injecting another person with their message, or interactional, as if we inject one another with meaning, the transactional view takes a step back to view the basic components in previous models in their context and environment. This model presents the view that our context and environment play a significant role in the understanding and sharing of meaning. Feedback links the receiver with the source, time, and setting and mediates the transaction. This model provides a foundation for studying communication with yourself, with others, or in group and public speaking contexts.

But what happens when you use a word your classmate does not understand? While context and environment may help us understand how miscommunication occurred, it brings us no closer to effective communication in this example. You may say the word is like this or that, using an example to create a context for your classmate until he or she "gets it." This process of coming to a common understanding of words extends to thoughts, ideas, experiences, and the central issue of meaning. What something means to you and your classmate may be entirely different. This process of coming to an understanding is much like a negotiation. When we *negotiate meaning,* we find ways around obstacles to communication in order to interact for the purpose of finding mutually satisfying results. Since we all discover the world through experience and communication interaction as we grow and age, we "construct" our view of the world. Sharing your perceptions with others requires negotiation and feedback to achieve a common understanding. In the *constructivist model of communication,* we focus on the negotiated meaning, or the common ground and understanding we create, when trying to describe the process (Pearce &

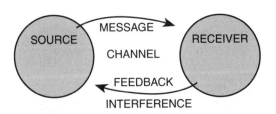

FIGURE 1.2 *Interactional Model of Communication*

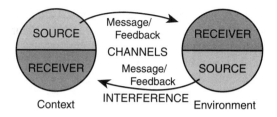

FIGURE 1.3 *Transactional Model of Communication*

Cronen, 1980; Cronen & Pearce, 1982). Look at Figure 1.4 and see if you can identify parts of the communication process.

Essential Components of Communication

Now that we've examined the four models of communication, you should begin to appreciate how complex this process can be. In order to better understand communication, the models we use to represent this dynamic process are comprised of components. Each component plays an integral function in the overall process. The linear and interactional models of communication presented a relatively simple view of the essential components, and the transactional and constructivist models introduced more complex models. How the individual components interact offers us insight into the process and also helps us gain an objective perspective. Now let's examine the eight components that comprise the communication process.

1. Source

The **source** creates and sends the message. Let's say you come home from a long day at work. Your problems from the day, ranging from a conflict with a co-worker to a headache, are on your mind. You enter the apartment and start to sit down when there is a knock at the door. Your friend and neighbor, who has had a great day and is full of energy, asks you how your day was as she comes right in. Before you have a chance to answer, she is talking about all the great things that happened today. She

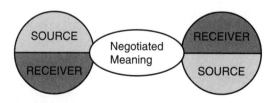

FIGURE 1.4 *Constructivist Model of Communication*

walks about the room, using gestures to emphasize her enthusiasm, while you look on and can only think of peace and quiet. She turns to look at you for the first time and stops mid-sentence, saying "Are you OK? You look terrible."

This scenario may sound in some ways familiar because we have all experienced miscommunication. Your friend chooses the time to talk, the words to convey meaning, even the gestures. She is called a source in this process because of the role she plays, intentionally or unintentionally choosing to share her experiences with you. A source both creates the message—preferring one word over another, for example—and chooses how to convey that message, through words and body language in this scenario.

2. Message

The **message** is the stimulus or meaning produced by the source for the receiver or audience. When your friend asks if you are OK, the words she chooses are part of the message. The way she says it is also part of the message. Her frame of mind, the time of day, the setting—all of these aspects of your interaction are part of the message. The words you choose to respond to her will convey the meaning of your message, and you may choose your response carefully. The message also consists of the way you say it, with your body, your tone of voice, and your appearance. Finally, part of the message may be the environment or context you present in and any noise that may make your message hard to hear or see.

3. Channel

The **channel** is the way in which a message or messages travel between source and receiver. When the other person turns to look at you, he or she notices the look on your face, how you are standing, and your overall body language. This nonverbal expression of how you feel may communicate more than words, and if the other person knows you well, he or she may be in tune with how you use body language. Nonverbal communication can be a channel, and so can words. Verbal communication includes the words people use and the order they use them in to express themselves. Perhaps you would've preferred that your neighbor call you instead of coming over, choosing the telephone and verbal communication as a channel. After giving it some thought, you may have preferred an email to this conversation, choosing words communicated electronically to convey meaning. Or perhaps your friend's presence and timing is welcome, and her support is appreciated. These are all examples of channels or ways we communicate with one another.

4. Receiver

The **receiver** receives the message from the source, analyzing and interpreting the message in ways both intended and unintended by the source. The other person receives your message via your body language and replies with both a question and a statement. You receive the other person's message and may respond to the words, the body language, or the person's sense of timing. This interaction is key to the process of communication. If the receiver is not ready to receive, then it is difficult to communicate. You might not be ready to listen to stories about someone's great day, or it might be just the ticket to pick you up. The source is sending you messages and perceiving your response. So are you. All of this happens at the same time, illustrating why and how communication is always changing.

5. Feedback

When you respond to the source, you are giving feedback. **Feedback,** by definition, is the messages the receiver sends back to the source. You give feedback through your voice and your eyes as you look at the other person. All of these signals in response to the source are called feedback. Feedback is a very important part of communication. It allows the source to see how well his or her message was received and gives the opportunity for the receiver to ask for clarification, disagree, or indicate misunderstanding. Your friend communicates feedback to your nonverbal messages by stopping mid-sentence and asking for clarification of those messages, telling you what she sees. One study found that as the amount of feedback increases, including spoken and unspoken responses, the accuracy of communication also increases (Leavitt & Mueller, 1951).

6. Environment

The **environment** is the atmosphere, physical and psychological, where you send and receive messages. It is the late in the day in this scenario as you have just come home from work. Your home environment contributes to the communication process. The environment can include the tables, chairs, lighting, and sound equipment that are in the room. The environment can also include psychological factors present, like whether a discussion is open and caring or more professional and formal. People may be more likely to have an intimate conversation when they are physically close to each other and less likely when they can only see each other from across the room.

7. Context

The **context** of the communication interaction, unlike the chairs, tables, or lighting of the environment, involves the setting, scene, and expectations of the individuals involved. Your friend was immediate and needed attention right away. She wanted to share her experiences with you. She may have interpreted that since you were physically close, you were ready to communicate. Context also involves whether you were emotionally ready to communicate. Your expectations of coming home may have involved crashing on the couch or taking a bath. Your friend's expectations are clearly different than yours, which can lead to miscommunication and interpersonal conflict.

The degree to which the communication environment is formal or informal depends largely on the context. A wedding or a church service may be a formal event, where there are certainly expectations on behavior. In a business meeting, who speaks first? That probably has some relation to the position and role each person has outside of the meeting. Your home and your friend's prior relationship with you may contribute to an informal context. Context plays a very important role in communication, particularly across cultures.

INTERCULTURAL COMMUNICATION 1.1 • *Cultural Context*

Cultural context involves the rules and customs, values and beliefs that are carried from one generation to the next. While there are different definitions of culture, many emphasize the processes and patterns of communication that are shared by a group of people. We learn our own cultural context(s) through a lifetime of experiences that guide us on how and when to communicate. For example, time, touch, space, and even eye contact are very important in interpersonal communication, but they vary in how and when they are used in cultural contexts around the world. By appreciating cultural differences, you can become more effective in your communication. One way to learn more about differences is to explore a single aspect of communication. What is the expectation for timing and punctuality (or touch, space, eye contact) where you come from? Compare your observations with classmates.

Source: Intercultural Communication Webpage, University of Hawaii at Manoa, http://www2. soc.hawaii.edu/css/dept/com/resources/Intercultural/Intercultural.html. Accessed 9/23/00.

8. Interference

The last part of the communication process that plays an important role is interference. Interference, also referred to as noise, can come from any source. **Interference** is anything that interferes or changes the source's intended meaning of the message. Psychological noise, or your own thoughts in response to your friend's comments, based on your own experiences or expectations, can prevent you from listening completely to another person's whole message. Preparing your own response and listening to yourself while failing to listen to the other person can interfere with the communication process. Perhaps you are hungry, tired, or just want to be left alone, and your attention to your own situation interferes with your ability to listen. Physical and psychological noise interferes with normal encoding, or preparing the message, and decoding, or understanding and making sense of the message carried by the channel between source and receiver. Noise is neither good nor bad independent of context, but noise by definition can interfere with the communication process.

Communication in Context

In the previous section we examined the eight components of communication. Let's examine these components together in context. Is a quiet dinner conversation with someone you care about the same experience as a discussion in class or giving a speech? Each context impacts the communication process, and all contexts can overlap and interrelate, creating an even more dynamic process.

Intrapersonal Communication

Just like in our scenario, has someone ever said something to you that you had choice words to respond with but did not? Perhaps you didn't want to say something you would later regret, or perhaps you didn't want to make a bad situation worse. As you "talk with yourself" about your possible responses, you are engaged in intrapersonal communication.

Intrapersonal communication involves one person and is often called "self-talk" (Wood, 1997, p. 22). We use language and thoughts to reflect on our own experiences and provide context in order to better understand a message from someone else or even ourselves (Vocate, 1994). We talk ourselves through situations all day long. Perhaps you had just talked yourself through rush hour traffic, up a long flight of stairs, and through finding your keys and approaching the couch when your friend came in to say hello. Your mental coaching of yourself is very important. Your intrapersonal communication can be positive or negative and directly influences how you perceive and react to situations and communication with others. If you say to yourself that you are not happy to see your friend, you may perceive her as a source of irritation. If, however, you tell yourself that you are glad to see her, then you open the door to the conversation. Your discussions with yourself will impact your discussions with others.

It is also important to note that what you perceive in communication with others is influenced by your culture and upbringing. Habermas (1984) wrote, "Every process of reaching understanding takes place against the background of a culturally ingrained preunderstanding" (p. 100). You may have certain expectations of time and punctuality, a need for specific rules, or a desire for freedom to complete a project in your own way, and your background plays an important part of intrapersonal communication. See Figure 1.5.

FIGURE 1.5   *Intrapersonal Communication*

Exercise

Learning to listen to yourself is as important as listening to others. What do you say to yourself when something goes right? Goes wrong? Write down when you notice what you say and bring it to class for discussion.

Interpersonal Communication

The second major content within the field of communication is **interpersonal communication**, communication that involves two people. Within the context of communication between people, there is considerable range, from intimate and very personal to formal and impersonal. Your conversation at home with your friend may be relatively informal, but your relationship provides context for the words and their meaning. If the next day at work your direct supervisor asks you a similar question about your health, the difference in relationships and roles establishes different expectations and interpretations. Both examples qualify as interpersonal communication but differ in terms of depth and levels of intimacy. The first example implies a prior knowledge, understanding, and trust established over time between two caring individuals. The second example level implies a lack of previous knowledge, little understanding, and concern for you more as a worker than a friend. See Figure 1.6.

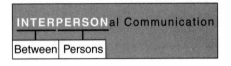

FIGURE 1.6   *Interpersonal Communication*

Group Communication

As you stand at the door thinking about how to respond to your neighbor's question, let's say another friend comes down the hall and starts to talk to you. He sees your friend in the apartment and walks right in. Your friends are now engaged in a conversation about the day's activities and where to go to celebrate, and you haven't said much of anything. What has changed? The context shifted from two people talking to a three-way conversation. Even if you aren't saying much, they are talking in your apartment and trying to engage you in the conversation.

    Group communication is a dynamic process where a small group of people engage in a conversation. In your apartment, there are two active people talking about the day and you looking on. As you hold open the door, a third friend enters and the volume rises. Group communication generally involves three to eight people, and the more people in the group, the harder it is to pay attention to any individual, unless one speaker steps forward and the group actively listens.

Public Communication

You watch as other friends walk down the hall and take interest in the conversation. You decide you have had enough and say out loud "OK, everybody out! I'm tired and there won't be a party here tonight." As your friends hear you raise your voice, they grow quiet and start to leave one by one. Your friend tells you to go relax and take a load off, to which you respond "My thoughts exactly."

In **public communication,** one person speaks to a group of people. The speaker may ask questions and engage the audience in a discussion, but the dynamics of the conversation are distinct from group communication, where different rules apply. In a public speaking situation, the group usually defers to the speaker. One person speaks to everyone, and the group or crowd listens. In our scenario, you spoke to the whole group at once, engaging them simultaneously.

Mass Communication

As you cross your living room you pick up the remote control and turn on the television. You hear the discussion of the news as you change into comfortable clothes and prepare dinner. You learn of problems that are not your own, in places you may have never been to, happening to people you may never meet. You may also recognize how their situations are like your own. The collection of words and images that come across your screen are essentially the same for everyone tuned to that channel. **Mass communication** is a form of communication in which a source addresses a large audience with the same or similar message. The **mass media,** ranging from television to newsprint, comprise a powerful force in modern society and our daily lives, adapting rapidly to new technologies. Mass communication allows us to communicate our message to a large number of people, but we are limited in our ability to tailor our message to specific audiences, groups, or individuals.

Principles of Communication

1. Communication Is Constant

> *The most important thing in communication is hearing what isn't being said.*
> —Author Unknown

There is no moment when you are not in the process of communication. This may first sound impossible, but let's look at a few examples. You are communicating with a co-worker over an issue on the job. You communicate with yourself as you replay and analyze the discussion you just had with the co-worker. Your friend communicates with you about her day, and you respond nonverbally. You are communicating whether you are talking or not. Your body language displays signals that express what you are thinking and feeling. Your face, your posture, your type of clothing, and even your choice of friends can send nonverbal messages that are open to interpretation. When you speak, the tone of your voice, when you take a breath, your pitch and volume all contribute to the message, combining to form expressions that attempt to convey your message. When you listen, to yourself or others, your internal monologue or self-talk comments on what you see, hear, think, and/or feel. Within the context of interpersonal relationships or small group discussions communication is always occurring, you cannot *not* communicate (Watzlawick, 1993).

Whether you communicate to yourself while you sleep is open to debate, but it is clear that in other contexts, the state of constant communication with self and others is less prevalent. If a patient is under anesthesia, communication may cease. The point is communication is constantly occurring, intentionally or unintentionally, in a range of contexts. Becoming more aware of communication in these contexts will contribute to a better understanding of the dynamic nature of the process of communication.

2. Communication Is Transactional

The most basic of all human needs is the need to understand and be understood.
—Ralph Nichols

In the previous scenario, you are tired from a long day at work. You may value peace and quiet. Your friend, however, is full on energy and values your interaction. The transactional model of communication takes the perspective that meaning and interpretation are part of the individual. Your frame of mind as tired and hers as energetic contribute to the transactional nature of communication between you. But we can't just limit our discussion to the here and now of the scenario. Where did you grow up? What language(s) did you learn? What did you learn to value? All of these factors and many more contribute to your interpretation of the message and your response to it.

One good example of transactional communication is the phenomenon of **understood meaning.** Understood meaning occurs when two or more people have in some way negotiated a common meaning for a word or phrase. Have you ever known two people who have been together for a long period of time? Could they finish each other's sentences? Did they have their own "words"? Their vocabulary held meanings they understood, drawn from years of experience together. An outsider might only guess at what they were talking about. The words themselves were only part of the picture. To fully grasp the understood meaning of the message you would have to have been part of the experience that led to the shared meaning.

Exercise _____

Can you think of words that have special meanings in your family, group of friends, or with someone you have known? Write down the words and their special definitions.

Outside of a small, close-knit group, do think this process occurs on a wider scale? If you travel from one part of the United States to another, do all of the words, phrases, and behaviors mean the same? You may come from the South where hospitality is an important social custom. Your expectation of yourself may be that you will be a gracious host regardless of how you really feel. Or, as someone from the North, you may have learned to raise your palms with a typical New Yorker's carefree shrug to easily communicate "No big deal" and go about your business. Where you come from influences the words you use with others. In order to understand the meaning of the words, we need more than just the words themselves.

3. Communication Is a Process

> *No one can step twice into the same river, nor touch mortal substance twice in the same condition. By the speed of its change, it scatters and gathers again.*
>
> —Heraclitus, Greek philosopher

The previous scenario involved you talking with yourself, a friend, and to a group of friends. Each time someone else entered the scene, the scene itself changed. Not only does the scene change and transform, but it is constantly changing. Your ability to adapt to this constant change impacts your ability communicate in a variety of settings and situations. Recognize that, like water running down a river, communication travels in one direction, and much as we would like to go back, we cannot. Communication is a dynamic process, where people come together, mingle, and then part. When you come together again, it is in a new context with a new set of conditions. We, too, as part of the communication process, are constantly changing and can learn new skills.

4. Communication Is Irreversible

> *They may forget what you said, but they will never forget how you made them feel.*
>
> —Carl W. Buechner

As soon as you heard yourself say the words "OK, everybody out!" you may have thought about what they sounded like. You might have felt bad about how you communicated your feelings and followed up with the disclaimer "I'm tired" to explain your tone. You might have wished, at least once in your life, that you could take back what you said or how you said it. Once something is expressed, it cannot be taken back.

Words and gestures can make an impact, and their impact can be felt for a lifetime. We simply cannot reverse the process of communication. However, by taking an active role in our communication with others, and recognizing that communication is irreversible, we can take a proactive approach to the words and gestures we use.

5. Communication Is Learned

> *Words are just words and without heart they have no meaning.*
>
> —Chinese proverb

When you said in the scenario "OK, everybody out!", did you stop for a moment and think that you sounded like your mother, father, or someone you looked up to while growing up? Have you ever heard yourself say or sound just like someone who was an authority figure during your childhood? While there is some debate as to the universal nature of language across cultures, most researchers conclude that our knowledge of communication is learned through interaction with others. Smiles and laughter may cross the language barrier, but words and many gestures require an understanding of the culture and context.

From the time of birth until around 9 months of age, babies make similar sounds and gestures regardless of the language of their primary caregiver. Usually

CASE STUDY 1.1 • *Language Deprivation and Development*

Like drinking or breathing, we often take our ability to communicate for granted. Because of language deprivation or limited exposure to meaningful interaction to establish rules and norms for communication early in life, for many children this gift is not a given. There is a window of opportunity to develop language skills that, if missed or underdeveloped, can make it much more challenging to acquire those skills later in life.

Consider a child's learning a second language where it is spoken in the home as opposed to learning it as an adult in a classroom. The child's brain is rapidly developing, and the acquisition of language helps facilitate the learning process, making it much easier while the child is young. Communication interaction stimulates the left side of the brain, which sets up rules for language and thought. As brain growth and development slows as we age, the learning process in terms of language development becomes more challenging.

Children who are born deaf to hearing parents provide us an opportunity to learn about this process. If the parents only talk and engage in limited gestures with their deaf children, the areas of the brain that involve language may not be adequately stimulated, limiting language development. In contrast, children who are raised in language-rich environments—where parents interact with children in American Sign Language—follow trends exhibited by hearing children with similar oral stimulation in terms of increased intelligence scores and the increased ability to communicate emotions. Language deprivation can inhibit the growth of the brain and language development in the same way vitamin deficiencies can limit the growth of the body.

The Northwest Regional Educational Laboratory offers four constructive ways to reinforce and enhance oral language development:

1. **Talk** to infants, giving lots of eye contact and giving time for verbal and nonverbal responses.
2. **Sing** to and with your children. Songs often help children learn challenging concepts, and the social interaction is positive.
3. **Tell stories** to your children. Make them up or relate what happened during your day at work. Help them make sense of their world through stories.
4. **Read aloud** to your children. Make a story before bedtime a habit, and don't rush your reading. Communicate your enthusiasm, and they will be excited to read with you.

Do your own survey of your classmates or friends. How many learned a second language as a child or as an adult? How hard was it for them to learn the language? Are there any differences in their responses?

Sources:
Lehmann, C. (2000, August 4). Clinical and research news. *Psychiatric News.* American Psychiatric Association. Accessed 9/23/00. http://www.psych.org/pnews/00-08-04/med.html.
Northwest Regional Educational Laboratory. (1998). *Paving the way for lifelong thinkers.* http://www.nwrel.org/pirc/hot5.html.
Swan, N. (2000, July 10). Hearing loss in children. *The Health Report.* Radio National. Accessed 9/23/00. http://www.abc.net.au/rn/talks/8.30/helthrpt/stories/s150097.htm.

between 9 and 12 months, babies start to imitate the vocalizations of their caregivers and start on a path toward using the language. At around 1 year, a child often uses his or her first word, and that word can mean many things. In addition to the use of words, the gestures and customs that are part of a culture are also learned as a child develops. A Chilean baby may raise his arms and say "Oopa" to communicate a desire to be held. A baby in the United States might also raise her arms but say "Up." As a child grows, social interaction and customs take on increasing importance. In Chile a child would learn to give a light kiss on the cheek to family friend or neighbor after saying "Hola." In the United States, a child learns to extend his hand for a handshake as he says "Hello." Issues of touch and space are as much a learned part of communication as words in distinct languages.

Summary

In this chapter, we discussed how important communication is in our lives. Employers prefer job candidates who have good communication skills. Relationships are formed through communication interaction and can be healthier when the participants actively work at effective communication. In addition, we looked at a definition of communication, and how process, understanding, and sharing relate to the definition. In our discussion of four models of communication, we examined how they incorporate the eight components of communication and become increasing complex in their representation of the communication process. We also examined the range of contexts in which communication occurs, from intrapersonal communication to mass communication. Finally, we discussed five principles of communication and how we learn to communicate. In the next chapter, we'll examine the concept of perspective, how we listen, and how these elements impact our communication with ourself and others.

> *Communication leads to community, that is, to*
> *understanding, intimacy and mutual valuing.*
> —Rollo May

For More Information

National Communication Association, **http://www.natcom.org/**

The National Association of Colleges and Employers, **http://www.naceweb.org**

Review Questions

1. Factual Questions
   a. What is the definition of communication presented in this text?
   b. What four models of communication are presented in this text?
   c. What are five principles of communication?

2. Interpretative Questions

    a. What assumptions are present in the Shannon and Weaver model of communication? What assumptions are present in later models?

    b. Do the principles of communication apply in all cases?

    c. How does our native language or culture influence our communication?

3. Evaluative Questions

    a. Does the definition of communication given work in all instances of communication? What might be a better or more accurate definition? Where does this definition place emphasis, and what does it leave out?

    b. Do the models of communication accurately present this dynamic process? What could improve these models?

    c. Can any of the four models of communication provided accurately depict the communication process? Why or why not?

4. Application Questions

    a. Observe two people talking. Draw a model of their communication.

    b. Find an example of a model of communication where you work.

    c. Find an example of one principle of communication.

References

Cronen, V., & Pearce, W. B. (1982). The coordinated management of meaning: A theory of communication. In F. E. X. Dance (Ed.), *Human communication theory* (pp. 61–89). New York: Harper & Row.

Habermas, J. (1984). *The theory of communicative action* (Vol. 1). Boston: Beacon Press.

Karnovsky, S., & Warner, C. (2002). An instant feedback learning environment. *Converge, 5*(5), 20–22.

Laswell, H. (1948). The structure and function of communication in society. In L. Bryson (Ed.), *The communication of ideas.* New York: Harper & Row.

Leavitt, H. J., & Mueller, R. (1951). Some effects of feedback on communication. *Human Relations 4,* 401–410.

Pearce, W. B., & Cronen, V. (1980). *Communication, action, and meaning: The creation of social realities.* New York: Praeger.

Pearson, J., & Nelson, P. (2000). *An introduction to human communication: Understanding and sharing* (8th ed.; p. 6). Dubuque, IA: McGraw-Hill.

Shannon, C., & Weaver, W. (1949). *The mathematical theory of communication.* Urbana: University of Illinois Press.

Vocate, D. (Ed.). (1994). *Intrapersonal communication: Different voices, different minds.* Hillsdale, NJ: Lawrence Erlbaum.

Watzlawick, P. (1993). *The language of change: Elements of therapeutic communication.* New York: W. W. Norton & Company.

Weekley, E. (1967). *An etymological dictionary of modern English* (Vol. 1). New York: Dover Publications.

Wood, J. (1997). *Communication in our lives.* Boston: Wadsworth.

2

Perception and Listening

Chapter Objectives _____

After completing this chapter, you should be able to:

1. Describe the relationship between perception and the communication process.
2. Describe the process of perception.
3. Determine how perception differs between people.
4. Describe the relationship between the components of perception and self-concept.
5. Identify the key components of self-concept.
6. Demonstrate the importance of listening skills
7. Describe the difference between passive, active, critical, and empathetic listening.
8. Identify and describe the stages of the listening process.
9. Describe similarities and differences between the three key barriers to listening.
10. Identify and describe ways to improve listening.

Introductory Exercise 1 _____

In order to communicate effective with others, it helps to know where you yourself are coming from. One way to learn more about yourself is to complete a personal inventory. The inventory is a simple list of what comes to mind in these five areas:

- **Your knowledge:**   What do you know?
- **Your skills:**   What do you do well?
- **Your experience:**   Where have you been successful?
- **Your interests:**   What do you enjoy doing?
- **Your relationships:**   Who do you rely on and/or care about?

Introductory Exercise 2 _____

Please find the hidden message(s):

D	U	E	O	E	F	T	E
L	O	C	Y	C	N	C	P
R	Y	R	W	N	I	E	R
O	E	E	O	E	E	P	U
W	V	P	H	U	V	S	O
R	I	U	S	L	I	R	Y

Introductory Exercise 3 _____

Please connect the dots with four straight lines, making sure you do not lift your pen or pencil from the paper or retrace lines.

O   O   O

O   O   O

O   O   O

Your mind is like a parachute. It works best when it's open.
—Anonymous

At the beginning of the first chapter you listed terms to describe yourself and your priorities. Building on your first responses, these exercises serve to highlight your knowledge, skills, experience, interests, and relationships. A personal inventory is a great way to begin to understand yourself better, and the degree to which you can see yourself reflected in your likes and dislikes, interests and experiences, and through your relationships will give you greater insight into yourself. Interpersonal communication starts with intrapersonal communication, and it is challenging to step outside of ourselves for a different perspective.

Perspective and awareness significantly impact communication with one another. If a friend strikes up a conversation about scuba diving, and you have never been but are interested, to what degree do you think you might be likely to pay attention? If, however, you have a fear a being underwater and had a traumatic experience as a child in a pool, how will your perspective influence your communication with your friend? In the first example, you may have paid particular attention, but in the second, you may have missed each other because you were not completely aware of each other's agenda or perspective. Awareness is a complicated and fascinating area of study. The way we take in information, give it order, and assign it meaning has long interested researchers from disciplines including sociology, anthropology, and psychology.

In the first chapter we learned about the basic models of communication and how the elements come together as a dynamic process. Your perspective is a major factor in this dynamic process. You bring to the act of reading this sentence a frame of mind formed from experiences and education across your lifetime. Learning to recognize how your perspective influences how you read this sentence as well as how you interact with yourself and others is a central goal of this book. We will explore the communication process from different perspectives, reinforcing more than one point of view, to help you be aware of how each element contributes to the process. The ability to examine communication with yourself and others is challenging, but as philosophers like Socrates and Descartes have long argued, it is central to our humanity. Your ability to view the communication process as a process gives you the possibility of influencing or changing it. If a conversation or relationship is challenging in some ways, your ability to recognize both the problem and possible solutions can empower you with the will and skill to improve the communication. Keep an open mind as we progress through our analysis of communication. Some of this material may seem very familiar. You may miss something that can offer new insight if you glance over passages you think you understand. Reflect on your own experience and this discussion and you will be amazed at how it changes the way you view your communication with yourself and others.

Did you solve the second exercise? If so, how did you solve it? By accident, or did you use a pattern, looking for common letter combinations or odd letter pairs. There are many ways to solve this puzzle but only one right answer. Reading right to left, not left to right, and bottom to top, not top to bottom, the puzzle reads: *Your perspective influences how you perceive your world.*

Most of us learn to read left to right, top to bottom. People who read and write Arabic, however, learn to write right to left. These are two distinct ways of reading, but the act of reading is similar. Another way to consider this issue is to ask a friend or classmate "What side of the road do the drive on in England or Australia?" A common response is "the wrong side," but this response involves a value statement that implies one culture is "good" and one is "bad." People in England or Australia simply drive on the other side of the road in comparison to drivers in the United States. The act of driving is similar, but the way we set up and follow the rules is different.

We can extend this concept in many ways. Consider you are having a conversation with a person who is much older or younger than you. Is their mental "roadmap" different than yours? In terms of words to use to communicate idea, references to music or movies, even expectations for behaviors when dating may be quite different. These differences in perspective influence communication and your ability to recognize not only your own point of view but theirs will help you become "other-oriented" and improve communication.

This exercise and example helps illustrate what Habermas calls "preunderstanding." We often enter a new situation, or solve a new problem, with a set of expectations, drawn from our experiences, already present to help guide us to our goal. Within our own community, language group, or culture, these expectations can facilitate communication with a common reference base as a resource. However, as we come into contact with groups, cultures, and puzzles that require different expectations and viewpoints, our ability to adapt to alternate perspectives becomes a key resource.

Finally, did you solve the third exercise? This exercise requires you to think outside of the "box." Looking at the solution, can you see how you had to go outside of the margins in order to solve the challenge? This puzzle, like the second exercise, requires you to explore alternate perspectives to discover a solution.

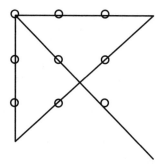

These exercises help introduce your perspective and highlight the importance of understanding the differences in perspective across age, gender, race and ethnicity, and cultural backgrounds. When we make false assumptions about what people are trying to say, particularly when we fail to account for differences in perspective, we open the door to increased misunderstandings.

- A young man comes around a corner and sees his girlfriend next to another young man. That young man has his arm around her. He gets angry, turns around and leaves.
- An employer responds to an employee's request for information via email, explaining an issue in simple terms. The employee perceives the tone of the email as condescending and replies with another email stating she is not stupid in less than professional language.
- A husband asks his wife to deposit money at the bank when she gets off work at 3:00 P.M. She deposits it in the ATM. He notices on the next statement a series of overdraft charges and, after a heated discussion, calls the bank. He confirmed that deposits via the ATM after 3:00 P.M. are processed the following business day, while deposits taken by the teller are recorded at the time of deposit.

What do these three examples have in common? Miscommunication that is influenced by perception. The young man later learned his girlfriend was hanging out with her cousin. The employer failed to see how the employee, who was already sensitive about how the employer perceived her skills, could interpret the tone as condescending. The husband failed to communicate how and why he needed the money deposited. All three examples impacted interpersonal relationships. We all have different interests and experiences, and we don't all pay attention to the same things. In this chapter we will examine how our individual perspectives and listening skills impact our communication.

Why Don't We All See Things the Same Way?

As the previous examples illustrate, we perceive things differently. The girlfriend in the previous example is Hispanic and was raised with her cousins. Touch is an important part of communication, and understanding the context, including the cultural norms, explains his familiarity. The employee read between the lines written in the email, and the lack of face-to-face communication to provide additional channels and cues contributed to an inappropriate response. The wife deposited the money but did not and could not know the importance of how to deposit the money because the husband failed to communicate it clearly. Each person interpreted parts of his or her communication with one another in distinct ways. Why is this? One reason is that we choose to select different aspects of a message to focus our attention based on what interests us, what is familiar to us, or what we consider to be important. Another reason that is often overlooked is that for many of us, our listening skills could use improvement. We spend may spend considerable effort thinking about a message and how to deliver it while someone is trying to communicate with us. We end up only listening to ourselves and the monologue we deliver once the other person has stopped talking. After we've said it, we spend time thinking about how we said it, failing to focus on the reaction and feedback. How much time do you spend thinking about how to best listen to what other people are saying? In order to better understand perception and the listening process, we will examine how you choose to pay attention, remember, and interpret messages within the communication process.

First we'll examine how you select, organize, and interpret communication, noting characteristics that influence your perception. Next we'll examine how your self-concept is formed and how communication with others helps form your image of how you see yourself. Finally, we'll examine the process of listening, identifying key barriers and ways to overcome them.

Exercise _____

When you watch a movie with a friend or friends, make a point talking about it afterwards and listen to how each person perceived aspects of the film. Did you see it the same way or differently? Did you catch all the clues, see how the characters formed relationships, or miss any information? What does this say about perception?

Perception and Awareness

> *To see an object in the world we must see it as something.*
> —Wittegenstein

Can you imagine what life would be like if you listened, saw, and felt every stimulus, or change or activity in your environment, that was around you all day long? It would be overwhelming. It is impossible to perceive, remember, process, and respond to every action, smell, sound, picture, or word we see, hear, small, taste, or touch. We would be lost paying attention to everything, being distracted by everything, and we would lack focus on anything. It is handy, therefore, that we as humans can choose to pay attention to specific stimulus while ignoring or tuning out others. This raises the question, however, of why do we choose to pay attention to one thing over another? Since we cannot pay attention to everything at once, we choose to pay attention to what appears to be the most relevant for us. This action of sorting competing messages, or choosing stimuli, is called **selection.**

Selection is one very important part of perception and awareness. You select what to pay attention to based on what is important to you, or what you value, and that is different for each person. Let's pretend you enter a movie rental business with your friend from across the hall. You've forgiven her for previously turning your apartment into grand central station and decided together to close a hectic workweek with a movie and dinner (she is cooking). As you look around, you will notice signs indicating movie genres, including horror, comedy, and adventure. You might go over to the horror section while your friend gravitates toward the comedy section. You may both select a film to watch together, and when you discuss your choices, may perceive the films as quite different. You may not be thrilled with her choice of films any more than she is with yours, but you both have selected a movie based on your own interests. Both individuals are involved in selecting what they want to watch based on their own interests and whatever catches their eye. The act of choosing one movie over another is an example of the selection process.

Selection has three main parts: exposure, attention, and retention (Klopf, 1995). **Selective exposure** is both information we choose to pay attention to and information that is either not available to us or information we choose to ignore. For example, you may have not seen many horror films and find them fascinating, while your friend has seen them all. Your levels of exposure influenced your decisions. **Selective attention** is when we focus on one stimulus, like a movie, and tune out a competing stimulus, like the radio playing in the next room. **Selective retention** is when you choose to remember one stimulus over another. Say we talk about the movie you watched together. What was it about? Who were the main characters? What was the plot? You may be able to answer all of these questions easily. Your friend, however, may be able to recall scenes from this movie that are similar to other horror films she has seen in the past. This illustrates how one aspect of selection, like exposure, can influence another aspect, like retention.

Now you if you both were asked to recall the songs on the radio that was playing in the next room, could you? Even if you recall the radio was playing, you may have a hard time remembering what songs you heard because you were focused on the movie you rented. Although you may have *heard* the music in the background, you may not have chosen to *listen* to it. Hearing means you heard music but listening implies you actively chose to listen to the songs, processing the sounds, making it easier for you to recall. This illustrates the point that you chose one stimuli over another, in effect selecting what to pay attention to, and if the radio was competing for your attention you probably just turned it off, in effect deselecting it.

Organization, the second step in the perception process, is when we sort and categorize information in ways that make sense to us. As the term implies, we organize what we perceive into categories based on what we have perceived previously. Think back to the movie rental business. The signs indicated horror, comedy, and adventure genres to indicate where you could find certain types of movies. These signs indicate that the movies are physically organized in groups that have common characteristics. Someone chose to put a movie under the horror sign, even though it may very well have aspects of comedy and adventure. Focusing on one aspect of the film, perhaps the main theme, allows us to organize the signs.

When you were younger and did not know the difference between a square and a circle, you saw little difference. As you grew, you learned the difference and saw squares and circles everywhere. Then you learned the difference between squares and rectangles. As an adult, you follow the same process you did as a child. You come across a situation where you are in unfamiliar surroundings, so you use clues to make sense of where you are and find your way home. You are in a conversation with someone and hear a topic that had been presented in one of your classes. You connect what you learned in class to this new conversation and have insight to offer. Your ability to organize information, taking information that you know and remember and applying it to new information, helps you make sense of your world and is key to communication.

Organization as a part of the perception process is often governed by principles, often called *gestalt principles.* Early psychologists thought we could examine parts of things, much as a scientist would examine an atom, and make a whole and complete picture regardless of context. Gestalt principles were developed in response to this view, asserting that context matters. The way our mind perceives a whole picture or perspective out of incomplete elements is fascinating, and a contextual process. These principles, which include proximity, similarity, uniformity or homogeneity, figure and ground, closure, area, symmetry, and continuity (Moore & Fitz, 1993), come from the perspective that context counts.

We often select, organize, and interpret information based on how physically close or to what degree things resemble one another. **Proximity** is the perceptual organization of information based on physical space between objects. In Exercise 3, we tried to connect nine dots with four straight lines and not lift our pencil. The physical proximity of each dot to one another contributed to the perception of the "square" and may have limited our ability to perceive possible solutions to the puzzle. The principle of proximity indicates that we will perceive things that are closer together as belonging together, whether they are related or not. We can extend this principle to our observation of others. If we see to people walking relatively close to one another, we might perceive they have a relationship. If we step back and perceive the context as a crowded sidewalk in a large city, our perception based on proximity might be in error. We perceive, intentionally or unintentionally, that if images, words, or shapes occur close to one another that they must be somehow related.

This perception of relationship extends to the concept of **continuation.** We appear to have a natural tendency to prefer the continuity of a figure over disconti- nuity. Examine Figure 2.1 and ask yourself what you see. Do you see two Xs or Vs? Or do you perceive two lines crossing one another? The principle of continuity pre- dicts that you would demonstrate a preference for continuous figures, meaning two lines crossing one another. This principle is related to our preference for familiarity and may certainly apply to our preference for people whom we know over people we do not.

We also tend to perceive that similar objects, ideas, and images are related. **Similarity** is the perceptual organization of information based on perceived points of similarity across distinct items. For example, a zebra is like a horse, and we may perceive them as similar. According to the principle of similarity, things that share visual characteristics such as shape, size, color, texture, value, or orientation we will perceive as belonging together. We can also use Exercise 3 to reinforce this concept, placing the emphasis on the similar characteristic of size instead of proximity as we did previously. We can also extend this principle in to the arena of human interac- tion. Do people who associate with one another dress in similar ways? This may be most noticeable in junior high or high school cliques or jobs that require uniforms like those in a hospital setting. All clothing in some way demonstrates group affilia- tion or self-concept. We can rationally understand that this tendency to group items physically close to one another or that resemble each other, like figure and ground and closure, can lead us to false conclusions.

Figure and ground organization is the act or organizing stimuli into catego- ries that receive extra emphasis, becoming more pronounced, while other categories are neglected and become less noticeable. In Figure 2.2, take a look at the picture. What do you see? Fish and birds? Anything else? The terms *figure* and *ground* help explain how we use elements of the picture, which are similar in appearance and shape, and then group the elements together as a whole. Similar elements (figure) are contrasted with dissimilar elements (ground) to give the overall impression of a complete picture. In the picture (Figure 2.2), the fish and the bird stand out as the

FIGURE 2.1 *Continuity*

FIGURE 2.2   *Talking about Fish and Fowl*

key figures, while the black background, which reveals the outline of someone talking, is perceived as ground. Would knowing the title was *Talking about Fish and Fowl* have helped you see things differently? To learn more about the use of figure and ground, do a search on information about "M. C. Escher" or "Tessellated Art."

Closure is our perceptual ability to fill in the gaps and connect the dots. Have you ever been in conversation with someone when something nearby drowns out some of his words? You might have automatically filled in the words if you anticipated what he was going to say next. Did you guess right? The principle of closure applies to perception when we tend to perceive complete figures or concepts even when part of the information is missing.

INTERCULTURAL COMMUNICATION 2.1 • *Slang*

People often use words to signal they are part of a group and often people who are not in that group fail to understand the understood meaning between in-group members. For example, which of the following words refers to sex? Can you match the rest of the terms to their slang meanings?

1. ace	A. sexual activity
2. ace boon coon	B. friend
3. action	C. a very good, trusted friend
4. afro	D. used after a word as an intensifier
5. ag	E. aggravated or upset
6. age	F. a large, almost spherical hair style generally attributed to people of African descent

If you want to learn more about slang and slang terms, check out the online slang dictionary on the University of California, Berkeley, website at: http://www.ocf.berkeley.edu/~wrader/slang/

Cover this answer key:

1-C, 2-B, 3-A, 4-F, 5-E, 6-D

Do you see a ring of "Pac-man"–like circles in Figure 2.3? Do you see anything else? What image(s) do the ring of "Pac-man" circles form? Do you see a star? Why?

The ability to mentally fill in the gaps, creating the perception that the shape of a star exists, is an example of closure. This ability is advantageous. Our minds predictably interpret patterns that are familiar, even though we often receive incomplete information. There is some speculation that this is a survival instinct, allowing us to complete the form, sound, or concept of a predator even when we have incomplete information. This advantage, however, can lead us to false conclusions. If we fill in the gaps incorrectly, or take a few words and interpret their overall meaning to be something other than it is, then our ability to close the gaps between information has steered us in the wrong direction. It can, however, help us make associations and solve problems everyday. If we know where 25th Street is and read that there is a new restaurant on 26th Street, our ability to build on what we know can help. Be aware of how you connect the dots and seek good information.

The third step in the perception process is called interpretation. **Interpretation** occurs when you assign meaning and value to what you perceive. There are two distinct processes that comprise interpretation: a blend of sensory input and prior expectations and knowledge. Your sensory input involves information received through your eyes and ears, for example. Your expectations, assumptions, and prior knowledge, however, also actively limit and contribute to how you interpret what you see, helping in the selection of what to focus on over other competing stimuli. Let's say you want to buy a car. You know you need to get from point A to point B, but you want to do it in style. You may value style over other features like mechanical reliability when you choose a sports car. You assign meaning and value to the car beyond its transportation usage. You take a test drive, and focus on how cool you look in the car rather than the handling of the car. You are, in effect, favoring the mental processing of information as it relates to prior expectations. You may be receiving sensory input that the car drives like a truck, but you might not pay attention to it. The interpretation process is important, and the alternative, involving a lack of ability to distinguish between what is important to you and what is not, would be

FIGURE 2.3   *What Do You See?*

chaotic, confusing, and possibly paralyzing. Being aware of how you perceive and interpret information is key to understanding yourself and others.

Each way of perceiving information highlights your ability to take what you perceive, together with what you know, and apply it to new situations. We always try

COMPUTER-MEDIATED COMMUNICATION 2.1 • *Information and Privacy*

We share information about ourselves everyday, but do we often consider that some of the ways we communicate may be stored and even transferred to people we don't know? Everyday we communicate our interests and by visiting websites. We indicate our preferences, our experiences, even our challenges in online forums and chat rooms. Our self-expression takes an interesting turn when you consider that every word you post online is stored. Every email has a copy somewhere. Your own computer may track your activities and report them to third parties. Everytime you download anything, like sharing programs such as Morpheus or Kazaa, there may be a "trojan horse" program inside that will hide in your registry files and open a "back door" to your computer. Some use of the information is used for marketing, or strategically targeting you with offers for services and products. Other information is used to generate a spam list, which corresponds to a ever-increasing number of spam, or junk email, that takes up your time. The programs that store and track your activities are often called "spyware." How do you control your information and prevent spyware from constantly watching, and reporting to others, what you do from over your shoulder?

One positive step is to recognize that electronic communication is for the most part public information, and you shouldn't write anything you don't want everyone to read, or be able to read years from now. Another is to learn about cookies, the tracking programs that install themselves on your computer and allow you to log on to websites easily. If you use a computer with Windows® by Microsoft®, there is a program called Ad-Aware that can help. Go to www.lavasoftusa.com and download the free utility. Once it is installed, watch it create a list of all the suspicious and malicious programs (cookies) on your computer. With the click of a box they are doomed for destruction.

Here are a few programs to watch out for:

B3D   When you download Kazaa, a common file-sharing program, Brilliant Digital installs a copy of B3D. This program then allocates your unused computing power and resources to a distant server to run other people's programs.

Red Sheriff   This program is a Java applet, like a cookie, that reports all your Web-surfing activities (time, length of visit at each site, in addition to web addresses of sites visited) as long as your browser is open.

Radlight   This program was designed to disable Ad-Aware.

Aureate   This is an older program that installs a back door that links to banner ads and records which ones you click on to tailor future ads to your preferences.

Source: Taylor (2002).

to make sense of our world, and as a general rule, we hardly ever have all the information necessary at one time. We often make decisions based on incomplete information, taking what we know and applying it to new and uncertain situations. How did you select this class? Your academic counselor may have recommended it as part of your degree program. Your friend may have taken the class from the instructor last semester. Perhaps the course description in the catalog sounded interesting. You made a decision to take the class, but could not know what it was really like until you actually started the first class.

Perceptual Differences

So why do we perceive things differently? There is no easy answer. As we've discussed previously, we all select what to pay attention to and remember things differently. While we organize what we perceive in some similar ways, our expectations and prior knowledge that contribute to this process are individual. How and what we interpret is also largely based on our individual experiences. Therefore, we'll explore how individual differences combine to influence our perception and our responses. Individual differences include:

- Physical characteristics
- Psychological state
- Cultural background
- Gender
- Media exposure
- Perceptual set

First let's look at **physical characteristics.** Some people are tall, others short. Some have excellent hearing (and some might say they have eyes in the back of their head), while others are hard of hearing. These individual differences greatly influence our sensory input. One example might be the door overhang. If I am short, going through doors is a matter of routine. If I am tall, it is part of my expectations based on prior knowledge to watch out for overhangs so I don't hit my head. If I hear within a normal range, I may not factor my hearing ability when I choose where I sit in a classroom. A person with hearing impairment may choose to consider this an important factor when selecting a seat in relation to the instructor. These examples illustrate how sensory input and the response we formulate are influenced by our physical characteristics.

    Psychological characteristics also influence perception. Are you happy to be in class? Are you distracted by something that happened before class? Are you frustrated? Your emotional state directly influences how you perceive your world. If you are in a good mood and something goes wrong, you are more likely to view it as a momentary setback (Covey, 1989). If you are sad or depressed, you may view the setback as more serious, even a defeating blow. This principle extends to personal traits like aggression, narcissism (self-absorption), and perfectionism, which are thought to be passed genetically from one generation to the next. It may also include personality traits and the degree to which you are, for example, shy, analytical, and/ or dextrous (good with your hands).

Cultural background includes more than just your nationality, race, or ethnicity. Did you grow up in a small town? A large city? Do you come from a large family? A small one? Is religion a part of your life? Do you speak more than one language? Cultural differences are expressed in many shades and are hard to define. They can, however, be observed, and their influence on communication has been clearly documented (Gage & Berliner, 1998). Geert Hofstede (1980) calls our cultural background *mental software* and compares the social codes and language you learned to computer software and your brain, like the computer, to the hardware. We can also see, in our discussion of selection, organization, and interpretation, how our cultural background can influence what we pay attention to and why.

Gender is another important factor that influences perception and awareness. Gender means the behavioral, cultural, or psychological traits typically associated with the sex of an individual. Gender concerns your sex role and what you perceive that role to be, as opposed to your sex, which is either male or female. There is significant debate over gender-related factors that influence perception. Some researchers argue there are biological predispositions linked to gender, while others dismiss this assertion as unfounded. Whether a child, for example, cares for a hurt friend because of his or her nature, or because of what he or she has learned, often called nurture, is a point of debate. There is a view among many researchers, however, that most behavior is a blend of both nature and nurture. Do a search using the keywords "nature" and "nurture" and explore this issue.

Gender is a factor when people have certain expectations for themselves and others. Who is going to fix the light? Who is going to make dinner? Who is going to stay home to take care of the baby? If you watched television shows in the 1950s, or caught them on many of the channels that feature "classic" programming, you will observe there were definite gender roles. For example, in a classic program entitled *Leave It to Beaver,* Ward Cleaver went off to work while June, his wife, stayed home. Their activities, experiences, roles, and responsibilities were clearly defined. Does television depict the 1950s accurately? No more than to say that as a cultural generalization, in the post–World War II United States, gender roles were more rigidly defined than we see today. Gender roles, like all roles in societies, are part of a constant, dynamic change. As people's individual perceptions and preferences change, so do expectations, and television has sometimes captured these societal changes. Popular modern programs often reflect different societal and cultural expectations than programs produced twenty or forty years ago.

Media exposure, from radio to television and newspapers to the Internet, also contributes to the way we see the world. How much television do you watch? What kind of television to you watch? Do you read a newspaper? How often? How about the radio? The Internet? Chat rooms? What you consume in terms of information

CASE STUDY 2.1 • *Groupthink*

You take in information about the world around you everyday, and choose how to respond and adapt. Usually, you choose a course that appear appropriate based on the information and your perception of the facts. Would you choose to act in a way that seems to contradict what you see and hear? People will sometimes be involved with actions and activities that they themselves would never choose on their own.

Dr. Irving Janis, a pioneer in the study of group dynamics, found individuals will go along with the group even when evidence to the contrary exists. He called this phenomenon groupthink (1982). **Groupthink** is defined as a phenomenon where people seek unanimous agreement even though there are contrary facts indicating another conclusion.

Common examples include the perception that the Japanese would never strike Pearl Harbor; the Bay of Pigs invasion of Cuba, involving 1,300 people, would prove successful; or even the NASA shuttle the Challenger would be a successful mission in spite of evidence and problems. Each assumption proved false, cost countless people their lives, and research into each case illustrates how people chose to ignore or downplay evidence that challenged their point of view.

Warning signs of groupthink include:

- Assertion of invulnerability
- Belief in the inherent group morality
- Rationalization of group views
- Stereotyping of out-groups or non-group members
- Self-censorship and group reinforcement
- Direct and indirect pressure on members who disagree

The response to groupthink is individual decision making and the freedom to challenge assumptions. We no longer consider the world to be flat or the Earth to be the center of the universe because explorers, philosophers, and researchers challenged the common views of their day.

We can prevent groupthink by:

- Establishing an open climate for the free exchange of ideas and perceptions.
- Avoiding the isolation of the group and its members.
- Assigning and valuing the role of critical evaluator(s).

Sources: Griffin (1997); Janis (1982).

through the media influences how you see the world. In many ways, "you are what you eat" holds true. You may be well informed through television or the Internet and be able to contribute insightful opinions in conversations. You may also consume the media equivalent of fast food and grow large on quantity but lack quality, losing time for other activities. What you choose to watch, listen to, log on to, or read influences how you perceive the world. See Case Study 2.2 for a related discussion on how television violence impacts individual behavior in children.

CASE STUDY 2.2 • *Television Violence and Group Interaction among Children*

Have you ever thought about how television influences children's behavior with peers, or how they perceive the world? Communication researchers have been investigating this issue for over forty years, and a leading researcher testified before Congress that "(t)here can no longer be any doubt that heavy exposure to televised violence is one of the causes of aggressive behavior, crime, and violence in society. The evidence comes from both the laboratory and real-life studies." (Eron, 1992, p. 1). Through these social science research studies, it has become possible "to predict some effects of violent viewing in conjunction with specific plot elements" (Aidman, 1997):

• **Aggressive Behavior**. Learning to use aggressive behavior is predicted to increase when the perpetrator is attractive, the violence is justified, weapons are present, the violence is graphic or extensive, the violence is realistic, the violence is rewarded, or the violence is presented in a humorous fashion. Conversely, the learning of aggression is inhibited by portrayals that show that violence is unjustified, show perpetrators of violence punished, or show the painful results of violence.

• **Fearful Attitudes**. The effects of fearful attitudes about the real world may be increased by a number of features, including attractive victims of violence; unjustified violence; graphic, extensive, or realistic violence; and rewards to the perpetrator of violence. According to the work of George Gerbner and his colleagues (1980), heavy viewers of violent content believe their world is meaner, scarier, and more dangerous than their lighter-viewing counterparts. When violence is punished on television, the expected effect is a decrease in fearful attitudes about the real world.

• **Desensitization**. Desensitization to violence refers to the idea of increased toleration of violence. It is predicted from exposure to extensive or graphic portrayals and humorous portrayals of violence and is of particular concern as a long-term effect for heavy viewers of violent content. Some of the most violent programs are children's animated series in which violence is routinely intended to be funny, and realistic consequences of violence are not shown. (Aidman, 1997)

The debate over to whether or to what extent television violence influences children's behavior is a fascinating topic to investigate. Research the topic online and share your results in class.

Sources: Aidman (1997); Eron (1992); Gerbner, George, & Gross (1980).

Finally, **perceptual set** is when we use a fixed perspective to view the world. One way to think of it is to imagine you are always wearing a set of sunglasses. Our sunglasses are formed from your past experiences and from all the characteristics we've discussed previously. Our use of just one set of "sunglasses" to view events, people, or objects, without taking into account how the glasses themselves color and shade the way we perceive the world, can limit or distort our perceptions. A common example is stereotyping, where we categorize events, people, or objects without taking into account individual or unique differences. "All pit bull dogs are mean." This is a stereotype, which generalizes an entire breed of dogs as one way, without taking into account individual differences in training or temperament.

Now that we have examined perception and ways of expressing and interpreting, let's examine one fundamental process that significantly contributes to our point of view. When we listen to one another, we take in not only the spoken works, but the way they were said, the context in which they were said, and most importantly, how they make us feel about ourselves and others.

Eyes, Ears, Heart

When you hear, you passively receive sound. When you listen, you actively focus on receiving and interpreting aural (heard) stimuli. According to the Chinese character for listening, when you listen you use your eyes, ears, and heart (Figure 2.4). With your eyes you may pay attention to nonverbal cues. With your ears, you may pay attention to not only the words but the tone of voice, pitch, rate of speech, and degree of fluidity of the words spoken. With your heart, you may pay attention to the emotional state of the speaker, and observe the context in which the message is spoken. Listening is an important skill, and we will examine the kinds of listening and ways to improve your skills.

Importance of Listening

If speaking is silver, then listening is gold.
—Turkish proverb

Why is listening so important? As we've examined previously in this chapter, your communication with others directly affects how you feel about and perceive yourself. Your ability to actively listen to the messages that are directed to you gives you the ability to control what you receive and how you interpret it.

Sometimes people mistake hearing for listening. Hearing involves the physiological process of recognizing sounds. Your ears receive and transmit the information to your brain. Once your brain receives the signals, then they start to make

FIGURE 2.4   *Chinese Character for "Listening"*

sense to you. This is the listening stage, where you create meaning based on previous experiences and contextual cues to make sense of the sounds. It's important to recognize that you spend a considerable amount of your time engaging in listening activities. One of the first studies on listening behavior found people are involved in listening activities—person to person or listening to mass media, for example—around 40 percent of the time (Pearson & Nelson, 2000). Werner (1975), for example, found people spend 55 percent of their time listening.

Kinds of Listening

> *Everyone hears only what he understands.*
> —Goethe

As stated previously, it is important to make the distinction between hearing and listening. Hearing is the passive reception of sounds while listening is the act of actively focusing on specific sounds with a purpose (Barker, 1971). The difference is easy to remember:

HEAR: You hear sounds all around you simply because they're *here.*
LISTEN: You make a *list* of exactly what you choose to hear when you listen.

There are three different kinds of listening: **active, empathic,** and **critical.** Each kind of listening, as its title implies, has a specific focus. We will examine the focus of each type of listening and then see how they relate to common listening barriers.

In **active listening,** you want to hear something. While the radio plays in the background, someone asks you a question. You want to hear that person, so you selectively attend to them, trying to listen to what they have to say. You want to give the person **feedback,** letting him or her know you are interested. If you nod to the person, he or she may understand that you have heard. This is called **positive feedback** and reinforces the listener's interest to the speaker. If you hold your hand to your ear and move your head back and forth, as in "no," you are indicating that you did not receive the message. This is also positive feedback, because you are still showing your interest. **Negative feedback** indicates that you did hear the message, but you don't like what you heard. Perhaps you show this negative feedback by glancing away or frowning. Your message to the speaker is one of frustration, or lack of interest, and it communicates an interest in not continuing the conversation.

In **empathic listening,** you take one more step. First, you listen with a purpose, wanting to hear the message. Second, you listen with the intent to understand the other person's point of view. In empathic listening, you pay attention to not only the words and nonverbal gestures, but also pay particular attention to the context, previous information that pertains to the present situation, and the speaker's emotional state. Is she excited? Angry? Why is she so worked up? You attempt to gain insight into where the message comes from and why it is expressed in a particular way.

In **critical listening,** you listen with attention to detail, listening for clear support of the statements, and trying to identify any inconsistencies. A salesperson may say, "this is our most exclusive (expensive) product—it is the best." He or she is using a logical shortcut that people often use: If something costs a lot, it must be good. Does this assertion hold up in all cases all the time? Of course not. It is up to you, the critical listener, to evaluate information for its accuracy and utility, then decide whether you can use it. This is called **critical thinking.** Where do people get information to support what they say? Do they have a financial interest in your decision? Examine what is said closely, paying attention to nonverbal as well as verbal cues. Examine even closer what is not said, because without all the information,

INTERCULTURAL COMMUNICATION 2.2 • *How Do You Show That You Are Listening?*

- You are the teacher. You are speaking to a student about a problem behavior you want him to change. The student looks at his feet.
- You are a student. Your teacher is talking to you about a problem behavior she wants you to change. You look her in the eyes as she speaks.

What is the difference? If you are a member of many Native American tribes or from many of the countries in Latin America, you learned to show respect by not establishing eye contact with an authority figure. In Native American cultures, eyes are often considered windows to the soul and not to be shared casually. If you were raised in the United States, you may have heard the phrase "Look me in the eye when I am talking to you!" This phrase underlines the importance of maintaining eye contact with an authority figure to signal attention. How people show they are listening, and how people are chosen—through social custom or ritual—to speak, varies around the world. Across cultures, however, the importance of showing you are listening, in a culturally appropriate way, is universal. Here are a few tips to help you if you find yourself in a new place, where people communicate in ways that are new to you.

1. **Check your perceptions.** It is necessary to ask if what you think the other person said is accurate or if what happens between you has the same meaning for him or her that it has for you. Wait until the other person has clearly finished speaking, and then wait an extra second to be sure.
2. **Look for feedback.** Remember to ask for more than a simple yes or no answer. In some cultures it is impolite to say no.
3. **Don't judge.** Reserving judgment while listening allows you to be more open to another's message and point of view, reducing defensiveness in intercultural communication.
4. **Be self-aware.** Be conscious of the way you behave; your verbal and nonverbal communication style; and your values, beliefs, and attitudes. Intercultural communication can be challenging. Start by examining your own cultural background.

your decision may be based on partial truths. As a critical listener and a critical thinker, your goal is to actively listen and decide whether the message gives you the information you need.

Active Listening	**1.** Choose to listen.
Empathic Listening	**1.** Choose to listen.
	2. Try to understand speaker's point of view.
Critical Listening	**1.** Choose to listen.
	2. Try to understand speaker's point of view or agenda.
	3. Pay particular attention to detail.

Listening Styles

Now that we've examined types of listening behavior, let's examine specific styles of listening. Perhaps you know someone who always listens for the details, or a friend who often fails to listen because he is busy figuring out what to say the moment you stop talking. These kinds of listening behaviors specifically impact interpersonal communication, and the degree to which you can recognize them in your own listening habits as well as those of others will help improve communication. Kitty Watson, Larry Barker, and James Weaver (1995) have researched this area extensively and have found four listening styles that we can learn to recognize.

1. People-Oriented Listeners. Listeners who tend to be comfortable listening to both the words and the way the words are communicated, including expressions of emotions and feelings. They can empathize with the speaker and often find common ground. They may exhibit less apprehension in communication interactions.

2. Action-Oriented Listeners. Listeners who tend to listen for information that is well organized, to the point, and without error. This type of listener may grow impatient when listening to a story that provides important background to a situation, instead preferring a brief summary and action points clearly listed. He or she may also be listening for cues as to how to use the information and fail to appreciate seemingly unrelated information if a connection in not clearly expressed.

3. Content-Oriented Listeners. Listeners who tend to listen to the content of the message, focusing on details and facts rather than context. This type of listener may do very well and picking out an unsubstantiated claim or an overall lack of supporting evidence, much like a detective or a debater, but may lack an awareness of the context of the message, including emotions and feelings.

4. Time-Oriented Listeners. Listeners who tend be very aware of time and commitments and typically prefer messages in brief and succinct formats. These listeners often appreciated list-making and prioritizing activities, and their mental template of this prioritization applies to their listening behavior. These listeners may ignore small talk and extraneous information, and they may lack awareness of the context of the message.

While humans exhibit a diverse range of listening behavior, these types of listening styles help highlight various listening strategies and their relative strengths and weaknesses. If you tend be a time-oriented listener, then perhaps paying a bit more attention to the context may provide a valuable strategy to improve listening skills. If you tend to be content-oriented listener, then recognize your strength in noting details but try to keep the context and environment in mind. If you are an action-oriented listener, attending to aspects of the messages that indicate feelings, like voice inflection and nonverbal communication, may improve listening skills. If you are a people-oriented listener, you may benefit from paying additional attention to detail or content when listening. Each style can learn from one another.

Stages of Listening

Now that we've discussed the importance of listening, let's examine the eight steps in the listening process (see Figure 2.5). These may seem familiar to you because you use them all the time, often without even thinking about it. Let's pretend you want to listen to the radio. You turn the power on and out of the speaker comes **noise.** The static that you **hear** tells you that you need to find a radio station signal. You tune the radio into a station and **select** the music coming out of the speakers rather than noise. You then choose to **attend,** or focus, on the music to see if you can **understand** which group is playing the music or determine the song. You then **evaluate** the music, deciding whether you like it by **remembering** if you have heard it before or by determining that the new song sounds interesting. Finally, you **respond** to the music, either by choosing to listen to it or by changing the station.

Noise	External interference
Hearing	Registering sound
Selecting	Choosing stimuli
Attending	Focusing
Understanding	Assigning meaning
Evaluating	Analyzing and judging
Remembering	Recall and thinking
Responding	Listener responds to message

In addition to the eight steps in the listening process, we need to keep in mind two important factors that influence this process. As we discussed in the basic elements of the communication process, **environment** and **context** play an important role. If the environment where you listen to the radio is quiet, then you may not need much volume to listen. If it is already filled with other sounds, like another radio, a television, or people talking, you may need to reduce the noise level to hear the radio. In terms of context, are you listening to the music by yourself? Then you can choose to listen to your favorite music, regardless whether it is rap or hard rock. If you share the space with other people, or they are trying to study, you might need to take this into account when you select the music.

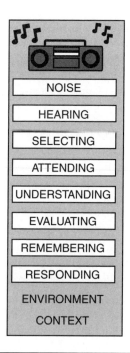

FIGURE 2.5 *The Listening Process*

Barriers to Listening

Barriers to listening are exactly what they sound like: things that get in the way of your hearing the message. The environment may be full of noise, which makes a message hard to hear. Or it might be right after lunch, when you've had a full meal, and you are feeling a little sleepy. Beyond environmental and contextual distractions, there are five key barriers to listening that can contribute to a failure to listen.

1. Lack of Interest

If you are not interested in what the speaker has to say, you are less likely to listen. In addition, if the speaker is not interested in what he or she is presenting and fails to show enthusiasm for the topic, the speaker's lack of interest may influence your decision to listen. Try to find one thing about the message that interests you or look for something within the speech that may come in handy later.

2. Dislike the Speaker, Disregard the Message

If you do not like the speaker because of his or her choice of clothes, manner of speaking, or other personal attribute, you may fail to listen to the speaker and lose the message. Aristotle discusses the importance of **ethos,** or credibility and proof of character, as an integral part of any speech (Covino & Joliffe, 1995). If the listener isn't receptive to the messenger, he or she won't receive the message. You also may make a spot judgment about a person and decide whatever he or she has to say does not interest you. The saying "Never judge a book by its cover" holds true when it comes to listening. You never know where the person is coming from until you listen, and you never know what he or she may share if you tune out.

3. Can't See the Forest through the Trees

You may focus on the details within the message (trees) and lose sight of the larger picture (the forest). Perspective is important, and attention to detail is as well. In critical listening as part of critical thinking, attention to detail can have a large impact on your ability to understand the message and its value to you. The key to critical listening, and not getting lost, is to take notes. Actively listen for points you find interesting or ideas and issues you want to address later. In order to not get distracted by thinking (internal monologue) about one detail and missing countless others, take a note and then actively listen to the speaker, letting go of the point you recorded. Imagine that sometimes you have the perspective of a mouse, low and close to the ground, where small things can be easily seen. Other times have the perspective of the hawk, with its precise eyesight from high above, where you can take in the larger picture. Both perspectives have value, and you need both to listen actively.

4. Faking Attention

Have you ever been listening to someone and seen him or her talking but your mind is thousands of miles away? The person asks you a question, but you are not listening. In order to answer the question, you have to ask him or her to repeat what was said. Faking attention is dangerous because the other person may not get that you missed what she was saying, and without checking, assume that you will use the information to get something done. Let's say a healthcare provider instructs a nurse to administer a shot to a patient, an important shot that contains medicine the patient will need throughout the day. If the nurse fakes attention, how will he know which drug to use? Perhaps he can go to the chart and check, and perhaps not. People depend one each other, emotionally and professionally, and more than feelings can get hurt. Try to quiet your own inner voice and be there for the speaker. Julia Wood (1997) relates this ability to quiet your own voice to the Zen Buddhist concept of mindfulness, of being fully engaged in listening (and not thinking about what you need to do next or what your response will be).

5. Being Self-Absorbed

An additional barrier to listening can be yourself and your orientation to the listening context and environment. If you are listening, much like a content-oriented listener, for only information that applies to you, and specifically your needs and wants, then you are engaging in conversational narcissism (Beebe, Beebe, & Redmond, 2002). Narcissism refers to self-love and goes back to the classical Greek man Narcissus, who fell in love with his own reflection. For our use, **conversational narcissism** refers to listening from the perspective that the only information that matters is that directly pertaining to you. In order to shift this emphasis, become other-oriented when listening and focus on others' needs instead of your own.

Improving Listening Skills

Now that we've discussed how important listening is as a part of the communication process, let's look at a brief list of some ways to improve listening skills.

- Be silent. Let the other person speak and wait until you are sure he or she is finished before you respond.
- Acknowledge understanding. Clearly communicate to the other person know that you have heard and understood what he or she is saying.
- Take turns. Balancing the time between speaking and listening allows each person to take a turn.
- Don't interrupt. Interrupting may prevent something from ever being said.
- Communicate acceptance. Be open to what your partner is communicating. Being open and accepting to communication does not mean that you have to agree with what is said.
- Confirm understanding. Make sure you understand what your partner is communicating. If you don't understand, say so and check for meaning.
- Be attentive. Focus on the words, the message, the ideas, the body language, the context, and the speaker's emotions as he or she communicates with you.
- Make time. It is important to take time to listen. Plan on it. If you know you will spend some of your time listening beforehand, it will help take the pressure off to move on the next activity. Also consider a special time for listening, for people you care about or have a relationship with, for communicating when you will not be disturbed or interrupted. Taking the time needed to get yourself understood and hear the other person's thoughts, ideas, and hopes will keep you connected and your relationship will grow stronger. (Adapted from Galanes, Adams, & Brilhart, 2000)

Now that we've discussed several ways to improve your listening skills, let's leave our discussion on perception and listening with a reminder to practice active listening. Hearing is a passive activity, but active listening requires your time and attention. At the beginning of this text we discussed the importance of communication and how much time you spend communicating throughout your lifetime. Communication is a powerful force in our lives, and active listening is a critical part of the process. Here is a short list of helpful hints to encourage you to practice active listening.

- Give positive eye contact.
- Smile and nod you head gently to give positive nonverbal feedback.
- Restate the speaker's main ideas when you take your turn to speak.
- Ask clarifying questions to better comprehend the message.

- Let go of resentments, issues, and your own agenda.
- Create environments to share feelings.
- Turn off your own internal monologue, refraining from "preparing" your response before the speaker has finished speaking.

Summary

We've examined the concept of perception, how our perspective is personal and how it impacts our communication with others. We've also examined how our self-concept is formed, and the differences between values, beliefs, and attitudes. We've discussed the importance of listening, looked at three kinds of listening, examined the eight stages in the listening process, and identified four key barriers to listening. Improving our communication skills can be challenging, but also rewarding, in terms of new relationships, understanding new concepts, and making sense of our world.

> *To listen well is as powerful a means of communication*
> *and influence as to talk well.*
> —John Marshall

For More Information _____

Perception: **http://www.perceptionweb.com/**

Rosie the Riveter: **http://www.library.csi.cuny.edu/dept/history/lavender/rosie.html**

Academic Survival Tips, provided by Edinboro University of Pennsylvania: **http://www.edinboro.edu/cwis/acaff/suppserv/tips/tipsmenu.html**

For a musical interpretation of personality traits, listen to Robyn Hitchcock's *Uncorrected Personality Traits* (CD), 1997, Rhino Records.

Review Questions _____

1. Factual Questions
   a. What are the three types of listening?
   b. What are the eight stages in the listening process?
   c. What are the four barriers to listening?
2. Interpretative Questions
   a. What is perception and how does it limit/expand our understanding?
   b. How does our self-concept impact our interaction with others?
   c. Do people hold similar values across cultures?
3. Evaluative Questions
   a. Is it really important to always listen? Explain your response.

   b. Can some listening cause harm to the listener? What types of harm? Provide an example.

   c. How do we account for hate speech or abusive language when stating it is important to listen?

4. Application Questions

   a. What do people value? Create a survey, identify a target sample size, conduct your survey, and compare the results.

   b. What laws pertain to the freedom of speech? Are there limitations and in which cases? Investigate the issue and share your findings.

   c. What does the field of psychology say about self-concept? Can you find one example of how self-concept impacts individual behavior? Compare the results.

References

Aidman, A. (1997). *Television violence: Content, context, and consequences.* Washington, DC: Education Resources Information Center (ERIC) at: http://www.ed.gov/databases/ERIC_Digests/ed414078.html

Barker, L. (1971). *Listening behavior.* Englewood Cliffs, NJ: Prentice Hall.

Beebe, S., Beebe, S., & Redmond, M. (2002). *Interpersonal communication: Relating to others* (3rd ed.). Boston: Allyn and Bacon.

Covey, S. (1989). *The seven habits of highly effective people.* New York: Simon & Schuster.

Covino, W., & Joliffe, D. (1995). *Rhetoric.* Boston: Allyn and Bacon.

Eron, L. D. (1992). The impact of televised violence. Testimony on behalf of the American Psychological Association before the Senate Committee on Governmental Affairs. *Congressional Record,* June 18, 1992, p. 1.

Gage, N., & Berliner, D. (1998). *Educational psychology* (6th ed.; p. 151). Boston: Houghton Mifflin.

Galanes, G., Adams, K., & Brilhart, J. (2000*). Communicating in groups: Applications and skills* (4th ed.). Boston: McGraw-Hill.

Gerbner, G., & Gross, L. (1980). The violent face of television and its lessons. In E. L. Palmer & A. D. (Eds.), *Children and the faces of television: Teaching, violence, selling* (pp. 149–162). New York: Academic Press.

Griffin, E. (1997). *A first look at communication theory.* New York: McGraw-Hill.

Hofstede, G. (1980). *Culture's consequences: International differences in work-related values.* Beverly Hills, CA: Sage.

Janis, I. (1982). *Groupthink* (2nd ed.). Boston: Houghton Mifflin.

Klopf, D. (1995). *Intercultural encounters: The fundamentals of intercultural communication.* Englewood, CA: Morton.

Moore, P., & Fitz, C. (1993). Gestalt theory and instructional design. *Journal of Technical Writing and Communication, 23*(2), 137–157.

Pearson, J., & Nelson, P. (2000). *An introduction to human communication: understanding and sharing* (8th ed.; p. 100). Boston: McGraw-Hill.

Taylor, C. (2002, October 7). What spies beneath. *Time,* 106.

Watson, K., Barker, L., & Weaver, J. (1995). *The Listener Style Inventory.* New Orleans, LA: SPECTRA.

Werner, E. (1975). *A study of communication time.* Unpublished master's thesis, University of Maryland.

Wood, J. (1997). *Communication in our lives.* Belmont, CA: Wadsworth.

3

Verbal Communication

Chapter Objectives _____

After completing this chapter, you should be able to:

1. Describe language and its role in perception and the communication process.
2. Identify and describe five key principles of verbal communication.
3. Demonstrate nine ways language can be an obstacle to communication.
4. Describe similarities and difference between nine key barriers to communication.
5. Demonstrate six ways to improve verbal communication.

Introductory Exercise 1 _____

Can you match each word to its meaning?

1.	A capella	____ **A.**	To sing words in nonsense syllables.
2.	Bar	____ **B.**	Choral music sung without instrumental accompaniment.
3.	Old School	____ **C.**	A way of dividing music into small, organized groups of beats.
4.	East Coast	____ **D.**	A slow, sad style of jazz.
5.	Verse	____ **E.**	The hip hop culture, from which rap music sprang.
6.	West Coast	____ **F.**	Making up music as it is being performed.
7.	Scat	____ **G.**	A group of words in a song.
8.	Hip Hop	____ **H.**	Generally more edgy and stripped down rap.
9.	Improvise	____ **I.**	Funk and gangsta imagery rap dominated by drum machines and synthesizer bass lines.
10.	Blues	____ **J.**	Vibe-based rap around sampled breakbeats and hard-edged rhyme styles.

Cover this answer key: 1-B, 2-C, 3-J, 4-H, 5-G, 6-I, 7-A, 8-E, 9-F, 10-D

Introductory Exercise 2 _____

Notice how your friends communicate with one another. Notice how you communicate with teachers or other authority figures. Do you notice specific words that you use with one group but not with another? Record your words and their meanings. Share with a classmate.

> *The meanings of words are not in the words, they are in us.*
> —Hayakawa (1978)

How do you communicate? How do you think? We use language as a system to create and exchange meaning with one another, and the types of words we use influence both our perceptions and others' interpretation of our meanings. What kinds of words to use to describe your thoughts, feelings, preferences in music, or other areas of interest? This chapter discusses the importance of verbal communication and examines how the characteristics of language interact in ways that can both improve and diminish effective communication. We will examine how language plays a significant role in how you perceive and interact with the world, and how culture, language, education, gender, race, and ethnicity all influence this dynamic process. Finally, we will look at ways to improve your awareness of miscommunication and focus on constructive ways to decrease barriers to interpersonal communication.

What Is Language?

Right now you are reading this sentence. Hopefully, it makes sense to you. You are reading by assigning meaning to each individual letter that is part of a specific grouping, called a word, brought together by a set of rules called syntax or grammar. How do you know what each word means? You know the code. The family, group, or society in which you were raised taught you the code, called language. We use this code to communicate via the written word, recording ideas to be read and interpreted. In spoken speech, we also use this code but in often much less formal ways. Does that mean everyone knows our code? Probably not. People are raised in different cultures, with different languages, values, and beliefs. Even people with similar languages, like speakers of English in the United States, Australia, or New Zealand, speak and interact using their own distinct code words. Within the United States, we speak in many distinct ways, with our own terms, and we even speak in several styles depending on the context and environment. This variation in our use of language is the creative way we create and build relationships and communities, but it can also lead to miscommunication.

   The words we exchange every day are directly and indirectly shaped by what we mean them to represent, and the person who receives them may miss our meaning entirely. This can be intentional and unintentional, and we'll look at how intentional manipulation of words and their meanings can be an obstacle to good communication later in this chapter. Languages have borrowed words and ways to organize them forever. Does the word "rodeo" make sense to you? It makes sense to a Spanish speaker as well. English adopted the word to express sporting events that involve horses, riders, and obstacles because there wasn't a word to describe these events. The letters come together to form an arbitrary word that refers to the thought or idea of the thing in the *semantic triangle* (see Figure 3.1).

This triangle illustrates how the combination of five letters refers to the thought, which then refers to the thing or event itself. Who decides that *R O D E O* means the sporting event? Each letter stands for a sound, and when they come together in a specific way, the sounds they represent, when spoken, express the "word" that symbolizes the event. The key word is "symbolizes." The word stands in for the actual event. Words allow us to talk about something that isn't right in front of us. The word stands in place of the event, representing it.

Principles of Verbal Communication

> *Words are just words and without heart they have no meaning.*
> —Chinese proverb

Verbal communication, through language, has certain basic principles. In this section, we'll refer to examples we have discussed previously, highlight the principles of verbal communication, and look forward to how knowledge of these principles can help us improve our communication.

1. Language Has Rules

> *Language is a code, a collection of symbols, letters, or words with arbitrary meanings that are arranged according to the rules of syntax and are used to communicate.*
> —Pearson & Nelson (2000)

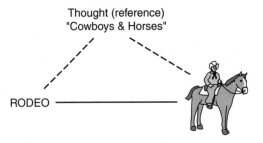

Thought (reference)
"Cowboys & Horses"

RODEO

FIGURE 3.1   *A Semantic Triangle*

Source: Adapted from Ogden & Richards (1932).

In the first exercise, were you able to match the terms to their meanings? Did you think of alternate meanings of the terms, or did you find that the definitions did not match your understanding of the terms? All of the terms are drawn from music. Some of the terms refer to universal principles in music, while others refer to various styles of music. African Americans have made significant contributions in music, but you may not be familiar with each style. Your lack of familiarity may have made the exercise challenging, or your understanding of each style may have enabled you to get a perfect score. The words themselves have meaning within their specific context. Without that context, "bar" may have brought to mind images of a place where alcoholic beverages are served, or "blues" may have been another word for "depression." The words themselves only carry meaning to you if you know the code and have context to interpret them.

There are three types of rules that govern or control our use of words, when we use certain words, and how to interpret these words when used. You probably use

INTERCULTURAL COMMUNICATION 3.1 • *Language and Music*

> *The hip hop culture is just like electricity.*
> *It can be used negatively or positively.*
> —Al Sharpton

Music is a language of expression. Music helps us make sense of our world and communicate that understanding to others. Combining words and rhythm is art in language, and African Americans have long made significant contributions to the musical landscape. Styles like jazz, blues, ska/reggae, hip hop, and rap in all its variations give a voice to groups of people to convey images and meaning in a memorable way. The songs of the Underground Railroad, including spirituals, were often adapted to speak to the experience of slavery and the search for freedom. Many of the working songs of the day would speak of abuse and suffering in ways to share the experience while hiding the real meaning of the songs from foremen and slave owners. From this tradition, blues combined rural roots, a simple acoustic style, and an improvisational form to continue to communicate expressions of experience. Reggae has also evolved from a simple music art form, known as Mento, to a diverse range of Jamaican r&b, ska, rocksteady, dub, and dancehall. Reggae, with its combination of traditional African rhythms, blues, and indigenous Jamaican folk music, and contemporary American rhythms, often speaks to social and political issues. Rap, with its stories of poverty, rape, murder, and cultural poisoning, also speaks to rebellion and perseverance found in traditional folk music. These themes, seen in music ranging from underground songs to blues and reggae, are expressed in new ways relevant to modern youth. The language of this expression contributes to formation of community and cultural identity. Before judging a musical style based on an individual artist or recent scandal, consider the long tradition of African American music and its influence on language in America today.

Sources: Rose (1994); Thomas (2001).

these rules all the time, but may not have given it any thought. Can you think of a word that is OK to use sometimes and not others? How about a word your friends understand, but other people do not?

Syntactic Rules: These are the rules that govern where words come in sentence. In English you would say "a happy person," but in Spanish you would say "una persona contenta."

Semantic Rules: These are the rules that govern the meaning of words and guidelines on how to interpret them. We agree "rodeo" means a sporting event featuring riders, horses, and cattle. If we didn't agree, we would all be making our words mean whatever we want them to when we say them, and communication would be impossible.

Contextual Rules: These are the rules that govern meaning and word choice according to context and social custom. The word "no" can mean many things, whether it is spoken by a judge, an instructor, or a 2-year-old child.

In this section we examined how language has rules and how even though we know the rules, we still may not get the correct meaning. Words represent the ideas we want to communicate, but often require us to negotiate their meaning, creating a common vocabulary.

2. Our Reality Is Shaped by Our Language

Have you ever thought of what it would be like if you were raised in China? or Greece? or Spain? You would have learned a language other than English, and your world would have been different. You would have eaten different foods, celebrated holidays that came from your religion or social customs, and perceived the world through your experiences. The same concept holds true if you were born in the southern United States, or the North, or on the West Coast. If you had born with different color skin, with different racial or ethnic tradition, or into a different socioeconomic class, your experiences and how you expressed your interpretation of those experiences would be distinct. The language you learned from those around helped shape the way you see the world and how you yourself perceive right and wrong and cultural or gender roles, and even how to communicate with one another. This raises the question: To what extent does the language you learned, including the cultural norms and values you learned growing up, determine your reality or the way you see the world?

Thomas Kuhn (1996) makes the point that **paradigms,** or clear points of view involving theories, laws, and/or generalizations that provide a framework for understanding, tend to form and become set around key validity claims, or statements of the way things work. These paradigms later become premises for scientific thought and inquiry. These premises act a lot like assumptions, and sometimes we need to return to our basic assumptions in order to see the paradigm from a new perspective, leading to alternate ways of understanding.

Can you think of an idea you once believed and later looked back and couldn't believe you thought, felt, acted, or dressed that way? Perhaps it was a picture of you with clothes long out of fashion, like the proverbial white polyester suit from the 1970s, that made you look at the picture and think "How could I think that was cool?" This is a shift or change in the way you see yourself in the world, and the way you dress, act, or even think may change when you go back and challenge some assumptions you made along the way. Now think about when people considered the world was flat like a table and if you got to close to the edge, that was it. It took time and effort to change the paradigm, or the way people saw the world. They came to that understanding not through satellite photos that wouldn't exist for centuries but through experience and the discussion of that experience through language. If no one ever thought the world might be anything other than flat, what would you think today?

Two researchers, Benjamin Lee Whorf and Edward Sapir, were among the first to investigate the nature of perception through language and culture. Whorf, employed by the Hartford Fire Insurance Company, found the conflict between science and religion fascinating. He started taking classes at Yale University and studied the Hopi language under the supervision of Edward Sapir. Whorf explored the world of linguistics and formulated what later became known as the Whorf/Sapir hypothesis. By relating culture and actions to language, he formulated the concept that states: "Our perception of reality is determined by our thought processes and our thought processes are limited by language and, therefore, language shapes our reality" (Whorf, 1956). Whorf died young and did not have time to fully support his ideas, but his hypothesis is well supported by most linguists and his writings are the source of continuing debate.

European scholars such as Jacques Derrida (1974) and Michel Foucault (1980), often referred to as "post-modern," take as a basic assumption that language creates reality and extend their application to the deconstruction of ideas, breaking them down to their elemental levels, to increase understanding. Concepts of "difference," "I" versus "you," and the nature of perception are open to question, in many ways examining those basic assumptions, or paradigms, that other philosophers, scholars, and researchers made along the course of human investigation and the search for meaning. Other scholars, like Jean Piaget, whose ideas contributed to our understanding of how people learn, or more currently, Steven Pinker, take the Whorf/Sapir hypothesis to task. There is a list of sources for further investigation at the end of this chapter.

Regardless of the debate over to what degree our reality is influenced by our language, researchers tend to agree that language is a major factor in our understanding of one another and our world. Gloria Anzaldúa highlights this point in her discussion of her experiences on the U.S./Mexican border in *Borderlands,* stating that "I am my language" (1987, p. 59). Anzaldúa uses the discussion on language to speak to cultural and social identity. Some Mexican Americans are ashamed of their nationality, at times represented by their use of the Spanish language, according to Anzaldúa. She was openly punished at school for speaking her first language, and her experience mirrors the experiences of Native Americans in mandatory boarding schools as well as several immigrant groups in the United States. In each case,

English was enforced as a way of imposing social identity and cultural expectations. English is the language that enables Mexican Americans to "fit in" and adopt new cultural norms, but learning it also involves the letting go or denial or their first language and, in the process, their loss of personal and cultural identities. "Until I can take pride in my language, I cannot take pride in myself," states Anzaldúa (1987, p. 59).

This example illustrates the importance of perspective and context. Our experiences become like sunglasses—tinting the way we see the world—or for some, as blinders, like on a horse, that create tunnel vision. To walk a mile in another person's shoes is an expression that asks you to put yourself in another's person's perspective.

Hall (1966) also underscores this point when discussing the importance of context. The situation in which a conversation occurs provides a lot of meaning and understanding for the participants in some cultures. In Japan, for example, the context, such as a business setting, says a great deal about the conversation and the meaning of the words and expressions within that context. In the United States, however, the concept of a workplace or a business meeting is less structured, and the context offers less meaning and understanding. Cultures that value context highly are aptly called **high-context cultures**; those that value context to a lesser degree are called **low-context cultures**. This ability to understand perspective and context is key to good communication, and one we will examine throughout the text.

> *Who is to say that robbing a people of its language is less violent than war?*
> —Ray Gwyn Smith

3. Language Is Arbitrary and Symbolic

Language is symbolic. This means the words stand for concepts and things but are not the things themselves. Words, by themselves, do not have any inherent meaning. We give meaning to them. The arbitrary symbols (letters, numbers, and punctuation marks, for example) stand for sounds and concepts in our experience. One way to think of this concept is to ask yourself: What is the value of a clay pot? The pot may have value to you because you made it or for its beauty, but one main function of the pot is to contain something. Its emptiness is, in effect, its value to you. Words, like that clay pot, are empty until you give them life and meaning by using them. Imagine yourself giving someone else a clay pot. Will he initially know what is inside? He may not be able to see in the shadows, and the meanings you have placed in the pot will have to be brought to the light by you. The person you give the pot to may also be able to reach inside and grasp some of the meaning, but when he brings the contents to the light of his own experience, he may perceive your meaning in new ways you did not plan on. By providing context, and explaining why you are giving him the pot as well as what it means to you, you help bridge the gap of understanding between you.

The letter "S" has a sound associated with it. The letter could just have easily have been reversed, or a different character entirely, when the alphabet was created.

Once it was created, it became a character we refer to as representing a sound or, in combination with other letters, a word that represents and idea or concept. Can you think of where our agreed-upon vocabulary is documented, for us to refer to as we need to clarify meanings or words and phrases?

Once we have an agreed-upon vocabulary, often stored in a dictionary, it is then possible to interpret words and refer to the denotative meaning. The **denotative meaning** is the dictionary meaning, or common meaning, that is generally agreed upon. Does everyone always agree on the meaning of words? Of course not. Take the word "cool," for example. At first it referred to temperature, as seen in a scale from cold to hot, or to describe a color, as in paintings from Picasso's Blue Period.

After World War II, the Beat Generation of the 1950s used the word "cool" to mean "hip" or "fashionable." Mainstream society still used the standard, dictionary meaning and had disdain for the slang meaning. Over time, the beat meaning came to be generally accepted, and now it is in common usage. Once, only a small group of "nontraditional" people used cool to refer to hip, but now aging "boomers" and dot.com CEOs alike use the word without fear of embarrassment. Take a moment and create a list of words that have a variety of meanings.

This example shows how a word can go from its denotative (dictionary) meaning to a **connotative meaning,** one that has meaning to an individual or group, and how that special meaning became common. Connotative meanings can also refer to emotions associated with words, but the association between the word and the emotion is an individual or personal one and not held by larger society.

It is important to note that while the arbitrary and symbolic nature of language is universal, culture plays a significant role in how language is used and interpreted. For example, as noted by *The New York Times* (reprinted in *Reader's Digest,* 2003), the title for the film *There's Something about Mary* proved challenging for many foreign audiences to understand. The movie was renamed several times to adapt to local audiences. In Poland blonde jokes are popular, and the film title became *For the Love of a Blonde*. In France, it was retitled *Mary at All Costs*, and for Thailand it became *My True Love Will Stand All Outrageous Events*. Each time, the title was changed to capture the meaning within the local culture of the audience.

4. Language Is Abstract

Words represent things and ideas in our environment. They simplify otherwise complex concepts. "Horse" can represent the four-legged animal without signifying the group of biological systems, from a system of muscles and bones to a well-developed respiratory system, which combined make a "horse." A "horse" for one person may mean recreation, but for another it may mean the standard form of transportation or power for farm implements. Both of these views look upon the horse as an object, just like a car or a motorcycle, and in some ways deny that the horse is a living animal. If you were raised with horses, you probably came to know their personalities and came to regard them as friends. The relationships you have or had with these horses (or dogs, cats, or other animals) involve interpersonal communication, typically nonverbal interaction. The relationship is real to both you and the horse, and when the relationship ends, the mourning process can be very real. To lose sight of how language itself is abstract is to lose sight of the levels of meaning and interpretation in inherent in language. The horse that is a lifelong friend may still be called a horse, but its meaning to you is quite distinct from that of the tourist driving by observing your horse through their car window and personal experience, only seeing the animal as object.

This ability to simplify concepts makes it easier to communicate, but we sometimes lose the specific meaning of what we are trying to say through abstraction. Take a look at the ladder of abstraction (Figure 3.2). Do you see how, at one level, "horse" can mean a concrete concept, but at another, the concept is abstract and removed from the original "horse"?

We can see how, at the extreme level of abstraction, the horse is like any other living creature. We can also see how, at the base level of Figure 3.2, the concept is most concrete. "Silver," the name given to the horse in the *Lone Ranger* television series, is a specific animal, with specific markings, size, shape, and coloring and a relationship with a classic television hero.

5. Language Organizes and Classifies Reality

Who wears the black cowboy hat? the white one? How do we distinguish between Luke Skywalker and Darth Vader? Our language organizes and classifies our realities in ways we may not normally notice. As we've discussed previously, we select, organize, and interpret information as we communicate. We tend to group words, concepts, shapes, and images, for example, by their physical proximity and/or their similarity to one another. Our ability to organize is handy, but we need to recognize that we impose categories on our world in order to make sense of it. Sometimes our categorizations can become habitual, without thought, or even unjustified. Western culture often reinforces the concept of opposites, such as good and evil, white and black, work and play, and the English language in particular lends itself to this dualism. For example, Robert Moore (1998) notes how the use of black and white polar-

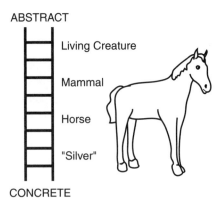

FIGURE 3.2   *Abstraction Ladder*

Source: Adapted from DeVito (1999, p. 119).

izes, or creates two extremes, in our everyday language. He discusses how people may "darken or blacken" your name with bad words or rumor, while others will look on the "bright" (white) side. The reference to black as bad and white as good is woven throughout the English language. The terms that we use to create categories that we then use to frame our experiences can lead us astray.

Have you ever noticed this or any type of classification in language that creates a superior and inferior group? Sometimes this classification is done by physical characteristics such as tall, short, or large, small, to create classifications. Sometimes classification, the organization of individuals into groups, happens on the basis of sex or religion. Can you think of an example when people choose to classify themselves according to a common characteristic? Can you think of an example where someone has imposed a classification on you or a friend without your consent? Organization and classification are natural parts of our daily lives. We relate what we don't know to what we do know, using lessons learned from the past to negotiate new situations. When we fail to question previous lessons learned or assumptions in light of new information or situations, we run the risk of making quick judgments that may not be fair to ourselves or others.

Language as an Obstacle to Communication

Now we have discussed the principles of verbal communication and examined how we use language to make sense of our world. You can probably see how many of the principles of communication can be a double-edged sword, meaning the principles can work both for and against you. Let's look at nine general ways language can be an obstacle to effective communication, and then find ways to turn the negatives into positives, making our communication even more effective.

1. Speech Is Not Like Written Language

Many people write well, but when it comes to speaking, they make all sorts of errors. These errors are often grammatical or involve semantics, the way words are put together, or word choice. Technically speaking, you are not supposed to say "Can I go to the bathroom?" to your teacher because the automatic answer is "I don't know—can you?" This response captures the "are you able to do something" sense of the word rather than the intended meaning, a request for permission. A more correct request would use the word "may." While the technical merit of which word to use may be the subject of debate, the intended meaning is clear. If the receiver/co-communicator focuses on the words, he or she misses, or chooses to miss, the intended meaning, creating an obstacle to communication. This may call to mind one of the basic principles of communication. Look back at Chapter 1 and see if you can make the connection.

In terms of grammar and semantics, sometimes "incorrect" grammar is actually correct within a regional dialect or comes from an adaptation in the language. Take, for example, the case of speech in some African American and Mexican American communities.

INTERCULTURAL COMMUNICATION 3.2 • *Gullah*

There is an island off the coast of South Carolina where a group of families speak a distinct variation of English. It wasn't until a linguist discovered, through a detailed examination of slave records from dealers, that their origins were in Sierra Leone in West Africa. A comparison of the native language of Sierra Leone to the type of English spoken by the Gullahs revealed striking similarities across grammar and syntax, blending African language patterns and words with English. Curiously, the language did not change much because they were left alone. The original Gullahs had a high resistance to malaria, ever present on the island, whereas the slave owners fell victim to the disease.

From Psalm 19:10,11:

The Sea Island (Gullah) Version
Gawd Wodmo sweeta den honey . . .
Wen A do wa E tell me fa do,
Gawd sen me great blessin.

The King James Version of the Bible
God's Words are sweeter than honey . . .
And in keeping of them there is great reward.

Source: Afrika (1990).

2. Slang

Slang is a word that takes the place of a standard or traditional word in order to add an unconventional, nonstandard, humorous, or rebellious effect. Slang words serve to bring us closer together, allowing us to share common meanings and better understand one another. Slang words also serve to divide us into groups of those who "get it" and those who don't.

Let's say you have come to know someone at college from Georgia. You both have come to know one another through a common class and interests. Perhaps you both like the same hobbies, music, or the same clubs. While walking on campus with him, you run into a friend from his same region of Georgia. You may hear "This your shorty? Hey—you been with your old boy? I remember him—he's cool—O.G." At first, you recognize the common words, but the meaning, even the grammar that brings the words together in a specific way, is somehow different. You may also wonder what "old boy" means. "Home boy" is a once slang but now common term for friend, and a variation on this is "old boy" or "old girl," which can refer to someone's mother, grandmother, or even a boyfriend/girlfriend, as in the use of "old lady." "O.G." can be a reference to an "old girl," but can also be a reference to an older member of the community, possibly an older gang member, who has been through a lot and can now share his or her "learning" with others. "Shorty" may also be a word that is unfamiliar, but if you knew it referred to you as a possible girlfriend, would it change your interpretation of the conversation?

Each of these terms is an example of slang, and if you are from certain places or from specific cultural groups, the language you learned may enable you to understand the meaning—making you the insider. If, however, you are from a different region or cultural group, your lack of familiarity with the slang words and their contextual meaning may impact your ability to understand what is being said. We are all familiar to some extent with slang, or words that mean something to us and the people we associate with, but may not be understood by people outside of our group. Being able to talk with "people like us" can often be interpreted to mean people who communicate like I do, where we share common symbols and values, and we use the same language, including slang. We discussed previously the word "cool," and how it transformed from a word among friends to one in everyday conversations across the nation. Other words have taken "cool's" place as slang terms, and as they become known, new words will take their place. Languages and co-languages, like cultures and communities, change and transform over time.

In addition to slang, **regionalisms,** or words and phrases that pertain to a particular area, can also create obstacles to effective communication. "O.G." may mean "old girl" to someone from Georgia, but might also mean an older, respected member of the community to someone from Chicago. As terms get used in the mass media and enter interpersonal conversations, both the person from Georgia and the person from Chicago can come to see multiple meanings of common terms depending on context and individual use.

3. Jargon

Jargon is a profession-specific language used by professionals. You probably speak some sort of jargon when you go to work or are aware of others, in a field that is not your own, speaking in their own language. Familiar television programs often use jargon to create the illusion of authenticity. On television shows based in a healthcare environment, for example, they speak medical-ese, discussing health conditions, procedures, and medications with jargon that makes it look like they know what they are talking about. Every field has its own terms and phrases that refer to specific concepts that group members understand. In the case of the medical professions, a common course offered at community colleges and universities alike is entitled "Medical Terminology." The purpose of the course is to teach the spelling, use, and interpretation of specific terms you will encounter daily in a healthcare environment. If you planned to work in healthcare, but did not take this course or have other relevant experience in the area, you might feel lost while established people in the industry communicate effortlessly.

Jargon can be used to communicate about technical or specific concepts quickly and accurately. It can also be used strategically to separate an outsider from a group, much like slang. It can facilitate effective communication and reduce everyone's errors if everyone understands, but if there is a gap in understanding, miscommunication can result. In the healthcare field, misinterpretation of specific jargon, particularly as it relates to administering medications, can have disastrous results. If you recognize that your current or future work environment features

COMPUTER-MEDIATED COMMUNICATION 3.1 • *Language in Computer-Mediated Communication*

The ability to chat with another person in real-time communication changes the way we use language. Rather than write "by the way," BTW is a common abbreviation. Here are a few "e-breviations":

What I meant was	WIMW	Have you heard	HYH
Face to face	F2F	Ta ta for now	TTFN
In my opinion	IMO	Laughing out loud	LOL

Like any new environment, the problem comes when the outsider doesn't know the meaning of the words the insiders use to communicate.

Real-time computer-mediated communication has also facilitated new types of communication, including process writing, active collaboration, and less logical linear writing. In process writing, the conversation participants engage in a James Joyce-like stream of consciousness, where spelling and grammar mean less than content and insight. In active collaboration, more than one person joins in the stream, and the collaboration can produce new and fascinating results. Finally, because the writing has no introduction, middle, or conclusion, and the point at which each participant joins in and departs varies, the writing loses its linear properties.

Have you ever participated in a chat room where process writing was used? How do you think active collaboration around a loosely formed topic engages the participants in new ways. Do these ways of communication empower people? How do they change the language?

jargon and you do not yet know the terminology, you have a clear goal for what you need to learn. One phrase often heard in business, which speaks to this point, is "Knowledge is power. If you don't share, it's a problem for everyone." Faking attention or pretending to understand can lead to unanticipated and dangerous results. It is better to ask clarifying questions to gain insight into the use and meaning of the terms.

4. Sexist and Racist Language

As we discussed in the section on how language organizes and classifies, language that creates a power position where one group is included or elevated and another group excluded or subordinated can be a serious obstacle to effective communication. Sexist language uses a person's gender identity as the discriminating factor. Racist language reinforces a power hierarchy, promoting a member of one group while degrading a member of another group.

Sexist language can have a corrosive effect on relationships. In the case of Stacey Maher, a former police officer with the City of New York, it made her work environment, a traditionally male-dominated field, hostile and dangerous (Raab,

1998). Maher was singled out on her first day of work with the words "That one, the blonde, is mine." A sergeant announced this in front of other officers and from across the room. Maher later fought off his groping advances, a complaint followed, and a work relationship soured. Sexist terms were used openly to describe Maher, and an internal investigation ensued. While there were many issues over time, the harassment continued and, according to the former head of the task force in which Maher served, he was ordered by his supervisor to give her undesirable work shifts and pressure for her transfer to another borough. "It was retaliation at its worst. And the cover-up was phenomenal," stated Lieutenant Thompson (Raab, 1998, p. 237). While not all sexist terms lead to similar lawsuits and retaliation, the terms divide and discriminate. The use of terms like "policeman" instead of "police officer" carry with them the association of masculinity where it may well not apply. **Gender neutral terms,** or the removing of this association of gender in relation to a job, role, or function, place the emphasis of the word on the task and not on personal characteristics like sex.

A relatively recent case that serves as an accurate example of racism in the work environment involves the events that led to the suit against American Eagle Airlines (McCartney, 1999). In a hangar in Miami occupied by mechanics for the airline, the walls often had to be repainted because of racially charged messages and pictures. On the bulletin boards in the hangar, meant to communicate common issues and information to employees, were cartoons depicting black mechanics as gorillas. A black supervisor found a stuffed gorilla with a noose around its neck and his name on it. Complaints went unheard and the climate became hostile (McCartney, 1999), leading to eventual resolution through a lawsuit. What takes an organization from a productive to a hostile work environment? While a variety of factors are involved, interpersonal communication and the use of racist language, including pictures and symbols, contributed to the change at American Eagle Airlines.

Racist language is part of the tradition of the English language. Obvious racial references, used in a negative sense to create a subordinate group, include "spook," "chink," "spic," and "wetback." Each term creates a classification, grouping people of similar racial and/or ethnic characteristics in a negative context. **Color symbolism,** as Robert Moore (1998) highlights in his essay on "Black" and "White" in the English language, creates a good/bad classification that segregates people.

Classification in language, where "policeman," once used for both male and female police officers, presumes the officer is masculine by default. Language is changing, and the title "police officer" replaces "policeman." It also changes what is interpreted as "in jest," and jokes and depictions once portrayed and tolerated are no longer considered appropriate. Being aware of sexist language can prevent it from becoming an obstacle to shared discussions and effective communication.

By extension, **ethnocentrism** is the viewpoint that one's own culture is the "ruler" by which all other cultures are measured and all fall short. Ethnocentrism creates a context in which the dominant group views itself positively, and other groups are viewed in relation to the dominant group, often negatively. The dominant group becomes the "norm," and other groups are evaluated in terms of their level of conformity. When you hear groups discussed as marginal or on the fringe, you see how, through language, they are viewed as removed or far from the "normal" or majority.

Beyond ethnocentrism, other terms create divisions based on class and privilege. The use of the term "third world" in reference to developing nations presumes a first world, which the third world could become. Development has, by its very nature, good and bad consequences, from the transformation of ecosystems to the change in social structures and interpersonal relationships. The ethnocentric viewpoint that industrial or information age infrastructure is the highpoint of human development is the source of considerable debate.

CASE STUDY 3.1 • *The Tuskegee Syphilis Study*

A joint study between the U.S. Public Health Service (PHS) and the Julius Rosenwald Fund was conducted to consider ways to improve the health of African Americans in the South. The Great Depression hit, and the Rosenwald Fund withdrew its financial support, leaving PHS unable to treat the patients.

Dr. Taliaferro Clark of the PHS suggested that the project could be partially "saved" by conducting a study on the effects of untreated syphilis on living "subjects." His suggestion was approved by PHS and the study continued with the focus on syphilis.

The PHS used the support of the local Tuskegee Institute to enroll participants in the study. At the time, many African Americans had almost no access to medical care. For many people, the examination by the PHS physician combined with the free food and transportation made participation attractive. Even though study participants received medical examinations, none were told that they were infected with syphilis. They were either not treated or were treated at a level that was judged to be insufficient to cure the disease, and PHS officials prevented other agencies from supplying treatment.

In 1943, while the study was ongoing, PHS began to administer penicillin to patients with syphilis as a standard treatment nationwide. Tuskegee study subjects did not receive penicillin treatments and their symptoms were observed and recorded as they got worse.

The study was stopped in 1972 when Peter Buxton, a venereal disease interviewer and investigator for the PHS, told an Associated Press reporter, who wrote a front-page story. Congressional subcommittee meetings were held in early 1973 by Senator Edward Kennedy. These resulted in a complete changes in laws, policies, and code of conduct for researchers, and a class action settlement.

The Tuskegee Syphilis Study stands as an extreme example of the effects of dehumanization of U.S. citizens and violates basic ethical principles established for prisoners of war. Among Heller's remarks were: "The men's status did not warrant ethical debate. They were subjects, not patients; clinical material, not sick people" (p. 179).

Source: Jones (1981).

Finally, words can be used to segregate people from their humanity. When we replace someone's name with a pronoun like he, she, or it, we begin abstracting the idea of that individual person. When we discuss others as *them,* and traits *they* have, we separate ourselves from other people as *us* and *them.* We can further replace their identity with language that confuses rather than clarifies, such as "collateral damage" for civilians killed in wartime. This separation of people from our connection to them or a sense of humanity has contributed to war crimes and tortures and has made some experiments on "subjects" sound almost respectable.

In the Tuskegee syphilis example, people were not referred to as human but as objects or things. The word "subjects" distances the speaker from personal involvement with the people he or she is discussing, viewing them in a more abstract context than a concrete one. The dehumanization of the people in this study led to serious consequences and changed the oversight and guidelines for U.S. research protocols forever.

5. Small Talk

Every day we say things like "How are you?" and respond to a similar question with "Oh fine, and you?" Are we really inquiring about each other's health or state of well-being? Of course not. We're just engaging in small talk, sometimes called "phatic communion" (Malinowski, 1935). In **small talk,** the meanings of the words are not literal, but understood, and the emphasis in the communication is on the interaction, not necessarily the content or information. It's a social custom, where we acknowledge each other's presence. To someone raised outside of Western culture, this may seem strange, but most cultures have similar rituals for greeting that focus on the context rather than literal meaning that people can relate to.

This concept takes on particular importance in interpersonal communication. Each person approaches a conversation from his or her own frame of reference, including language and culture. If you were to communicate with someone from Mexico regarding a business deal, the small talk at the beginning of the meeting is quite important. Questions will range from family to children, but will generally avoid "getting down to business" right away. This small talk lays an important foundation of trust and follows certain cultural expectations. These expectations can come into conflict and lead to misunderstanding when misunderstood. If the North American provides short answers to the small talk and pressures the Mexican to "get to the point" or "down to business" right away, an important opportunity for building trust may be lost. The interpersonal interactions may become awkward and an important relationship can be jeopardized. In most communication we naturally move from superficial to more personal levels, and this form of small talk plays an important role. When you decide to travel abroad or even engage in conversation with the international student you met in class, consider that there may be different expectations in terms of small talk.

Colloquialisms are like small talk in that words and phrases are used in social contexts as part of a ritual. When someone says "Have a nice day," she is often not communicating her genuine wish that you indeed have a pleasant day, but instead using the phrase to signal the close of a conversation or exchange of information.

COMPUTER-MEDIATED COMMUNICATION 3.2 • *Technical Jargon*

Computers are everywhere today, but do you speak their language? Please match the terms with their definitions:

1.	Biotech	**A.**	Rethinking or starting a project over
2.	Nanotechnology	**B.**	Reconnaissance drones with military applications
3.	Nano	**C.**	The integration of biology and technology
4.	Drill down	**D.**	The technology of building at the atomic level
5.	Bandwidth	**E.**	To contact someone, typically via instant messenger
6.	Ping	**F.**	Identifying an individual by a unique physical characteristic (eye, iris)
7.	Assistive tech	**G.**	One-billionth of a specific unit
8.	Biometrics	**H.**	The amount of time you devote to a task
9.	Reset button	**I.**	To complete a tedious or challenging task
10.	Scalable	**J.**	The number of people a place or event can hold
11.	Value added	**K.**	Using artifical intelligence in devices to assist elderly or disabled
12.	Unmanned craft	**L.**	A side benefit

Cover this answer key:

1-C, 2-D, 3-G, 4-I, 5-H, 6-E, 7-K, 8-F, 9-A, 10-J, 11-L, 12-B.

6. Clichés

You may have heard the phrase "The squeaky wheel gets the grease." What does it mean? That people who take the initiative get the reward or attention? Yes, but does the idea carry much weight or power? Probably not. Why? To answer the question, ask yourself—Do you know anyone who uses a phrase or word repeatedly? Does the frequent use of the word or phrase make it more powerful and impacting? For most people, words and phrases that are frequently used lose their originality and effectiveness, making the listener tune them out or ignore them. A **cliché** is a phrase that, through overuse, has lost its impact. Can you think of an example? Try a search on www.google.com for "cliché" and see what you find. There are thousands of sayings that use a metaphor to mean a specific idea, but that have lost much of their meaning or impact through overuse and abuse. As a general guideline, clichés, while often instantly recognizable, are often ineffective in communicating your idea with its intended impact or meaning. You may refer to them, but also consider how you can best communicate your thoughts and ideas effectively without clichés.

7. Profanity

Words that offend can create obstacles to effective communication, and when they are abusive or vulgar, they are called **profanity.** In Latin "pro" means *before* or *outside,* and "fanum" means *temple,* which became "profane," or profanity as it is commonly known.

Profane refers to "outside the temple," implying a sacred space and a place outside of that sacredness. In modern day, certain words are considered outside the boundary of good, civil taste for normal or professional conversation, and are therefore considered profane. Use of words that could be potentially offensive to the receiver can create an obstacle to clear communication, as well as a hostile climate where listening breaks down.

One general guideline in interpersonal communication is that when you really want to communicate something, a profane term will probably be an ineffective choice. For example, if you try to have a conversation about a point of conflict, the use of a profane term can change the climate of the conversation and negatively impact listening and sharing. Terms can be taken personally, your partner may reciprocate with a few choice words of his own, and the conversation can take a turn for the worst. When you want to fight fair, refrain from using profanity.

Also consider your choice of words when communicating with people who are unlike you culturally, linguistically, or even in terms of age. If someone comes from a different culture or has a language other than English as their first language, profanity may not communicate what you intended. In intergenerational communication, where the conversation participants are of different ages, speech may reflect socialization and learned expectations in the use of language. Profanity has not always been used openly, and people not accustomed to your words may take offense. In the work environment, where intergenerational communication is often an aspect of interpersonal communication, this concept is particularly true. Just as you would dress well for a job interview, consider how your speech reflects you as you interact with others.

8. Euphemisms

When you go to a funeral, do people say the person has died or passed away? When someone needs to eliminate personal waste, does he say he has to urinate or that he has to go to the bathroom? In each case, the second option is more socially acceptable than the first. People often prefer to refer to something perceived as unpleasant by using a euphemism. A **euphemism** substitutes a more polite term or phrase for one that is blunt or insensitive. When talking with someone about a sensitive issue, euphemisms can help you refer to the sensitive points without being abrupt or even insensitive. They can also be misunderstood. When using euphemisms to allude to issues, make sure your communication is effective while communicating your sensitivity through your choice of words.

9. Doublespeak

Doublespeak is an extension of the concept of a euphemism, but implies the intentional misleading of the listener. **Doublespeak** is language that is intentionally ambiguous or misleading. By saying "downsizing," the listener is not asked to contemplate the workers who are losing their jobs. By saying "collateral damage," the listener is not asked to contemplate the civilians who were killed alongside soldiers. Sometimes we use words to communicate an unpleasant idea in a more socially acceptable way, but doublespeak involves an intentional abstraction from a concrete reality that the speaker does not want the listener to think about. Books such as *1984,* by George Orwell, and *Fahrenheit 451,* by Ray Bradbury, both address this intentional manipulation and control of language to create an inaccurate sense of reality.

When you read an article like "Big Brother Is Back" (Barry, 2002) in *Newsweek* that states the government will engage in "super data mining," to prevent domestic and foreign terrorism, your first thought might be that national security is a worthy goal and the events of September 11th should never be repeated. If you consider, however, this phrase also means that the government will also be able to legally monitor your computer, your use of the Internet including websites visited and degree of frequency, and your purchases, media rentals, and other related personal activities, you may then consider the issue of privacy. At first glance doublespeak can may make an issue sound straightforward, but by taking a closer look at the meaning and its consequences, you are better able to grasp the impact of a policy decision or action on your own life.

You can observe how each of these nine obstacles to communication can create walls rather than bridges. If you are aware of each obstacle, you can successfully negotiate the conversation away from words and phrases that will distract the listener to a negative point, and focus instead on using clear, concrete terms that further mutual understanding.

Barriers to Interpersonal Communication

William Seiler and Melissa Beall (2000), in the book entitled *Communication: Making Connections,* note three key barriers to communication that combine elements of the obstacles we have discussed, but also offer unique insight to habits that act as barriers to effective communication. We'll also discuss additional barriers and how they can negatively impact interpersonal communication.

1. Bypassing

Bypassing happens when "what is meant by a speaker and what is heard and understood by the listener are often different" (Seiler & Beall, 2000, p. 93). Simply stated, bypassing is a misunderstanding that occurs when two people use the same word or term to mean two different things. They each interpret the word or term in their own way, and a miscommunication is the result.

Let's say you get asked out to dinner and will go to a party and meet their friends after the dinner. You agree to meet at the restaurant at 7:00 P.M. and your friend arrives on time. Dinner goes well and when it is time to pay the bill, your friend calculates your half and says "A $20 should cover it and your share of the tip." You may be annoyed because he asked you out and you thought that meant he would be responsible for the bill. Then you go to the party and find everyone is quite drunk, the music is loud, and that this type of party was not what you expected. Your friend doesn't see a problem and says "I said we'd go to a party." While you may not have expected a group of people playing games like Scrabble® or Twister®, you also may not have thought of the party as a wild environment where getting to know friends was next to impossible.

Here we have two examples of bypassing. You interpreted getting asked out as meaning you would be treated to dinner. Your understanding of getting asked out to dinner and your friend's interpretation were quite different. You both interpreted the meaning of "party" in different ways. What was said and what was heard were two different things. Has that ever happened to you?

2. Indiscrimination

Indiscrimination occurs when we emphasize or focus on similarities, but neglect or fail to acknowledge differences, considering all things similar essentially the same (Seiler & Beall, 2000). When we ignore differences, and lump things together, we fail to discriminate and discern key differences. The tendency to make untrue and unqualified statements in general is also called **allness** (Beebe, Beebe, & Redmond, 2002).

Let's say you decide it is time to replace your old car or pickup that requires frequent repair for a new one. You may ask your friends what they think and no doubt you'll hear Ford® stands for "Found on the Road Dead" or that Chevy® makes disposable cars. These unqualified generalizations indicate that all cars made by these manufacturers are not good. These statements are not true because they lack any support and group all cars and trucks together, regardless of where or how they were made. Applying this concept people can be achieved by simply completing these statements:

Tall people are _____.

Short people are _____.

Fat people are _____.

Thin people are _____.

Any of the statements you use to complete the sentence cannot be true for all people based on one single characteristic, and they can be considered indiscriminate statements.

There can be times when ignoring individual characteristics, differences, or qualities can be harmful, and even dangerous. Consider how people talk about one another. Do people ever make generalized statements about people based on race, ethnicity, language, or culture? These statements can lead to discrimination, or prejudicial actions based on perceptions of difference.

Racial profiling is the marking of a person based on his or her race or ethnicity within a specific context as suspect. For example, driving a Porsche® in a nice neighborhood and being African American or Hispanic may label you as a potential suspect if you are racially profiled. While studies may show that some crimes in certain communities may feature certain ethnic or racial groups with a certain degree of frequency, by targeting all members of these racial or ethnic groups, indiscrimination occurs. When a police officer pulls a driver over because he or she failed to signal a turn, did the officer notice the infraction because of the violation? Or was the car "marked" by the police officers because of the driver's individual character-istics, making the infraction an opportunity to learn more about the situation and see whether the vehicle is stolen? This is a complex issue that involves the effects of indiscrimination.

3. Polarization

The concept of **polarization** is the tendency to view issues, ideas, and the world around us in extremes. She is rich; he is poor. He is thin; she is fat. I am right; you are wrong. This view of the situation in absolute terms leaves little room for in-creased understanding and leads to conflict and debate. We do this naturally to save the mental effort of having to evaluate every little thing during the course of the day. For example, "We like our laundry detergent. The same manufacturer has a new product. Oh, it must be good." Or if you have to decide between two products, "Oh, I know this brand. I'll choose it." Or finally, another mental shortcut: "If it costs more, it must be better." All of these strategies can help us make decisions, but with-out reevaluation periodically, we may fall into habits that have no basis or our as-sumptions may be old and outdated.

The phrase "I am right and you are wrong" features polarization where, rather than being open to another's point of view or considering new evidence to support the other person's opinion, you stay with your "I'm right" attitude. This is called the **pendulum effect,** where like a pendulum in a grandfather clock, you perceive things in extreme terms. By using terms that polarize the conversation—such as "You never take out the garbage"—the conversation is negatively impacted. When trying to discuss a point or issue with someone, focus on specific actions and maintain a perspective where you can see both sides. Aristotle said the mark of an educated person was his or her ability to see, and be able to argue for, both sides of an issue. Now let's examine additional barriers to effective interpersonal communi-cation.

Exercise _____

Can you think of three examples from your own experiences where bypassing, indiscrimina-tion, or polarization led to miscommunication? Discuss with a classmate or friend and com-pare notes.

4. Limited Frame of Reference

Think of the pictures that hang on your wall. Do any have frames? The frames serve the purpose of presenting the picture or painting in a specific way, but they also limit your view of the picture. By using a software program like Adobe Photoshop® you can focus on specific people or objects in a picture and delete others. This action selectively focuses the attention on certain aspects of the original picture and ig-nores or eliminates other aspects. Our own understanding of the world, as we discussed in the perception and listening chapter, involves this same act of framing, where we focus on certain elements or actions in our world and ignore others. If you have not had a specific experience or lack the language to express your interpretation, your view may be limited. This viewpoint is your frame of reference and understanding. Understanding is shaped by the communication climate you were raised in, the specific context and setting of the communication interaction, your own background, experiences, knowledge, and even moods, as well as your values, beliefs, and your culture or co-cultures.

We all have limited frames of reference in many areas, and when we communicate with one another, this limitation can impact our ability to communicate effectively. If you go home with a friend on Christmas break and his family celebrates in ways you were not raised with, your lack of familiarity may influence your perception and communication. One age-old way to address this barrier is to become "other-oriented," or to try to walk in another's shoes for a day. By trying to focus on not only the words but why they are said, you gain insight into new experiences and expand your own frame of reference.

5. Lack of Language Skills

As we've discussed previously, language both enables us to communicate with one another and also shapes our perceptions. If you are a patient in the emergency room, you may experience a degree of anxiety simply because you do not understand all the terminology used between the healthcare professionals. You may also experience a degree of anxiety if you are with friends who communicate in a way that you are not familiar with, or if you lack the knowledge of their slang words. Children and even adults sometimes find expressing themselves to be challenge, and often indicate they can't find the words. This lack of language skills may mean that people communicate in nonverbal ways, including fighting, to communicate their feelings. By expanding your language skills and learning how to express yourself, you can reduce anxiety and improve relationships. Art therapy is often used with children and battered women who have experienced trauma and lack the language skills to express their feelings and emotions, allowing them to communicate more effectively.

6. Lack of Listening Skills

Listening skill development is critical to maintaining positive interpersonal relationships. As we discussed in the listening section of this text, there are several associated barriers—including a lack of interest, disliking the speaker and missing the message, focusing on details and losing perspective of the overall issue, and faking attention. By improving your listening skills, you can improve your relationships.

7. Emotional Interference

Emotional interference refers to the thoughts, feelings, or ideas that arise when presented with a stimuli that can distract the listener from the message. In the first chapter we examined interference and noted that **psychological noise** is a relevant issue in the communication model. Most distractions come in through our senses of sight, sound, taste, touch, and smell, stimulating a response from us. In many ways the **physical barriers** are the easiest to eliminate. If the noise outside the room or the smell of popcorn from down the hall is distracting, you can simply get up and leave that environment. You may find, however, that your thoughts wander while listening because of your own beliefs, values, or personal experiences. While in conversation with a friend, he or she may refer to an idea that you don't believe in, or say something that makes you recall an unpleasant experience. The emotional interference that arises can impact your listening skills. The first step to improving your listening skills in this area is to acknowledge your own emotional response. Then try several strategies to communicate your response—and don't dwell on your emotions—including writing down your thoughts to either share with the person at a later time or possibly making time for you and the friend to talk the issue out. It is important to express your thoughts and feelings, but it is also important to recognize that your own thoughts and feelings can inhibit your listening skills.

8. Fear of Reprisal for Honest Communication

Fear is a powerful emotion and one of our most basic emotional responses learned early in life. It features a physical response—an increase in pulse, breathing rate, and even sweating—and an emotional one, including emotional interference. If you fear that you will be hurt if you communicate your thoughts and feelings, then you cannot communicate openly and effectively. Trust is the foundation of all communication interactions and requires sharing and mutual understanding. Building trust into a relationship is important and, as we've discussed previously, is earned over time. We move naturally from superficial to personal levels as we come to know one another, and by self-disclosing too quickly and failing to allow trust to develop over time, we risk rejection. The fear of rejection is a powerful force in relationships, and there are no easy answers. Consider if the fear of reprisal or rejection is from past experience and whether it applies to your current context. By making time for one another, and placing an emphasis early in the relationship on the value of honesty, you can build trust and reach a point where you can discuss personal issues.

9. Self-Interest

If you approach communication with others strictly from the perspective of how relationships will meet your needs, you are viewing others as simply objects. This view is essentially **narcissistic,** or characterized by self-love that becomes the over-riding emphasis and motivation in your view of the world. While everyone is concerned to a degree with himself or herself, if your communication is limited to self-interest, your relationships will suffer. In order to effectively communicate in interpersonal relationships, we need to consider other's motivations, the context, and not only what it is said but why it is said. By becoming other-oriented, we can gain understanding into what others are trying to communicate to us, and we may gain new insight into ourselves and the world around us. We will also gain an understanding of others needs and be able to develop mutually satisfying relationships.

Principles of Emotional Communication

Emotions are a psychological and physical reaction, such as fear or anger, to stimuli that we experience as a feeling. Our feelings or emotions directly impact our own point of view and readiness to communicate, but also influence how, why, and when we say things. Emotions directly impact verbal communication. They not only influence how you say what you say, but also how you hear and what you hear. At times, it can seem like emotions are challenging to control. DeVito (1999) describes five key principles to acknowledge the role emotions play in communication and offers guidelines for their expression.

1. Emotions Are Universal

Emotions are a part of every conversation or interaction that we have. Whether you experience them while communicating with yourself or with others, they influence how you communicate. By recognizing that emotions are a component in all communication interactions, we can place emphasis on understanding both the content of the message and the emotions that influence how, why, and when the content is communicated. The context, which includes your psychological state of mind, is one of the eight basic components of communication. Expression of emotions is important, but requires tact, timing, and trust. If you find you are upset and may be less than diplomatic, the timing is simply not right. If you are unsure about the level of trust, then consider whether you can effectively communicate your emotions at that time. By considering these three "Ts," you can help yourself express your emotions more effectively.

2. Emotional Feelings and Emotional Expression Are Not the Same

Experiencing feelings and actually letting someone know you are experiencing them are two different things. We experience feeling in terms of our psychological state, or state of mind, and in terms of our physiological state, or state of our body. If we experience anxiety and apprehension before a test, we may have thoughts that correspond to our nervousness. We may also have an increase in our pulse, respiration (breathing) rate, and even sweat more. Our expression of our feelings by our body signs influences our nonverbal communication, but we can complement, repeat, replace, mask, or even contradict our verbal messages. Remember that we can't tell with any degree of accuracy what other people are feeling simply through observation, and neither can they tell what we are feeling. We need to ask clarifying questions to improve understanding.

3. Emotions Are Communicated Verbally and Nonverbally

You communicate emotions through your choice of words, but also by how you say those words. The words themselves communicate part of your message, but the nonverbal cues, including inflection, timing, space, and paralanguage can modify or contradict your spoken message. Be aware that emotions are expressed both verbally and nonverbally, and pay attention to how verbal and nonverbal messages reinforce and complement each other.

4. Emotional Expression Can Be Good and Bad

The expression of emotions can be a healthy activity for a relationship and build trust. This expression can also break down trust if it is combined with judgment. We're all different, and we all experience emotions, but how we express our emotions to ourselves and others can have a significant impact on our relationships. Expressing frustrations may help a partner or friend realize your point of view and see things as he or she has never seen them before. Expressing frustrations, combined with blaming, can generate defensiveness and decrease effective listening. When you're expressing yourself, consider the other person's point of view, be specific about your concern, and focus on your message that the relationship is important to you.

5. Emotions Are Often Contagious

Have you ever felt that being around certain people made your feel better, while hanging out with others brought you down? When we interact with each other, some of our emotions can be considered contagious. If your friends decide to celebrate, you may get caught up in the energy of their enthusiasm. Joiner (1994) noted that when one college roommate was depressed, it took less than three weeks to spread to the other roommate. It is important to recognize that we influence each other with our emotions, positively and negatively.

Improving Verbal Communication

> *Good communication is as stimulating as black*
> *coffee and just as hard to sleep after.*
> —Anne Morrow Lindbergh

Now let's take a look at five ways we can use our knowledge of the obstacles to communication to improve it.

1. Actively listen to the speaker. This means when someone is speaking to you, listen to what he or she is saying and how it is said. Don't listen to yourself thinking about your response to what's being said.

2. Check your understanding. "Did you mean _____ by saying this _____?" "What I heard you say was you are concerned about _____, " or "What do you mean by _____?" are all phrases that check meaning. You may think you "got it" the first time, but by checking your understanding of what's been said, you reduce the possibility of miscommunication.

3. Define your terms. "By this, I mean _____." Make sure the person or persons you are speaking to understand your meaning of a word before you use it. We all may understand the denotative (dictionary) meaning of the word, but the connotative meaning varies. It is better to clarify terms up front than to define and redefine terms later.

4. Use concrete words. "Silver" is a horse, but he was a specific horse within a specific context. "Black Beauty" is also a specific horse, but the context is different. If you have not watched *The Lone Ranger* television program or read Anna Sewall's book *Black Beauty* (or seen the movie), the use of concrete words about each horse can give meaning and understanding to your discussion of horses in general. You or your audience may not be familiar with "Silver" or "Black Beauty," so discussion in detail with concrete terms will improve everyone's understanding of your examples.

5. Know the difference between objectivity and subjectivity. Objectivity is "just the facts," documenting just what is observed. Subjectivity is recording not only the facts, but also your interpretation of the facts. For example, let's say you are involved in a car accident. The law enforcement officer will listen to both drivers and write down what each person states as objectively as possible. This is called a statement. Then the officer will compare the driver's stories to the visible signs of the accident, the damage, the tire marks, and interview witnesses to the accident. All of this information, collected and recorded as objectively as possible, helps the officer make a fair report of who is at fault in the accident, what contributing factors if any were present. This report will be an important part of the insurance claim process.

You would expect that the officer would hear both drivers out fairly and equally. You would hope that difference in the style, make, and model of your car would not influence perceptions. If you were driving an expensive car while the other car was built in 1974 and is three shades of rust, you would hope that the officer would not assume you could afford to pay for the accident when considering your degree of fault. Being objective is difficult, but critical thinking requires the ability to stand back and look at all the details before making an assessment or decision.

As we saw in the discussion on language and how it influences our perception of reality, it is challenging to be objective. At the same time, recognizing that objectivity is a goal and not a state easily achieved lends itself to the critical evaluation of information and its source. If conclusions are already provided in the discussion of information, who made these conclusions and why? Were they right? Did they have all the facts? Would I make the same decision? All of these questions apply as ways we can improve communication through critical thinking and examining what is said and heard for misunderstandings and errors. Jumping to the wrong conclusion leads you down the wrong path, but the well-placed question and the information it elicits may steer you down the right one.

Summary

In this chapter we have examined how language influences our perception of the world and the verbal principles of communication. Building on each of these principles, we examined nine obstacles to effective communication, nine barriers to interpersonal communication, the principles of emotional communication, and discussed six ways to improve communication. Throughout the chapter we have visited examples and stories that highlight the importance of verbal communication. To end the chapter we need to remember how language can be used to enlighten or deceive, encourage or discourage, empower or destroy. Recognizing the power of verbal communication is the first step to understanding its role and impact on the communication process.

For More Information

On B. L. Whorf, visit: **http://grail.cba.csuohio.edu/~somos/whorf.html**

On J. Piaget, visit: **http://www.piaget.org/**

Steven Pinker's books on the subject include: *Language Learnability and Language Development, How the Mind Works,* and *The Language Instinct*

Review Questions

1. Factual Questions
    a. What is language?
    b. What are the principles of communication?
    c. How can language be an obstacle to effective communication?
    d. What is one way language can be used to improve communication?

2. Interpretative Questions
    a. From your viewpoint, how do you think that thought influences the use of language?
    b. What causes emotional interference?
    c. What is meant by *conditioned* in the phrase "people in Western cultures do not realize the extent to which their racial attitudes have been conditioned since early childhood by the power of words to ennoble or condemn, augment or detract, glorify or demean" (Moore, 1998)?

3. Evaluative Questions
    a. To what extent does language help us communicate?
    b. To what extent does verbal communication limit communication?
    c. Who controls or regulates verbal communication?

4. Application Questions
    a. How does language change over time? Interview someone older than you and someone younger than you, then identify words that have changed.
    b. How does language affect self-concept? Explore and research your answer, finding examples which serve can as case studies.
    c. Can people readily identify the barriers to communication? Survey ten individuals and see if they accurately identify at least one barrier, even if they use a different term or word.

References

Afrika, L. O. (1990). *The Gullah.* Beaufort, SC: Llaila Oela Afrika.

Anzaldúa, G. (1987). *Borderlands/La frontera* (p. 59). San Francisco: Aunt Lute Books.

Barry, J. (2002). Big Brother is back. *Newsweek,* December 2, p. 33.

Beebe, S., Beebe, S., & Redmond, M. (2002). *Interpersonal communication: Relating to others* (3rd ed.). Boston: Allyn and Bacon.

Derrida, J. (1974). *Of grammatology* (G. Spivak, Translator). Baltimore, MD: Johns Hopkins Press.

DeVito, J. (1999). *Messages: Building interpersonal communiation skills* (4th ed.; pp. 119, 193–194). New York: Addison, Wesley, Longman.

Foucault, M. (1980). *Power/knowledge: Selected interviews and other writings: 1972/1977* (C. Gordon, Ed.). Brighton, UK: Harvester.

Hall, E. (1966). *The hidden dimension.* New York: Doubleday.

Hayakawa, S. I. (1978). *Language in thought and action.* Orlando, FL: Harcourt Brace Jovanovich.

Joiner, T. (1994). Contagious depression: Existence, specificity to depressed symptoms, and the role or reassurance seeking. *Journal of Personality and Social Psychology, 67,* 287–296.

Jones, J. (1981). *Bad blood: The Tuskegee syphilis experiment: A tragedy of race and medicine.* New York: The Free Press.

Kuhn, T. (1996). *The structure of scientific revolutions* (3rd ed.). Chicago: University of Chicago Press.

Malinowski, B. (1935). *The language and magic of gardening.* London: Allen & Unwin.

McCartney, S. (1999). What some call racist at American Eagle, others say was in jest. In P. S. Rothenberg (Ed.), *Race, class and gender in the United States* (2001) (5th ed.; pp. 223–232). New York: Worth Publishers.

Moore, R. (1998). Racism in the English language. In P. S. Rothenburg (Ed.), *Race, class, and gender in the United States* (4th ed.; pp. 465–466). New York: St. Martin's Press.

Ogden, C., & Richards, I. (1932). *The meaning of meaning: A study of the influence of language upon thought and of the science of symbolism.* New York: Harcourt Brace and World.

Pearson, J., & Nelson, P. (2000). *An introduction to human communication: Understanding and sharing* (8th ed.; p. 54). Boston: McGraw-Hill.

Raab, S. (1998). Lawsuits depict a police culture of sexual harrassment and cover-ups. In P. S. Rothenberg (Ed.), *Race, class and gender in the United States* (2001) (5th ed.; pp. 234–238). New York: Worth Publishers.

Reader's Digest. (2003, August). Lost in the translation, p. 121.

Rose, T. (1994). *Black noise: Rap music and black culture in contemporary America.* Middletown, CT: Wesleyan University Press.

Seiler, W., & Beall, M. (2000). *Communication: Making connections* (4th ed.). Boston: Allyn and Bacon.

Thomas, V. (2001). *No man can hinder me: The journey from slavery to emancipation through song.* New York: Crown Publishers.

Whorf, B. L. (1956). Science and lingusitics. In J. B. Carroll (Ed.), *Language, thought, and reality* (pp. 207–219). Cambridge, MA: MIT Press.

4

Nonverbal Communication

Chapter Objectives _____

After completing this chapter, you should be able to:

1. Demonstrate nonverbal communication and describe its role in the communication process.
2. Describe similarities and differences between six principles of nonverbal communication.
3. Identify and describe eight types of nonverbal communication.
4. Demonstrate three ways to improve nonverbal communication.

Introductory Exercise 1 _____

Play "What's Going On?"

In this exercise, the class should be randomly divided into four groups. One group will be taken from the class and presented with a script or scenario, where each of the characters play an active role but no sound is allowed. When the acting group re-enters and performs its nonverbal scenario or scene, the remaining three groups should record the major plot points (who does what to whom, when, why, and how is it resolved).

Observers: Record how you can tell what's going on. Record what you think of each character, and why you think that. Describe the relationships between the characters and note how you arrived at your conclusions. Compare with another student (watch the same program but keep separate notes, for example) and notice any patterns. Consider how much of your results came from what you saw and how much came your own background and interpretation.

Introductory Exercise 2 _____

Play with Space and Signs

Have you ever felt uncomfortable because someone has "invaded" your space? Or felt awkward because someone was "just too close"? Sometime we don't even notice how important space is to communication, and it produces some interesting results. Sometimes signs or nonverbal signals have different meanings in different places. As an objective observer, pick three friends or relatives and make a conscious effort to notice how far apart they stand from people they talk. Record the results (approximations are fine, and you don't have to tell people you are watching them to observe space). Are there differences in male/female conversations? Are there differences in same sex conversations? Are there generational (age) differences. Complete a survey with the people you watched, asking them to give one guideline or rule for nonverbal conduct if you were to go to their hometown for the first time. For example, you could ask about how people greet one another where they come from. Discuss your results with another student and see if together you can see any patterns.

If you enjoyed the second exercise, repeat the process, this time focusing on touching in conversation, how often and where people touch each other while in conversation.

> *Communication is something so simple and difficult*
> *that we can never put it in simple words.*
> —T. S. Matthews

What Is Nonverbal Communication?

In order to arrive at a definition, let's first examine what happened in the first exercise. Did you understand the program? Could you figure out how the characters were related? Could you tell who liked and disliked each other? How? You couldn't hear a word they said. "Body language," or more technically "nonverbal communication," was the key to your understanding.

You are already aware to some extent of how we communicate our thoughts, hopes, ideas, and feeling in ways other than words. People cry in pain and cry for joy. They hold both arms up in victory after winning a sporting event. We can tell what they are communicating through their nonverbal communication. So, like the term itself implies, **nonverbal communication** is communication that is not verbal. This may sound simple, but let's examine the principles of nonverbal communication and discover how complex it can be.

Principles of Nonverbal Communication

1. Nonverbal Communication Is Fluid

The first principle of nonverbal communication involves the nature of its process. In English class we can focus on nouns, verbs, or adjectives and how they come together to create meaning. If we don't like a particular order or word choice, we simply hit "delete" and start over. In conversation we lack the useful "delete" button and have a hard time distinguishing where one nonverbal act begins and another ends. This process, where one nonverbal act flows almost seamlessly into the next, is a challenge to interpret.

Nonverbal communication keeps moving and is never the same twice. It is irreversible. In verbal communication, once something is said, it is out there, and you can't take it back. With nonverbal communication, the same concept holds true. Once something is expressed, with a smile or frown, a shrug of the shoulder or a cold shoulder, you can't take it back. Nonverbal communication is fluid in the sense that it is always occurring. If someone drives in front of you suddenly, your surprise and frustration is communicated through your facial gestures, by how tightly you grip the steering wheel, and in the tenseness of your jaw. The passenger can observe your cues and guess that you are stressed.

In conversation, nonverbal communication is continuous in the sense that it is always occurring, and because it is so fluid, it can be hard to determine where one nonverbal message starts and another stops. Words can be easily identified and isolated, but if we try to single out a gesture, smile, or stance without looking at how they all come together in context, we may miss the point and draw the wrong conclusion.

2. Nonverbal Communication Is Fast

As in the driving example, nonverbal communication gives away our feelings before we even complete the thought or speak a word. Wrinkled eyebrows or wide eyes, white knuckles, or posture all communicate our feelings at that moment. This makes catching signals that are expressed through body language difficult, but we do it every day.

In conversation, we often look each other in the eye for a time to express interest and maintain contact, but we usually don't stare at one another. If someone looks away, over your shoulder, or looks away with increasing frequency, what does that mean to you? But what if the other person looks at you with a "glassy-eyed" stare or a "bright-eyed" gaze, hardly ever looking away? All these types of eye contact communicate interest in communicating with you, and while interpretation requires context, we can observe these fast nonverbal displays and learn from them. We can also note that people are often unaware of their nonverbal signals, and their quick responses often express their initial reactions. When asking someone out on a date, if that person looks down and away and shies away from eye contact, you might interpret that he or she is not interested but nonetheless unsure of how to communicate that to you. Nonverbal communication contributes to the message, and intentionally or unintentionally, it can happen quickly. We have to be alert to nonverbal communication to get the whole message.

3. Nonverbal Communication Can Add to or Replace Verbal Communication

You have no doubt heard the phrase "actions speak louder than words," and in conversation this is particularly true. We communicate all the time, every day through our body motions and nonverbal cues. We communicate nonverbally far more than we engage in verbal communication, and we often use it to add to or actually replace verbal communication. If we want to add emphasis to what we're saying, adding nonverbal communication to reinforce out point, we use a nonverbal gesture called an **illustrator** to communicate our message effectively. This can be as simple as a nod accompanied by a smile and the word "yes" in response to asking someone out. We may also use a nonverbal gesture called an **emblem** when we signal "OK" with the OK sign after the other person has indicated comprehension of where to meet.

In addition to illustrators or emblematic nonverbal communication, we also use regulators, affect displays, and adaptors to communicate our messages nonverbally. **Regulators** are nonverbal messages that control, maintain, or discourage interaction. Let's say you are in conversation with your date at a club and the music is so loud you can't hear each other. If you nod your head in agreement on important points and maintain good eye contact, you are encouraging your partner to continue speaking. If he or she asks you a personal question you're not ready for, you may also look at your feet or the floor and indicate an unwillingness to respond. **Affect displays** are nonverbal communication that express emotions or feelings. Raising your arms toward the person as you move toward the dance floor may indicate your interest in dancing. Your arms and body language communicate your emotions. **Adaptors** are displays of nonverbal communication that help you adapt to your environment and each context, helping you feel comfortable and secure. With a **self-adaptor,** you may play with your hair or make sure it is not sticking up to meet your need for security or to feel comfortable. An **object-adaptor** is the nonverbal communication with the use of an object in a way that it was not designed for. Tapping your pen on the tabletop communicates impatience—not a typical use for the pen.

Illustrators	Reinforce a verbal message	Indicating where the library is located with words and gestures
Emblems	Have a specific meaning and can replace or reinforce words	The "OK" sign substituted for the word
Regulators	Control, encourage, or discourage interaction	Nodding your head in agreement
Affect displays	Displays express emotions or feelings	Arms over your head to signal victory
Adaptors	Help us feel comfortable or indicate emotions or moods	Grooming your hair Tapping a pen on a table

These types of nonverbal communication can complement, repeat, replace, mask, or contradict verbal communication. In the case of the first example, indicating "yes" with a smile **complemented** the verbal message. If the person you asked out did not understand the first time, because he or she was distracted or the music was too loud, he or she might shrug the shoulders to indicate confusion. You may then ask again, but this time point in the direction of yourself as you state, "Do you want to go out tonight with me?" verbally. This effectively **repeats** the verbal message with a nonverbal one. As the person gets it, he or she may smile back at you for confirmation. You may then point toward the door, but say nothing. You have **replaced** your verbal message with a nonverbal one.

We also mask or even contradict our thoughts, feelings, or words with nonverbal communication. **Masking** involves the substitution of appropriate nonverbal communication for nonverbal communication you may want to display. Let's say you didn't get the response you hoped for when asking the person out. You may mask disappointment with a laugh or a shrug of the shoulder, as in "no big deal." This also applies to formal interpersonal interactions. If you are at work and a customer is really upset and letting you and everyone know about it, you may mask your emotions with a calm, professional demeanor more appropriate to the work environment. If the customer picks up on your frustration, or the frown on your face contradicts "no big deal," then your nonverbal communication may have been in disagreement with your spoken words. **Contradiction** is the communication of nonverbal messages that conflict with verbal communication.

Complements	Reinforces verbal communication.
Repeats	Repeats verbal communication.
Replaces	Replaces verbal communication.
Masks	Substitutes more appropriate displays for less appropriate displays.
Contradicting	Contradicts verbal communication.

4. Nonverbal Communication Is Universal

The statement that nonverbal communication is universal is relatively straightforward, but have you considered nonverbal communication among people who cannot hear, people who cannot see, or people from a culture other than your own? Do they communicate nonverbally in similar or distinct ways? How does context and culture impact our interpretation of nonverbal communication, and does our interpretation of distinct context take away from the claim that it is universal?

The claim that nonverbal communication is universal means that all people use it, but not that it is the same for all people. There are some signs and signals that may be universal in the sense that they are passed from one generation to the next and not learned. The classic example is the blind child who smiles the same as a sighted child, even though no one has shown the blind child how to smile. We don't have conclusive answers for this behavior, but many researchers have observed and documented similar types of behaviors expressed across cultures. We also know that a great deal of nonverbal communication is learned through interaction with one another, and what is a perfectly acceptable sign in one culture may get you into a fight in another culture.

Have you ever traveled to a country other than your own, where people spoke a different language and had a distinct culture? How did you communicate? Besides having a friend who spoke the language, how did you communicate and get your needs met? Did you refer to your dictionary and try to pronounce words? Perhaps you just said one word in the local language and hoped they would understand: "Bano?" Then someone points you in the direction of the bathroom. Many people who do not speak the native language find that gestures and even pantomiming get the point across quite effectively. Pretending to eat shows the listener you want to eat. Rubbing your tummy and pushing your plate away indicates you are full. We all use these gestures in our daily lives, but when we are thrust into a situation where verbal communication just doesn't work, nonverbal communication often saves the day.

One word of caution, however. You will find in the Intercultural Communication chapter a discussion about how gestures are different in many countries. You wouldn't want to give the "OK" sign if you knew it was an insult to the local community members. Ask people from a culture other than your own if they can give you examples of gestures they see used in the United States that are different from their own. Nonverbal communication itself is universal, but specific gestures vary greatly in their meaning and interpretation. See Figure 4.1.

5. Nonverbal Communication Is Confusing and Contextual

Nonverbal communication can be very confusing. What one person thinks he or she is conveying may not at all be related to what the receiver perceives. A gesture may have multiple meanings, depending on the context in which it is used. Raising a hand in class communicates a far different message than raising your hands while being arrested. One communicates a wish to speak, the other submission or surrender. A crossing guard may raise her hand to indicate traffic is to stop, or an athlete may raise arms to stretch before an event. Each action is similar, but through our perception of the context, we can draw different conclusions. Is the hand raised in a

Gestures mean different things to different people, particularly if they come from different cultures, languages, or traditions (Axtell, 1991). What may mean "A-OK" to you is a serious insult to many people in Latin America, or means "zero" to someone from France. The universal thumbs-up isn't so universal. In the United States it commonly means "good going," but in many Islamic countries it's equal to the upraised middle finger. Make a "V" sign and ask your classmates what it means. Some may say "peace," but the "V" for victory sign, which has been adopted by a telecommunications company as its sign, can be an old insult to an Englishman. Years ago, when the English fought with the French with bows and arrows, to disable captured archers, the victor would cut off the middle and fore fingers. The signal with two fingers upthrust came to mean triumph and the ability to fight another day. Can you think of any gestures that may be misinterpreted? Think twice before demonstrating them to a classmate.

FIGURE 4.1 *Watch What You Do*

classroom? Does the crossing guard have a fluorescent vest and a hand-held sign? These clues help us make sense of nonverbal communication.

6. Nonverbal Communication Can Be Intentional or Unintentional

If we go back to the earlier driving example, where another car suddenly pulled in front of you, would your actions be intentional or unintentional? Your wrinkled eyebrows, white knuckles, or wide eyes may have been unintentional. Nonetheless, they clearly communicate your feelings at that moment. Your passenger asks you about the incident and you shrug your shoulders and say "No big deal," but the stress of the moment is still "written" on your face. Your intentional shrugging of your shoulders contributes to your message, but your wrinkled eyebrows or the memory of your white knuckles may contradict your message. Can we tell when people are intentionally or unintentionally communicating nonverbally? Ask ten people this question and compare their responses. You may be surprised. It is clearly a challenge to understanding nonverbal communication in action.

In addition to the six general principles of nonverbal communication, Beebe, Beebe, and Redmond (2002) offer us three principles of interpersonal nonverbal communication. While each of these principles in some way relates to the six we have previously discussed, they offer us additional insight into areas of nonverbal communication that we can use to guide our interpretation and understanding of one another.

7. Nonverbal Messages Communicate Feelings and Attitudes

Nonverbal communication is fast, as we've discussed, and we demonstrate our feelings and thoughts quite quickly through our facial gestures and body movements. Albert Mehrabian (1972), a noted psychologist, conducted a comprehensive study and found that we communicate emotional messages through the spoken word as little as 7 percent of the time, indicating that up to 93 percent of the time we communicate our emotions nonverbally. This leads us to the natural question, "If we communicate so much of our emotions nonverbally, how do we express them?" Mehrabian would answer that question "through facial gestures, about 55 percent of the time." He would no doubt follow up with the qualification that the other 38 percent of the time, we use vocal cues and voice inflection to communicate emotional messages. While this study is not the only study on the topic, it is an often-cited study that has served as a benchmark in the field, underlining the common sense assertion that nonverbal communication is a very important factor in how we communicate with each other.

8. Nonverbal Communication Is More Believable Than Verbal

Perhaps you have seen a program on television where a character is taking or being subjected to a lie detector test. The person administering the tests asks questions and records responses. Wouldn't it be nice to be able to have our own lie detectors for everyday conversation? At first it sounds promising, but as the character Matt, a lawyer with a gift for "bending the truth," found out in the film *Liar Liar* (1997), you can upset people and hurt relationships when you can't use euphemisms to soften discussions or choose to not state your complete thoughts, reserving some issues for a later day. Matt's (Jim Carrey) son makes a wish as he blows out his birthday candles that his father will go just one day without telling a lie. When the wish comes true, the movie becomes both tragic and hilarious as others try to deal with his frank honesty. We mask our nonverbal responses to display tact and grace all the time, and some of the social customs we use help us get along as a couple, community, or society. That said, if we know someone well, we can follow certain clues to determine if that person is indeed lying. Zuckerman, DePaulo, and Rosenthal (1981) indicate that there are several behaviors that we can tune into and discern whether people are being deceptive:

- Reduction in eye contact while engaged in a conversation.
- Awkward pauses in conversation.
- Higher pitch in voice.
- Deliberate pronunciation and articulation of words.
- Increased delay in response time to a question.
- Increased body movements like changes in posture.
- Decreased smiling.
- Decreased rate of speech.

Do any of these signs alone indicate lying? Do all of these signs together indicate lying? The answer to both questions is a "maybe" to indicate that we cannot lose sight of context, individual personality, and the importance of culture in nonverbal displays. By observing someone over time we learn his or her patterns of speech and behavior. Variation in this pattern, combined with the clues above, will help you better discern whether he or she is misleading you.

The focus on patterns of speech and behavior also has a connection to our physiological, or body, responses to stress and behaviors like lying. Lie detectors, while used extensively in movies to create the illusion of credibility, seek to focus on these patterns and demonstrate anomalies. There is significant debate whether lie detectors measure with any degree of accuracy. They are not admissible in court or allowed by the U.S. government in private workplaces because the science is far from proven and the results are highly unreliable (Koerner, 2002). This has not stopped many law enforcement agencies from using lie detectors to screen future employees or even current employees. You may ask yourself why, if a test is so controversial or even unreliable, do people keep using it to determine if nonverbal behavior and body responses reveal lying? There are no easy answers, but there is a lot of research on the topic. Investigate the controversy and use the information for a class project or presentation.

9. Nonverbal Communication Is Key in Relationships

Have you ever encountered two people who have been together as a couple for a long time and watched them communicate? Notice how they seem to be in tune with one another, able to finish each other's sentences, even appearing as if they are reading one another's thoughts. Their understanding of each other's verbal and nonverbal communication patterns and habits enables them to communicate in this way. Verbal and nonverbal communication work together as we simultaneously create meaning through conversation and interaction with one another. We examined this transactional nature of communication in Chapter 1, but here it takes on a new dimension. Do we have this same level of trust and intimacy in the first few minutes of knowing each other? Of course not, but what is different?

When we first see each other, before anyone says a word, we are already sizing each other up. Within the first few seconds we have made judgments about each other based on what we wear, our physical characteristics, even our posture. Are these judgments accurate? That is hard to know without context, but we can say that nonverbal communication certainly impacts first impressions, good or bad. When two people first meet and get to know one another, they typically verbalize to talk about lots of things, including likes/dislikes, attitudes, family, and themselves. Soon, however, as they learn to "read" one another, which is another way of saying they learn to listen to each other, they can see whether their friend likes something or not by stance or facial expressions. As they get to know each other and develop new levels of trust, they may also develop a better understanding of nonverbal communication, which can lead to better communication, better understanding, more trust, and the cycle continues. They can also lose sight of the nonverbal cues and hurt each other, negatively impacting the relationship. Regardless of how we approach this central principle, we arrive at the same point: Nonverbal communication is key to interpersonal relationships.

Now that we have discussed the general principles that apply to nonverbal communication, let's examine eight types of nonverbal communication to further understand this challenging aspect of communication.

Types of Nonverbal Communication

1. Space

Take a moment and "people-watch." This means to observe others' behavior but not stare or invade their sense of space. Consider whether you see women or men, young or old, whether people seem familiar or unfamiliar with one another. Do you notice any patterns? Were people who knew each other well standing any closer than people who were not as familiar with each other? Was gender a factor in the differences? How about age? All of these issues relate to how important space is in our everyday communication.

Edward T. Hall served in the European and South Pacific Regions in the Corps of Engineers during World War II. As he traveled from one place to another, he kept a record of his observations and noticed that in different countries, people kept different distances from each other. In France, they stood rather close. In England, they stood farther apart. Hall wondered why that was and began to study what he called **proxemics,** or the study of the human use of space and distance in communication.

INTERCULTURAL COMMUNICATION 4.1 • *Cultural Differences in the Use of Space*

Americans overseas were confronted with a variety of difficulties because of cultural differences in the handling of space. People stood "too close" during conversations, and when the Americans backed away to a comfortable conversational distance, this was taken to mean that Americans were cold, aloof, withdrawn, and disinterested in the people of the country. U.S. housewives muttered about "waste space" in houses in the Middle East. In England, Americans who were used to neighborliness were hurt when they discovered that their neighbors were no more accessible or friendly than other people, and in Latin America, ex-suburbanites, accustomed to unfenced yards, found that the high walls there made them feel "shut out." Even in Germany, where so many of my countrymen felt at home, radically different patterns in the use of space led to unexpected tensions. (Hall, 1963, p. 422)

As you can see in Hall's observations, space can play an important role in communication across culture. Find your International Student Programs Office on campus and learn where and when international students get together. Make the effort to learn more about the importance of nonverbal communication within the context of intercultural communication. You may be amazed at what you find!

He gathered his observations and conclusions together and published *The Hidden Dimension* in 1966. Hall placed the spotlight on aspects of communication that people hadn't studied in depth previously.

In *The Hidden Dimension,* he indicated there are two main aspects of space that are necessary to study it. The first was **territory.** Hall drew on cultural anthropology, or the study of people in cultures, to get at the concepts of dominance and submission. People claim space all the time, but who gets the big corner office and who gets the broom closet office? The more powerful person often claims more space. Within everyday life we often establish territory as a matter of routine and have customs to accommodate this. When you sit at a cafeteria table, your space may be established by your tray. What's on your tray is yours. Let's say the salt and pepper are to your right, and someone sits next to you on your left. That person could easily reach across the table and take the salt and pepper, but his or her awareness (hopefully) of you and your territory means he or she will not reach across your tray, and your space, to get them. Instead the person will ask, "May I have the salt and pepper?", in which case you simply pass them to the person, respecting the boundaries you've established for yourself and reinforcing your territory.

Exercise _____

Do a www.google.com search on "participant-observation research." What are its key elements, strengths, and weaknesses? How does it impact your view of "people-watching"?

The second is **personal space.** Initially, this may sound like territory, but there is a key difference. Power. Territory implies the ability to control a space and mark that space as owned by you. You may do this with fences or walls around your house or a poster on the door of your own room. This sense of ownership, or the right to control that space, is implicit in territory.

Personal space moves with you like a bubble all around you. It is the space you need to carry out your business. In a lecture hall, people often sit quite close together. In an aerobics class, people stand or dance with more distance between them. You need a little personal space in which to write in the lecture hall, but need more personal space (so you don't hit each other) on the gym mat. Hall was a pioneer in the field of proxemics, and the first to categorize the types of space used in communication.

Consider the last time you stepped into an elevator. Where did everyone look? Did people speak to one another? Typically, people will give each other space by standing apart in the elevator and facing forward, noting the changes in floors as they approach their destinations. As more people enter the elevator, space between individuals decreases. People may be more tolerant of shoulders rubbing in this situation than other contexts.

Exercise _____

Note where people sit on the first day of class and for each class session thereafter. Do students return to the same seat? If they do not attend class, do the classmates leave their seat vacant? Compare your results.

Figure 4.2 features the four main categories of distance that Hall (1966) used in communication. **Intimate space** is generally up to 18 inches away from you, while **personal space** can range from 18 inches to 4 feet. **Social space** can range from 4 to 12 feet and can usually be found in more formal settings like workplaces.

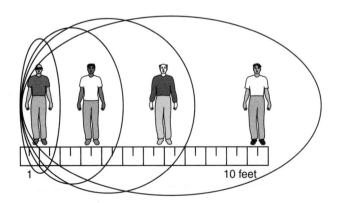

FIGURE 4.2 *Categories of Space*

Finally, **public space** is usually over 12 feet and can often be found in public speaking situations in the classroom, courtroom, or church.

2. Time

Look around the room and see how long it takes you to find out what time it is. Is there a clock on the wall, your wrist, the nightstand? Devices that measure time are all around us because we consider time important, often stating that "time is money" or "time is precious." Time is quite important to everyone, though people in different cultures express their awareness and its level of importance in diverse ways. One key way we demonstrate the value of time to us is how we share it with others. By sharing time, or spending time with someone we care about, our nonverbal gesture communicates "I value you." Conversely, to spend little time on something may reveal where it ranks on our own personal "priority list."

Have you ever gone to a doctor's appointment and not been seen on time? Many people wait for varying lengths of time before seeing, or gaining audience to, the doctor. Why do they wait? Because the doctor is in a position of power because they need the information that he or she has. Have you ever called someone who has been too busy to talk right at that moment? Have you ever talked to someone who speaks English as his or her second language? Can you see how in each case, time is a relevant factor in the communication process?

The study of how we refer to and perceive time is called **chronemics.** Researchers have long found time in verbal and nonverbal communication to be an extremely important factor to consider. Tom Bruneau, of Radford University, is a pioneer in the field and has spent a lifetime investigating how time interacts in communication, particularly in intercultural communication (Bruneau, 1974, 1990; Bruneau & Ishii, 1988).

For example, in western society, time is considered the equivalent of money. The value of speed is highly prized in our society (Schwartz, 1989) and can be seen all around us in the way we buy our food (drive through or, lately, ordering it online to be delivered), the way we want faster computers, cars, and instant gratification, and the decrease in the time between access to communication devices (like pagers, cellular/digital telephone, email). Some people use all the technology to "stay in touch," and end up being "on call" all the time. How has this need for speed affected your life or habits?

This idea about time, however, is not universal. Some Orthodox Jews observe religious days in which they use no electricity and do not work. Some Mexican American citizens say a barbeque is at eight, but it is understood that it really doesn't start until nine, and then goes on until after midnight. Some Native Americans, particularly elders, speak in well-measured phrases and take long pauses, not hurrying their speech or competing for their turn. Cultures have different ways of expressing value for time.

Now consider how you perceive your time and where you devote your energies. Make for yourself—in the left margin if you like—a short list of what you do every day, with what you spend the most time on at the top of your list. Once you've listed your daily activities, switch to the right-hand column and list what you value

INTERCULTURAL COMMUNICATION 4.2 • *Time Orientations*

Edward T. Hall and Mildred Reed Hall (1987) state that **monochronic time-oriented cultures** (the United States, Germany, and Switzerland, for example) schedule one thing at a time, while **polychronic time-oriented cultures** (Greece, Italy, Chile, and Saudi Arabia, to name a few examples) schedule many things at one time. In monochromatic time, it is one thing at a time (no interruptions), and everything has its own time. First work, then play. Polychromatic time looks a little more complicated, with business and family mixing with dinner and dancing. People in monochromatic time-oriented cultures often view time seriously (time is money), while people in polychromatic time-oriented cultures view schedules as more flexible. Understanding the value and treatment of time in different cultures can help you communicate more effectively.

most. List an equal number of items on each list. Do they match? If not, where are you spending your time on something you do not value, and where could you spend more time on what is important to you?

3. Physical Characteristics

Have you ever heard that taller people get paid more, or that people prefer symmetrical (equal sides) faces over asymmetrical (unequal sides, like a broken nose or having one eye slightly higher than the other)? There is a fair amount of debate in both the popular press and the scientific community over the impact of physical characteristics on our lives. To some degree we have control over our weight or our length of hair, but we also can't control our DNA and its expression in terms of body type, skin tone, height, or predisposition for disease or recovery from illness. Researchers indicate people often make judgments about a person's personality or behavior based on physical characteristics. They also point out that those judgments are often inaccurate (Wells & Siegel, 1961; Cash & Kilcullen, 1985).

We may try to change or manipulate our physical characteristics to communicate with each other. If someone feels too tall, he or she may stoop to appear shorter, in the same way someone who is short may use lifters in the shoes to gain an extra inch of height. Both of these expressions of our physical characteristics communicate something about us. Do people ever change their physical characteristics in more permanent ways to communicate something about themselves? Cosmetic surgeons would certainly say yes, and the patients who reduce, enlarge, or otherwise manipulate their bodies to then present to others are certainly communicating. Can the manipulation of physical characteristics in permanent ways ever harm an individual? Conduct your own investigation with a web search and see what you find. You may find a compelling class project or presentation.

4. Body Movements

The movement in a dance, the shrug of a shoulder, or the turn on an ankle can all communicate volumes without one word. Human expression often uses body movements to express ideas, thoughts, and feeling that escape words. The study of body movements, formally called **kinesics,** is key to understanding nonverbal communication in a variety of ways. Let's examine four distinct ways body movements complement, repeat, regulate, and replace our verbal messages.

Body movements can complement the verbal message by reinforcing the main idea, like points while giving directions. They can also reinforce the message by repeating it. If you first say "take a right at the end of the street," and then motion with your hand to the right, your repetition can help make sure the listener understood your message. In addition to repeating our message, body movements can also regulate our conversations. Nodding your head to indicate you are listening may encourage the speaker to continue speaking. Drawing your hand across your throat or giving the time-out "T" sign with your hands might signal them to stop. Finally, body movements may actually substitute or replace verbal messages. "Which way to the library?" can be answered with just a pointing gesture.

On an interesting note, Ekman and Friesen (1967) found that when studying the communication of emotions, facial features communicate to others our feelings, but our body movements often reveal how intensely we experience those feelings. For example, if the nurse draws blood from your arm and your face shows your pain but you remain still, we could discern that while it hurt, it wasn't that bad. If, however, you pull back or worse, try to stand up, we know that what you feel, you feel intensely.

5. Touch

Can you remember a time when someone placed a hand on your shoulder or gave you a hug, and it meant more to you than any words could say? How long did that person hold you? Did his or her touch communicate to you what words could not at that moment? For many people, across cultures and language, touch is an important aspect of nonverbal communication. Touch in communication interaction is called **haptics,** and Seiler and Beall (2000) identify five distinct types of touch, from impersonal to intimate.

The first involves the most impersonal type, the **functional-professional touch.** This is exemplified by a doctor touching you during an exam. The touch only serves to fulfill the professional function and is generally brief. The next level of touch is called the **social-polite touch.** We shake hands in western society, while in other cultures people may briefly kiss each other on the cheek as a form of polite greeting. Beyond these two levels of impersonal touch comes a more familiar touch that conveys trust and familiarity. The **friendship-warmth touch,** like a hug when greeting, is used between conversation partners who know each other. They have formed bonds of friendship and express it through a familiar touch like a hug. A more intimate type of touch, as you may guess, involves a more intense degree of relationship and is called the **love-intimacy touch.** People hold hands, hug, kiss, and caress in ways that communicate their love. Finally, the most intimate form of touch between two consenting adults is the **sexual-arousal touch.**

6. Paralanguage

Where there are rules, there will always be exceptions, and paralanguage serves a great example. We define nonverbal communication by stating it is not verbal communication. We can observe, measure, and analyze types of nonverbal communication like touch, time, or space and gain insight into each other. We also learn a lot by how we express ourselves between words, or even how we say them. Did your parents ever say "It's not what you said but how you said it"? Your inflection, tone or even a sigh can communicate your meaning in ways other than the spoken word.

"Uh-huh," "Ohhh (yawn)," and "Arrggh!" are all no doubt familiar verbal fillers that you hear people use all the time. "Uh-huh" may serve as an indication of agreement, and encourage the speaker to continue talking, like a head nod. A yawn may show disinterest or reveal the listener is tired. "Arrggh!" may express frustration without using words. All of these cues, both vocal and silent, are called **paralanguage.** The inflection in someone's voice may communicate that he or she is nervous or happy. If someone says "I saw him at the *store*," the emphasis on *store* gives it importance in relation to the other words. The entire meaning of the same sentence can change if we change the emphasis on one word. "I saw *him* at the store," shifts the emphasis from the *store* to *him*, and it changes the meaning of the sentence.

Silence or vocal pauses can communicate hesitation, need to gather thought, or a sign of respect. Keith Basso (1970) quotes an anonymous source as stating "it is not the case that a man who is silent says nothing." Sometimes we learn just as much, even more, from what a person does not say as what he or she does say. In addition, Basso and Philips (1983) and McLean (1998) found that traditional speech among Native Americans places a special emphasis on silence.

7. Artifacts

Three rings in the ear, one in the nose, and a stud through the tongue. While some people find the prospect of having their bodies pierced uncomfortable, others view it as a way to express their sense of self. According to *The San Diego Union-Tribune* (Kinsman, 2001), body art or tattoos are more or less likely to be accepted in the workplace depending on who you interview.

- 20 percent of workers indicated their body art had been held against them on the job.
- 42 percent of employers said the presence of visible body art lowered their opinion of workers.
- 44 percent of managers surveyed have body art.
- 52 percent of workers surveyed have body art.
- 67 percent of workers cover their body art or remove piercings during work hours.

Tattoos, however, can carry significant meaning to those who choose them. For example, look at the tattoo in Figure 4.3. Miguel Sandoval, of Tucson, Arizona, has a tattoo of a family tree, illustrating his mother and their family. This tattoo, like many similar tattoos across cultures, communicates significant meaning to both the owner and those who see it. Its significance, however, may go unnoticed by an employer or other observers who do not value self-expression in this way.

FIGURE 4.3   *Miguel Sandoval's Family Tree Tattoo*

Men's Health magazine (2003, p. 18) discussed this topic with interesting results from a *Cosmopolitan* magazine survey of 400 female respondents to a survey on the perceptions of tattoos on men. Fifty-nine percent of respondents indicated tattoos were still very popular, but 37 percent indicated they would find them creepy on a male over the age of 36. Sixty-eight percent indicated the best tattoo is one that involves a "mysterious symbol or sign" about the size of a beer coaster (70%). In terms of location for tattoos, 65 percent indicated they would like to see them on the biceps or shoulder blades. Before you go looking for your nearest tattoo shop, consider that 72 percent of respondents indicated that men who do not choose to have a tattoo often think of themselves as "cool enough to not care what others think" and skip the tattoo.

Artifacts include rings and tattoos, and also things like clothes, cars, watches, briefcases, purses, and even eyeglasses. All of these objects somehow relate to the owner, and the owner uses them to project gender, role or position, class or status, personality, and group membership.

When is someone expected to wear a tie? More than likely in a formal situation. Artifacts may be culturally acceptable adornments that are associated with specific contexts, like a wedding dress, or they can be expressions of self and individuality. Can you find an example of an artifact that is marketed or advertised to people your age? How is it shown as making you a member of the group? Young people may pay attention to artifacts like clothing labels, and parents of children may compare notes about minivans. Artifacts serve to express individuality and group affiliation and play an important role in communication.

8. Environment

The physical and psychological aspects of the communication context are called **environment.** As we discussed in Chapter 1, it is an important part of the dynamic

CASE STUDY 4.1 • *Noise Pollution*

Noise in the environment can actually contribute to hearing loss, a problem that costs Americans over $56 billion a year. Our ears hurt when the noise levels reach 140 decibels, but damage can occur with much lower levels that are part of our everyday environment.

Noise	Decibels	Length of Exposure Necessary to Cause Measurable Hearing Loss
Jackhammer	90	8 hours
Ride in a convertible on freeway	95	4 hours
Subway train	100	2 hours
Power lawnmower	105	1 hour
Live rock concert	110	30 minutes
Car horn	120	7.5 minutes

Source: USA Weekend (1999).

communication process. In Chapter 2, we observed how perception of one's environment influences his or her reaction to it. In Chapter 3, cultures that place a high degree of emphasis on context were highlighted. Our environment influences and plays a role in our communication. Within the realm of nonverbal communication, this takes on additional aspects: the type of furniture you select for your room; the type of lighting you give a space; the smells of freshly baked bread or old socks in a room; the music playing on the radio. These elements combine to form the environment in which communication occurs, and the degree of formality/informality, temperature, and even lighting can be an element in the communication process. Think about how you might change the environment where you live if you wanted a romantic evening, have a birthday party, or host a family reunion.

All of these elements combine to contribute to nonverbal communication, a powerful force in the communication process. What happens when the nonverbal message and the verbal message that you receive or demonstrate do not match? Let's say we meet and I say what a pleasure it is to meet you while looking over your shoulder and gently moving away to greet someone else. Can you think of an example where the nonverbal and verbal messages did not match? When this happens, which communication do you believe? According to Seiler and Beall (2000), most of us tend to believe the nonverbal message over the verbal message.

Improving Your Understanding

By now you are more aware of both the principles and types of nonverbal communication. Taking this one step further, apply your knowledge that you had when you started this chapter to the insights and connections you made to the material. How can you do this? Here are three ways to examine nonverbal communication, in yourself and others, in order to improve communication.

1. Watch reactions. Pretend you are a researcher. Document what you see objectively. Take detailed notes and make sure to note context and environment. Compare your results with other students. This can be done as "people watching" or possibly as part of a classroom exercise. You decide where and when to watch reactions, but now that you are more aware of the different types and how they work, you'll notice them in new and fascinating ways.

2. Enroll an observer. If the goal is for you to assess your own nonverbal communication, enroll a friend to act as the objective researcher. If you prefer to see it for yourself, have a friend videotape you in conversation, and then repeat introductory Exercise 1 (watch your movie, this time of yourself).

3. Focus on a specific type of nonverbal communication. How do others use their hands to communicate? Does this change or differ based on a variable (gender, age, ethnicity, cultural background, context, environment, etc.)? Through observing others, you will learn more about how people communicate and more about how you yourself communicate nonverbally.

Summary

In this chapter we have related nonverbal communication to the dynamic process of communication, the perception process and listening, and verbal communication by examining the principles of nonverbal communication and specific types of nonverbal communication. After defining nonverbal communication, we examined the nine principles and eight types of nonverbal communication. We then looked at three ways to improve our understanding, improving awareness and understanding in order to communicate more effectively.

For More Information

http://www.wheaton.edu/Missions/Courses/561Camp/simulations.htm

http://carla.acad.umn.edu/IS-resources.html

Nonverbal Communication Research Page, Louisiana College: **http://socpsych.lacollege.edu/nonverbal.html**

Review Questions

1. Factual Questions
    a. What is nonverbal communication?
    b. What are the principles of nonverbal communication?
    c. What are the types of nonverbal communication?

2. Interpretative Questions

   a. What are the assumptions (explicit or underlying) about nonverbal communication in this chapter?

   b. To what degree is time a relevant factor in communication in the information age?

   c. Does it limit or enhance our understanding of communication to view nonverbal communication as something that is not verbal communication?

3. Evaluative Questions

   a. Is nonverbal communication accurate? Why or why not?

   b. Can you effectively study nonverbal communication? Explain.

   c. Can the study of nonverbal communication be separate from the study of intercultural communication? Explain.

4. Application Questions

   a. Create a survey that addresses the issue of which people trust more, nonverbal or verbal messages. Ask an equal number of men and women and compare your results.

   b. See how long and how much you can get done during the day without verbal messages.

   c. Interview international students about nonverbal communication in their native languages and cultures. Compare to your local customs and traditions.

References

Axtell, R. (1991). *Gestures: The do's and taboos of body language around the world.* New York: John Wiley & Sons.

Basso, K. A. (1970). To give up on words: Silence in Western Apache culture. In D. Carbaugh (Ed.), *Cultural communication and intercultural contact* (pp. 301–318). Hillsdale, NJ: Lawrence Erlbaum.

Beebe, S., Beebe, S., & Redmond, M. (2002). *Interpersonal communication: Relating to others* (3rd ed.). Boston: Allyn and Bacon.

Bruneau, T. (1974). Time and nonverbal communication. *Journal of Popular Culture, 8,* pp. 658–666.

Bruneau, T. (1990). Chronemics: The study of time in human interaction. In J. DeVito & M. Hecht (Eds.), *The nonverbal reader.* Prospect Heights, IL: Waveland Press, pp. 301–311.

Bruneau, T., & Ishii, S. (1988). Communicative silence: East and West. *World Communication, 17,* 1–33.

Cash, T., & Kilcullen, R. (1985). The eye of the beholder: Susceptibility to sexism and beautyism in the evaluation of managerial applicants. *Journal of Applied Social Psychology, 15,* 591–605.

Ekman, P., & Friesen, W. (1967). Head and body cues in the judgment of emotions: A reformulation. *Perceptual and Motor Skills, 24,* 711–724.

Hall, E. T. (1963). Proxemics: The study of man's spatial relations and boundaries. In *Man's image in medicine and anthropology.* New York: International Universities Press, pp. 422–445.

Hall, E. T. (1966). *The hidden dimension.* New York: Doubleday.

Hall, E. T., & Hall, M. R. (1987). *Hidden differences: Doing business with the Japanese.* New York: Doubleday (Anchor Books).

Kinsman, M. (2001, August 20). Tattoos and nose rings. *The San Diego Union-Tribune,* p. C1.

Koerner, B. (2002, November/December). Lie detector roulette. *Mother Jones, 27*(6), 56–59, 92.

McLean, S. (1998). Turn-taking and the extended pause: A study of interpersonal communication styles across generations on the Warm Springs Indian Reservation. In K. S. Sitaram & M.

Prosser (Eds.), *Civic discourse: Multiculturalism, cultural diversity, and global communication.* Stamford, CT: Ablex Publishing Corporation, pp. 213–227.

Mehrabian, A. (1972). *Nonverbal communication.* Chicago: Aldine Atherton, p. 108.

Men's Health. (2003, September). Tattoo? You?, p. 18.

Philips, S. (1983). *The invisible culture: Communication in the classroom and community on the Warm Springs Indian Reservation* (pp. 58–61). Chicago: Waveland Press.

Schwartz, T. (1989, January/February). Acceleration syndrome: Does everyone live in the fast lane? *Utne Reader, 36–43.*

Seiler, W., & Beall, M. (2000). *Communication: Making connections.* Boston; Allyn and Bacon.

USA Weekend. (1999, October 15). p. 22.

Wells, W., & Siegel, B. (1961). Stereotypes somatypes. *Psychological Reports, 8,* 77–78.

Zuckerman, M., DePaulo, D., & Rosenthal, R. (1981). Verbal and nonverbal communication of deception. *Advances in Experimental Social Psychology, 14,* 1–59.

5

Interpersonal Communication

Chapter Objectives _____

After completing this chapter, you should be able to:

1. Describe the similarities and the differences between intrapersonal communication and interpersonal communication.
2. State and provide examples of interpersonal needs.
3. Describe the process of self-disclosure.
4. Construct models to explain theories of interpersonal needs.
5. Demonstrate five ways to improve interpersonal communication.

Introductory Exercise 1 _____

Communication researchers have long documented the importance of trust in developing productive, healthy relationships. Within our normal range of relationships, we have different levels of trust, involvement, and commitment to the relationship. Consider what kinds of relationships you have with others. Think of examples from your own life. Write a short list of relationships that are important to you, from most important to least important. Sharing with another student or friend may prove interesting.

Introductory Exercise 2 _____

How you view yourself and others is important part of interpersonal communication. Please consider what groups you belong, particularly in terms of race, ethnicity, or culture. Imagine you had to communicate your perception of just one group to someone. Please choose five terms from the list below and circle a corresponding number to indicate the degree to which you consider it to be accurate (1 is *completely disagree* and 5 is *completely agree*).

Independent	1	2	3	4	5
Dependent	1	2	3	4	5
Hard working	1	2	3	4	5

Lazy	1	2	3	4	5
Progressive	1	2	3	4	5
Traditional	1	2	3	4	5
Sophisticated	1	2	3	4	5
Simple	1	2	3	4	5
Creative	1	2	3	4	5
Practical	1	2	3	4	5

Now consider a group that you have little or no contact with. Please choose five terms (same or different) and again circle the number. Use a different color or a pencil instead of a pen to make sure the difference is clear. Once you are done, you can easily see a representation of the stereotypes you hold both for your own group and a group that you do not know well. If the second group numbers are lower or the descriptive terms are the negatives of other terms you chose for your own group, make sure you read about ethnocentrism in this chapter. It discusses how we see each other and examines values and judgments we make based on our perceptions.

Source: Adapted from Gudykunst (1994).

> *To the world you're just one person, but to one person you could mean the world.*
> —Anonymous

Relationships are complicated but are often the most rewarding experiences in our lives. We spend our lives communicating and sometimes find communication with others difficult or even frustrating. As we discussed in Chapter 1, communication has several principles and models that serve to help us improve our communication with others. Now we'll build on these principles as we focus on the context of inter-personal communication, adding another layer of principles to guide us and examining our motivations to form and maintain relationships. In this chapter we will first examine how we communicate with ourselves and how relating to ourselves is connected to how we relate to others. Within the context of relationships, we'll explore the range of wants and needs we hope to meet, look at expectations, and discuss some guidelines for self-disclosure.

In the first exercise, did you find it relatively easy to find examples of relationships in your own life? For each of us the answers may be different, but the answers we give and why we give them have common threads we will observe throughout this chapter.

In the second exercise, what did you observe? Were your scores of a familiar group higher than the scores you gave an unfamiliar group? We often approach interactions with one another using stereotypes to guide us, but when we consider our own culture to be the benchmark and engage in the tendency to judge the customs of other societies by the standards of our own culture, we're being ethnocentric. This concept directly applies to interpersonal communication, because we often communicate with people different than we are everyday. If we approach interactions with others only from our own point of view and fail to try to understand not only what is

said but also why it is said, then we may miss important information, and our relationships will suffer. You will read the phrase "become other-oriented" several times in this text, and the idea is central to effective interpersonal communication. If you really want to communicate with someone, you need to learn how to consider things from his or her point of view.

This may sound familiar to you—and indeed other information in this chapter may sound familiar. Some of the discussion may even sound like a page out of your own life. There is a clear reason for it. You have been communicating all your life and have come to know yourself and the rules of your culture—including the expectations for yourself and others—and have already come to know quite a bit about interpersonal communication through experience. Take what you've learned from a lifetime of observation and experience and see how it relates to the material in this chapter. Some of the discussion, however, may not sound like something you've experienced. Throughout this chapter keep your own experiences in mind and see how looking at interpersonal communication through a formal, theory-based approach can give insight into everyday conversations. Also keep in mind that conversations and relationships do not fit well into categories, and unlike words in boxes, they are dynamic and ever changing.

FIGURE 5.1 *Intrapersonal/Interpersonal Communication*

In Figure 5.1, there is both intrapersonal communication and interpersonal communication. Each person is talking to himself, and one asks the other if they should have coffee. In a conversation where the other person is talking, have you ever let your mind drift only to get caught when the other person asks you a question? Your discussion with yourself is interrupting your active listening. Let's first look at intrapersonal communication and how it relates to self-concept and listening to others.

We look in the mirror and see one facet of ourselves but also recognize that there is more to us than other people, or even ourselves, know about us. People treat us in distinct ways, and we respond to them, and ourselves, through communication. This process over time contributes to our self-concept, or how we perceive ourselves. How we see ourselves plays an important role in what we expect from ourselves, as well as what we expect others to expect from us.

Self-Concept

> *Identity is the essential core of who we are as individuals,*
> *the conscious experience of the self inside.*
> —Kauffman

Our self-concept is what we perceive ourselves to be. This involves the mental picture you have for yourself and how you judge yourself. How you see yourself, to a large extent, is based on how you think others see you. This involves aspects of race, gender, ethnicity, class, and status in addition to your self-image, social comparisons, and your evaluation of your own thoughts and behavior. You gather a sense of how others see you through communication, interacting with others.

Trying to define what is the term *self* means is a challenging task. What makes you *you*? Or, from another perspective, what is not you? We can no doubt see that we are independent of one another to a certain extent, but what makes us unique?

For our purposes, we'll define **self** as one's own sense of individuality, motivations, and personal characteristics. What, then, can we point to, in terms of individuality, motivations, and characteristics, that makes us who we are?

One way is to examine our attitudes, beliefs, and values. An **attitude,** or a learned predisposition to a concept or object, can vary from one another. You may have learned to love broccoli, but someone else may have learned quite the opposite. Next, we can examine our beliefs. Our **beliefs,** or ideas based on our previous experiences and convictions, can serve a frame of reference through which we interpret our world. Finally, **values,** or central concepts and ideas of what we consider good and bad, right and wrong, worthy of our effort and attention or unworthy, guide our interpretation of our world.

Term	*Definition*	*Example*
VALUES	Ideals that guide our behavior—generally long lasting.	Education is important.
BELIEFS	Convictions or expressions of confidence that can change over time.	This class is important because I may use the skills I'm learning someday.
ATTITUDES	Your immediate disposition—can change easily and frequently.	I liked the game in class today.

We learn our values, beliefs, and attitudes through our interactions with others. By listening to others, we learn what is important to us.

A second or alternative way of examining our concept of self is to integrate context and interaction into the discussion. Do you communicate with everyone in exactly the same way regardless of context? Do you make exactly the same choices in different situations? The answer, of course, is no, and no one exactly the same in all contexts or interactions, but we do have our central values, beliefs, and general attitudes that do influence our behavior. William James, a philosopher, discussed this issue in three ways (Beebe, Beebe, & Redmond, 2002). He looked upon our **material self** as the physical objects and artifacts that we surround ourselves with to define and reflect our self-concept. This material self is often contrasted with the **spiritual self,** which focuses on intangible aspects of ourselves, including values, morals, and beliefs, that make us who we are. The third aspect of self, according to James, is the **social self,** involving the informal and formal interactions with others, which emphasizes a person's constantly changing nature in these interactions.

Your self-concept is comprised of two main components: **self-image** and **self-esteem.**

Self-Concept = Self-Image + Self-Esteem

Your self-image is just like it sounds—the image you have of yourself. Self-esteem, however, has to do with how you feel about yourself and your attributes. Have you ever known someone who has an eating disorder? These deadly diseases have everything to do with self-image and self-esteem. If someone's image of himself or herself is as an overweight person, and he or she feels that is negative and wants to change, he or she may exercise more and control diet. If someone who is already thin sees him- or herself as fat and feels bad about body image, this person may also diet and exercise, even though he or she might be below ideal weight or body mass. Anorexia and bulimia are two eating disorders characterized by a self-concept that reinforces dangerous behaviors, which can have life-threatening results. Being aware of your self-concept, and how you form that concept of yourself, is very important.

Self-concept is a process where what we sense in communication with others becomes internalized. From the time we are born, or even in the womb, we hear others. In our first year of life we learn faces of those close to us and start to imitate sounds. By our second year of life we are using some words and many gestures to communicate our needs and wants. We develop communication skills by doing as we grow, trying new words and phrases, participating in conversations with people our own age or of different ages. According to Cooley's (1922) concept of the **looking-glass self,** we look to others and how they view us, treat us, and interact with us to gain insight into our own identity. It is important to recognize that we do not regard everyone the same in this search for self. We place more weight and emphasis on the reactions of others who are important or are significant to us, such as parents, caregivers, and teachers. As they reflect a positive image of you to you, you will internalize it and in many ways reflect this view. If the view and resulting interaction is negative, then your view of yourself will, over time, incorporate this image.

> *Dime con quien andas y te dire quien eres.*
> —Mexican saying

As we broaden our communication skills, we also reflect more on how others communicate with us. According to Festinger (1954), we engage in **social comparisons,** or our own evaluation of self in relation to peers of similar status or qualities. The saying above, which speaks directly to this concept, can be translated as "Tell me who your friends are and I'll tell you who you are." We often measure our own degree of competency, intelligence, desirability, and self-worth in relation to how we perceive others. We spend more time noticing what others wear, how they present themselves, and how we fit into groups. It is important to recognize this process and in particular, who we tend to relate to in terms of comparison. If we compare ourselves to someone who has outwardly different characteristics than us—for example, height—then we may miss the inner characteristics we share in common. By focusing on our perceived similarities, we also may miss the distinct differences that contribute to our unique personalities and potential. We all have different talents, and how people celebrate them or put them down makes a significant impact on our self-concept as we grow and develop. This process continues throughout our lives.

When people encourage you, it affects the way you see yourself and how well you perform. In a well-known study, teachers were told that specific students were expected to do quite well because of their intelligence, while other students were described to the teachers as "late bloomers," or developmentally delayed. Researchers observed the students during the course of the school year, and the students that were expected to do well actually did. Those that were expected to not do as well also lived up to the expectation. The students were chosen at random at the beginning of the study, so there was, in fact, no reason to expect that students would demonstrate either better than average or worse than average academic abilities (Rosenthal & Jacobsen, 1968; Insel & Jacobson, 1975). According to the researchers, the differences probably came from the teacher's expectations of the students

COMPUTER-MEDIATED COMMUNICATION 5.1 • *Internet Marketing and Personal Information*

Have you ever thought of how the Internet can serve you better? Rather than reading the same newspaper everyone else does, would you like just the information you want? How about your very own web page, where you pick exactly what news you want to receive, for free? What information are you willing to share about yourself to receive this information? All of this is now possible, but the process, called mass personalization, has a price.

In exchange for providing information like your name, address, zip code, and age and spending a little time on selecting what you want to read, you get your own "virtual newspaper," complete with short video and sound files. What does the Internet company, like Yahoo! or AltaVista, two personal content page providers, get in exchange? Information about you—and that's worth money.

Building relationships with customers has been a dominant phrase in many business circles for years. John Hagel and Arthur Armstrong, in their text *Net Gain: Expanding Markets Through Virtual Communities* (1997), detail how businesses must move beyond individual relationships (shopkeeper and customer) to building communities, where people come to interact and feel like they belong. The long-term goal is increased customer loyalty and increased sales.

Cookies are small identification markers placed on your hard drive. These markers can simply identify you, track every website you link on and how long you stay, and report the information to third-party computers, allowing people to gather information on what you see and do. Under the category "preferences" on Internet Explorer you'll find the "privacy and security" option. There you'll find a tab for cookies, and, depending on your preference, you can restrict their use.

By combining elements of mass communication with customization based on expressed interest areas, businesses can better target people who might buy their products. Do you think consumers are receiving a service or that they are involved with whole new level of marketing? Discuss your comments with a classmate.

Source: Hagel & Armstrong (1997).

and the extra attention and the communication, nonverbal as well as verbal, of those expectations. Have you ever lived up to someone's expectations of you? How about your expectations for yourself? Write down one example for each situation.

The Pygmalion effect, otherwise known as a *self-fulfilling prophecy,* is quite powerful. As Ovid (43 B.C.–17 A.D.), a Roman philosopher and poet, told the story in the tenth book of *Metamorphoses,* the sculptor Pygmalion, a prince of Cyprus, sought to create an ivory statue of the ideal woman. He named the statue Galatea. She was so beautiful that Pygmalion fell hopelessly in love with his own creation. He prayed to the goddess Venus to bring Galatea to life, and she did. The couple, as the story goes, lived happily ever after.

A modern version of this story is told in the film *The Princess Diaries* (2001), a Disney film starring Julie Andrews and Anne Hathaway. Mia Thermopolis, a shy 15-year-old, lives in San Francisco with her mother, an artist. She learns that her father, recently deceased, was the Prince of Genovia, and she is now the sole heir to

---

CASE STUDY 5.1 • *Gender and Self-Disclosure*

Who talks more about themselves, men or women? The answer depends on whom you ask and what underlying factor(s) might be considered. According to some researchers, women disclose more private, emotional information than men, stating that men risk getting hurt (Rosenfeld, 1979; Pearson, West, & Turner, 1998). Others state it depends on who they are talking to. For example, Stokes, Fuehrer, and Childs (1980) indicated their studies showed that men are more willing to talk about personal information with strangers, while women are more likely to talk to someone they know well. Do women prefer to disclose to other women more than men (Pearson, West, & Turner, 1998)? Are women more accepting, more likely to view people as connected (Gilligan, 1982)? Do males view self-disclosure from females as seduction (Abbey, 1982)? What do you think?

The importance of the gender (the role or behavioral aspects) as opposed to the sex (biological) of the person is a hotly debated issue. Which carries more weight, nature (biology) or nuture (environment; observation of others)? Add to this the dynamics of communication and the important process of self-disclosure, and the area of study gets quickly complicated. Isolating variables (that are themselves quite complicated) such as culture, language, or background from your gender within the context of communication is difficult. Some researchers have spent considerable effort in this area, but many have contradictory conclusions. We cannot take general statements as fact, but we can observe how they have elements of truth in them. Some men may disclose feelings more than some women. Some women may reveal more to strangers. We must be careful to avoid stereotyping, reducing a complex process to simple labeling, on the basis of biological traits.

Try this: Write five questions concerning gender and self-disclosure. Ask an equal number of men and women, within a defined age range, the questions separately. Compare your results.

the throne. Before our eyes, she transforms from an awkward teen to a poised princess through interaction with her grandmother the Queen. We, as the audience, watch as outward signs of this awkwardness are chiseled off by the modern Pygmalion sculptor, her grandmother. Mia's transformation is mirrored through her conversations and interactions until her self-image and self-esteem approach a mature interpretation of a modern princess. She becomes the princess, as she was in the eyes of others but not her own until now, when she accepts the throne and travels to her new country, Genovia.

From Ovid to Mia Thermopolis, we can see how people have expressed an interest in this effect for a very long time. We can also see how this process can work in a similar, yet negative way. Can you think of a similar story from a television show or movie? What was necessary for the effect to work?

To summarize the process of self-fulfilling prophecies, let's introduce four key principles that Robert Rosenthal (Rosnow & Rosenthal, 1999), a professor of social psychology at Harvard, has observed while studying this effect:

1. We form certain expectations of people or events.
2. We communicate those expectations with various cues, verbal and nonverbal.
3. People tend to respond to these cues by adjusting their behavior to match the expectations.
4. The outcome is that the original expectation becomes true.

What Is Intrapersonal Communication?

You may recall we briefly addressed intrapersonal communication in the first chapter. The word *intrapersonal* means within one person. **Intrapersonal communication** is communication with one's self, including self-talk, imaging, and visualization. Shedletsky (1989) discusses intrapersonal communication within context of the basic transactional model of communication, but all components of the model, from sender to receiver and so forth, happen within the individual. Pearson and Nelson (1985) discuss this interpretation, adding that intrapersonal communication is not limited to just internal monologue. They point to aspects of intrapersonal communication that include planning, problem solving, internal conflict resolution, and the evaluation of others and ourselves. Let's look at a practical example. Your friends come in and say they are going to the club and want to know if you want to go. Your speech book is in front of you and you know the instructor reminded everyone of an upcoming quiz. You probably consider your different options in your own mind before deciding what to do. All the mental problem solving, including the internal aspects of talking yourself through the decision, is intrapersonal communication in action. If we look at this process objectively, we can identify the eight components of communication and the mental dialogue. We engage in intrapersonal communication all the time, and how we do this impacts our communication with others.

Who you are and how you view yourself are in many ways within the context of your individual experiences. Once you learned how to use language, you began to implement on various levels the principles of communication, such as classifying and labeling. Did you perceive that an experience was a problem that caused you harm, or did you perceive it as a challenge to be learned from, or both? The way you interpret situations and circumstances, conversations and information, actions of others and yourself, all contribute to your knowledge and understanding of the world and your place in it. If you learned that staying out late the night before a quiz can negatively impact your performance, you may choose to focus on your studies. How you talk to yourself, based on everything you've learned so far, makes a big impact.

Let's say you are taking a test, and there are four answers to choose from. You choose how to respond to the question. You may eliminate two options that don't make sense and choose the best option from the two remaining answers. Each step in that complicated process involves intrapersonal communication, where you talk to yourself and talk yourself through a problem, applying your previous knowledge to this new challenge.

Speaking of challenges, have you ever been in a competitive event like a sport or a debate, or perhaps in an extracurricular activity like theater or band? You may have had moments where the spotlight, even if no one was watching, was on you. You are on the line in a race. You just recovered the ball and are pushing for a drive down the court. You take a breath and hit a high C on your trumpet as you begin a solo. Regardless of the challenge, the situations are in many ways the same. You are in a tense moment, and what you say to yourself makes a big impact. If you say "I can do it," you probably will hit close to your goal. If you say to yourself "There is no way I can do this," what effect do you think this has on your performance? You would be right if you say it certainly doesn't help and probably hinders your ability to focus on the task rather than pay attention to the nagging doubts.

Your intrapersonal communication, your conversation with yourself, is a significant part of your conversations with others. You seek affirmation that people see you as you want to be seen, perhaps how you see yourself. You look for actions, gestures, words, and attitudes in others that you relate back to how you see yourself and how you feel about yourself. This emphasis on feedback from others relates to your self-concept, which is comprised of two main aspects, your self-image and your self-esteem.

Some researchers call it internal monologue, others self-talk. Both terms point to the same general idea—that you talk with yourself in a running monologue that may be coherent and logical but can also be disorganized and illogical. Alfred Korzybski (1933), a scholar and philosopher of language best known for his system of linguistic philosophy and expression (general semantics), considered the first step for becoming conscious of how we think (and, by extension, how we talk to ourselves) was to achieve a degree of inner quietness. This means you learn to be quiet inside and listen to others, without a running monologue in response to what they are saying as they say it. It allows you to be open to others and not miss important information or nonverbal cues. Think of your skills and experiences as tools in a toolbox. You have all the tools accumulated through your lifetime that help you cope and adapt to new situations and experiences. If you are closed to others and let your internal monologue run interference while others try to share, you might miss a valuable new tool. We all need new tools or ways of adapting to our world. By becoming other-oriented, we improve out listening skills and our relationships.

We recognize that though communication with others we see ourselves and how we view our strengths and weaknesses. In this way, we come to recognize the importance of intrapersonal communication. By understanding that our conversations with ourselves can interrupt with conversations with others, we can learn to control who we are listening to and to downplay our internal monologue. By accepting that we can choose what messages to say to ourselves, we can encourage ourselves to achieve our goals.

What Is Interpersonal Communication?

We've all had a conversation with someone where we needed to listen or offer support. Through this interaction, you already have gained a working knowledge of interpersonal communication. For our purposes, interpersonal communication is defined as communication interaction typically between two people. This is a broad definition, primarily a comparison to other forms of communication, such as group communication or mass communication. This emphasis on the number of people, usually referred to as a contextual definition, helps us understand interpersonal communication but lacks a discussion of the types of relationships between people. The developmental view of interpersonal communication places emphasis on the relationships and draws a distinction between a conversation with a store clerk and someone you care deeply about. In the developmental view, interpersonal communication involves people who have known each other previously.

Relationships with others are formed through communication, particularly interpersonal communication, and come in all sorts of shapes and sizes. A relationship with a parent or caregiver, a husband or wife, boyfriend or girlfriend can be impersonal or close, professional or personal. Relationships can be enhanced (or not) though interpersonal communication. Can you recall a time when you noticed someone whom you did not already know and wanted to get to know him or her? How about a time when you knew someone, but wanted to get to know that person better? Why do you suppose you wanted to know more? Curiosity? Attraction? Possibly, but underlying your interest was the need to feel more confident and less uncertain about the person and the relationship. **Uncertainty theory** states that we seek to know more about others with whom we have relationships in order to reduce the anxiety created by the unknown (Berger & Calabrese, 1975; Berger, 1986; Gudykunst, 1995). Another motivation theory points to what we *want* from others. **Predicted outcome value theory** asserts that not only do we want to reduce uncertainty, but we are also interested in the rewards that will result from the association (Sunnafrank, 1986, 1990; Kellermann & Reynolds, 1990).

Why do you do what you do? Is it to reduce uncertainty? To get something? Certainly this has something to do with your need to communicate with others, but is there more? Although each of us has different needs and wants, there is some

common ground for all of us. We need to eat and stay warm. We need to feel safe and know that we belong to a group and have a place in a world. We may even want to make a difference in our world. If we look at the issue of uncertainty within the context of security, we can see how we may want to learn more about others to feel safe and secure. Researchers Abraham Maslow and William Schutz offer two frameworks for us to consider when examining the question: What makes us want to communicate?

Why Should We Engage in Interpersonal Communication?

Interpersonal communication is one form of communication we use to meet our needs and the needs of others. We engage in interpersonal communication to gain information, get to know one another, better understand our situation or context, come to know ourselves and our role or identity, and meet our fundamental interpersonal needs. In this section we will examine the functions of interpersonal communication, examining the many ways we choose to communicate with each other and why.

Maslow's Hierarchy

If you have taken courses in anthropology, philosophy, psychology, or perhaps sociology in the past, you may have seen Maslow's hierarchy (Figure 5.2). Maslow (1970) provides seven basic categories for human needs and arranges them in order of priority, from the most basic to the most advanced.

In this figure we can see that we need energy, water, and air to survive. Without any of these three basic elements, which meet our physiological needs (1), we cannot live. These are our most basic needs, and we normally need to meet them before we can do anything else. Once we have what we need to survive right now, we seek safety (2). Perhaps this once came in the form of a cave or shelter; in modern days this may be a job or a safe place where your basic needs are met. Victims of domestic violence and abuse are sometimes given shelter (safety) at a facility designed to protect them from their abusers. There are also examples of sacrifice,

FIGURE 5.2 *Maslow's Hierarchy of Needs*

where someone places the well-being and safety of another over his or her own needs and places himself or herself at risk. Can you think of any profession that involves heroism? Individuals who work in public safety often risk their own safety and basic needs in order to save others.

Once we have the basics to live and feel safe from immediate danger, we seek affection from others, looking for a sense of **love and belonging** (3). This need builds on the foundation of the previous needs and focuses on our need to be a part of a group. This is an important step that directly relates to interpersonal communication. If a person feels safe, he or she is more likely to be open to communication. Researchers have also spent considerable energy studying the dynamics of bullying and the impact of fear on children and their education. If you don't feel safe, it is hard to learn and interact in the classroom. This analysis has extended to classroom dynamics, particularly the impact of preferential treatment by the teacher on one group of students over another. In the essay "Failing at Fairness: How America's Schools Cheat Girls," the authors Myra and David Sadker (2001) provide significant evidence to support their assertion. What was it like where you went to elementary school? Did bullies impact the learning environment, or did a teacher demonstrate preferences for one group over another? By recognizing that we need to feel safe in order to form interpersonal relationships and meet the need for love and belonging, we come closer to creating safe spaces where children are free to learn.

Once we have been integrated in a group, we begin to assert our sense of self and self-respect, addressing our need for **self-esteem** (4). Self-esteem is essentially how we feel about ourselves, and in the previous example, the authors detail how girls' self-esteem is diminished and the danger of depression increases over time (Sadker & Sadker, 2001). This progression also involves changing body images. Coupled with the frequent portrayal of very thin women in advertisements and magazines specifically designed for preadolescent and developing teens, the question "Am I thin enough yet?" becomes central to girls and young women. Sharlene Hesse-Biber (2001), in an article with that question as the title, provides a quote that captures this viewpoint.

> Ever since I was ten years old, I was just a very vain person. I wanted to be the thinnest, the prettiest. 'Cause I thought, if I look like this, then I'm going to have so many boyfriends, and guys are going to be in love with me, and I'll be taken care of for the rest of my life. I'll never have to work, you know?
>
> —Delia, college senior (p. 527)

While we can recognize that not everyone shares Delia's view as expressed in this quote, we can also acknowledge through observation that the image of a thin woman as an object of desire is common and contemplate the consequences. There are numerous studies on the increase about anorexia and bulimia and other related eating disorders that relate to self-concept, the combination of self-esteem and self-image. By reinforcing unhealthy body ideals in materials that target girls early in life, we impact self-esteem.

Maslow discusses the next level in terms of how we feel about ourselves and our ability to assert control and influence over our lives. Once we are part of a group and have begun to assert ourselves, we start to feel as if have reached our potential and are actively making a difference in our own world. Maslow calls this level the need for **self-actualization** (5). Self-actualization can involve feeling accepted for who you are, accepting yourself, and perceiving a degree of control or empowerment in your environment.

Beyond these levels, Maslow points to our basic human curiosity about the world around us. When we have our basic needs met, and do not need to fear losing our place in a group or access to resources, we are free to explore and play, discovering the world around us. Our **need to know** (6) drives us to grow and learn. Perhaps you've taken an elective class that sparked your interest in a new area or started a new sport or hobby. If you work at a low-paying job that barely meets your basic needs, or your class load in your major is significant, you might not be able to explore all your interests. For example, celebrations of our humanity in areas of art, music, and architecture all represent expressions of our drive to explore and create, but we must first meet our basic needs.

Finally, beyond curiosity and the desire to know what makes things happen or why things work, we have an **aesthetic need to experience beauty** (7) for its own sake. Beauty takes many forms for many people, and the experience of sky-diving or bungee-jumping may for some rival the experience of seeing a famous painting or listening to music. The key is appreciating form, design, or experience for its own sake, not just focusing on its function or ability to meet basic needs.

We can see in Maslow's hierarchy how our basic needs are quite concrete, but as we progress through the levels, we increase our degree of interconnectedness with others, relying on our relationships with others to support our level and, in turn, helping others achieve their goals.

It should be said at this point that Maslow's hierarchy, though in many aspects universal, nonetheless focuses on individual needs. Western cultures typically promote the individual, and by extension the individual's needs and wants, from concrete to abstract, are regarded as important. Other cultures see things differently. The Confucian concept of *Jen,* for example, holds that "benevolence" or "humaneness," or our treatment of others, is the highest form of virtue or excellence to which one can aspire (Kessler, 1998). This emphasis on the group, as opposed to the individual, promotes the meeting of the needs of all. Through meeting everyone's needs, individual needs are then met. Rather than getting "my fair share" first, some cultures value the giving of your "share" to the group, through your effort and creativity; by this giving, your needs will be met by the group.

Exercise

Looking at Maslow's hierarchy, how might understanding this help you if you are a supervisor responsible for a shift? a parent? a counselor? Write down one use of the information for each example.

Schutz's Interpersonal Needs

William Schutz, like Abraham Maslow, provides a useful framework for the discussion of interpersonal needs. In his theory (1966), Schutz points to three key interpersonal needs that are largely universal: affection, inclusion, and control.

The need for **affection,** according to Schutz, is the need we have to feel that people like us, or we, ourselves, can be loved and wanted. Can you see where this need may connect to one of Maslow's needs? Schutz takes this need one step further with his discussion of what happens when this need is not met and indicates two opposite categories. If a person does not feel liked, he or she may withdraw and not let others get close. Schutz describes people who exhibit these behavioral characteristics as **underpersonals.** The opposite of this withdrawn approach to interpersonal relationships is the **overpersonal** individual, who has such a strong need to be liked that he or she constantly seeks approval from others. The middle ground is where a person, called a **personal individual,** is mature and balanced in his or her approach to interpersonal relationships, both meeting the need for affection and understanding that not being liked by everyone is normal.

After our need for affection, Schutz discusses the need for **inclusion,** the need for us to belong to a group. Our need for inclusion drives us to communicate with others, much as belonging is a basic human need according to Maslow. In new situations, where the majority of people already know each other, people can feel out of place. Take, for example, a chat room or bulletin board group on the Internet. The new person, or newbie, can read the rules of the group and even "lurk," or read messages without ever posting a reply, in order to gain information and understand how to communicate in this context. This alone, however, will not prepare anyone adequately to leap into the group and post his or her opinion. As in group communication, the members will come to know one another through interaction, and until that step occurs, the newbie won't truly understand the chat group or bbs community. Nonetheless, our need to be included is fundamental across all cultures and languages, and meeting that need through interpersonal communication is important.

In terms of this need to be included or belong, Schutz outlines three major categories: **undersocial, oversocial,** and **social.** As in the case of an underpersonal individual, an undersocial one does not seek out communication interaction with others. When presented with a situation where communication occurs, he or she tends to be shy and withdrawn. The opposite of an undersocial person is an oversocial person, who can be characterized by the need to constantly communicate, often dominating the conversation by taking the speech turns from others. A social person is balanced and both says what needs to be said and also listens to others.

Related to this is the idea that interpersonal communication can involve messages on more than one level in varying social settings. **Content messages** focus on the superficial level meaning of the message. Let's say you ask your friend for help, and she replies in an upbeat way "sure," maintaining eye contact and waiting for you to relay how she can help. The literal meaning of her response is affirmative or yes, but the way she says it conveys meaning about your relationship. **Relationship messages,** which happen at the same time as content messages, focus on how the message was said. In this case, the upbeat tone of "sure" combined with clear eye contact communicates that the participants have a relationship. By paying attention to both types of messages, we can come to understand the degree to which someone is social and discern relationships within conversations.

Finally, Schutz discussed our need for **control,** which also relates to one of Maslow's levels. Can you find which one? In our drive to control our surroundings, we at times may control others, the situation, or type of interpersonal relationship. This need for control can be for some—called **abdicrats**—a burden of responsibility they would rather shift to others. For others, called **autocrats,** there is a need to control without input from others. **Democrats** share the need for control between the individual and the group.

Can you think of people you know who fit these categories? At the same time, can you remember an obstacle to communication that applies to these categories? People are not categories or labels, and though they exhibit similar behavioral characteristics, they do so in different ways to varying degrees. They are also involved in the dynamic process of communication, where self-concept is constantly redefined through interaction. This means people can get caught in cycles where, for example, they withdraw from interpersonal relationships. It also posits that people change over time, allowing for the possibility that people improve their relationships and strike a healthy balance.

Johari Window

At the end of the 1960s, when the relationship between a person and the world was a frequent topic of discussion, some individuals advocated building bridges (lines of communication) between people and countries rather than walls. Joseph Luft (1970) and Harry Ingram investigated the realm of individual growth and the development of relationships with others. They presented their now famous Johari Window (the name was created by combining their two first names, Joe and Harry). In this window, or table, they present four types of information that are relevant to the self. In the first quadrant (1), as you can see in Figure 5.3, is the open quadrant, where information is known to both you and others, like how tall you are and your name. The next quadrant (2) the window presents is that information that others know about us that we don't even know. Perhaps someone notices something in your hair

FIGURE 5.3 *The Johari Window*

you didn't know was there, or your supervisor recognizes in you potential that you didn't know you had. The third quadrant (3) focuses on information you hide from others, considering the information private. Finally, the unknown quadrant (4) covers information about you that no one, including you, knows. How would you handle an emergency? How would you do in a certain job? You haven't done it yet, so no one knows.

Social Penetration Theory

The field of communication draws from many disciplines—in this case, from two prominent social psychologists. Irwin Altman and Dalmas Taylor (1973) articulated the social penetration theory, which describes how we move from superficial talk to intimate and revealing talk. They discuss how we attempt to learn about others so that we can better understand how to interact. With a better understanding of them through more information, we are in a better position to predict how they may behave, what they may value, or what they might feel in specific situations. We usually gain this understanding of others without thinking about it through observation or self-disclosure. In this model, often called the onion model (Figure 5.4), we see how we start out on superficial level, but as we peel away layers, we gain knowledge about the other person that encompasses both breadth and depth.

We come to know more about the way a person perceives a situation (breadth), but also gain perspective into how he or she sees the situation through an understanding of their previous experiences (depth). Imagine these two spheres, which represent people, coming together. What touches first? The superficial level. As the two start to overlap, the personal levels may touch, then the intimate level, and finally the core levels may even touch. Have you ever known two people who have been together for a very long time? They know each other's stories and finish each other's sentences. They might represent the near overlap, where their core values, attitudes, and beliefs are similar through a lifetime of shared experiences.

In the onion model, we also move from public to private information as we progress from small talk to intimate conversations. The outer surface can be peeled away, and each new layer reveals another until you arrive at the heart of the onion. People interact on the surface and only remove layers as trust and confidence grows.

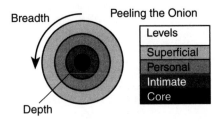

FIGURE 5.4 *The Onion Model*

Source: Adapted from Altman & Taylor (1973).

Another way to look at social penetration theory is to imagine an iceberg. What can you see from the surface? Not much. But once you start to go under the water, you gain an understanding of the large size of the iceberg and the extent of its depth. We have to go beyond superficial understanding to know each other, and we have to progress through the process of self-disclosure to come to know and understand one another. See Figure 5.5 for an illustration of an iceberg model. This model has existed in several forms since the 1960s and serves as a useful illustration of how little we perceive of each other with our first impressions and general assumptions.

Review	***Why Do We Engage in Interpersonal Communication?***
Gain information	We engage in interpersonal communication to gain information. This information can involve directions to an unknown location or a better understanding about another person through observation or self-disclosure.
Understand communication contexts	We also want to understand the context in which we communicate, discerning the range between impersonal and intimate, to better anticipate how to communicate effectively in each setting.
Understand our identity	Through engaging in interpersonal communication, we come to perceive ourselves, our roles, and our relationships with others.
Meet our needs	As Maslow and Shutz discuss, we meet our needs through interpersonal communication.

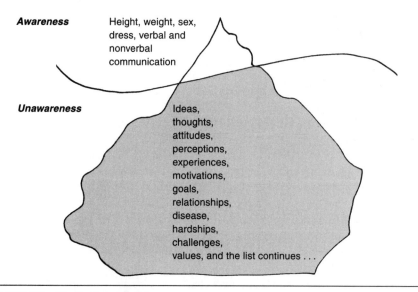

FIGURE 5.5   *The Iceberg Model*

Source: American Field Service (1997).

Self-Disclosure

> *I am afraid to tell you who I am, because, if I tell you who I am,*
> *you may not like who I am, and that's all I have.*
> —John Powell (Woods, 1997)

With this framework in mind, let's examine the process of self-disclosure. **Self-disclosure** is information, thoughts, or feelings we tell others about ourselves that they would not otherwise know. For example, if you tell someone that you liked or disliked a particular website, your discussion of your attitudes is self-disclosure. However, if you tell someone you are tall or short, large or small, or wear eyeglasses (and you have them on), then your discussion of information is already apparent to the listener and therefore not self-disclosure.

As we discussed previously, in order for us to meet our needs, we need people, and for them to know what our needs and wants are, we have to communicate them. In addition, we have basic human needs such as affection, inclusion, and control that are met through interpersonal relationships. One way we try to get our needs met and build relationships is through self-disclosure.

Can you recall a time when you met someone new whom you wanted to get to know better? What did you talk about? Could some of what you discussed with the person have been considered small talk? You may have told him or her your name or what you do. Where do you think this type of conversation falls within the framework of the Johari Window?

Let's say the person also wanted to get to know you better. How did he or she respond? Probably with similar information, like name or area of study. Where did your conversation go from there? If it stayed on small talk for long, you may have felt you were not getting anywhere. That's because you are playing a game, and it takes two to play. You disclose something about yourself, and the other person reciprocates, or also discloses something. Your conversation is off and running, and you both play the game.

Sometimes, however, conversations go awry and don't seem to work out. One key denominator across conversations is that the degree to which we adapt to one another impacts our communication. Roderick Hart (1972; Carlson, Hart, & Eadie, 1979), in his Rhetorical Sensitivity Theory, discusses three different conversational styles and how they interact to cultivate or discourage communication. Conversational participants Hart calls **noble selves** stand by their personal beliefs without adapting to others' attitudes, beliefs, or values. **Rhetorical reflectors,** however, change their messages to meet others' expectations. Between the firm stance on principles and the ability to change in conversation like a chameleon, the **rhetorically sensitive** find common ground with others. People often exhibit behaviors associated with all three categories, depending on the context and environment. Rhetorical sensitivity theory demonstrates the principle that effective communication is facilitated with sensitivity by adjusting what you say to the listener and how you say it. It also underscores the importance of the ability to understand and develop appropriate responses to situations based on concern for yourself, your concern for others, and your knowledge of the context and environment.

Looking back at our previous example, you may recall that, through self-disclosure, people get to know one another. Taking into account the need to be rhetorically sensitive, you may discuss likes and dislikes, but you may also talk more about thoughts, ideas, or feelings that you don't share with everyone. As you do this, the other person may disclose information about himself or herself, and you both get to know each other better, forming bonds of trust. As the trust grows, the level of intimacy can deepen.

Satisfactory communication involves a mutual understanding and agreement on whether or how much to self-disclose. If one person self-discloses a thought or feeling that is too personal, the other person may not be ready to handle it. For example, let's pretend you have known a new co-worker for only a day, and the next day you see him and ask "How are you?" He then responds with great detail about his personal problems, and you begin to look away. Your greeting was a social ritual, and the communication was meant to establish a connection but not gain information, with a person with whom you have not developed a significant relationship. The other person, being rhetorically insensitive, missed the nature of your inquiry and instead self-disclosed information you did not request. By focusing on the types of self-disclosure that occur in a relationship, you can better reach that understanding or mutual agreement and avoid pitfalls. Which quadrant in the Johari Window are we now talking about?

Principles of Self-Disclosure

Now that we've examined self-disclosure, let's focus on five principles of self-disclosure (Beebe, Beebe, & Redmond, 2002) that can help guide us in our own interactions and provide insight into why other people tell us about themselves.

1. Self-disclosure usually moves in small steps. We usually disclose small bits of information about ourselves in relatively small steps, and, as our trust increases with one another, the degree to which we are likely to disclose more personal information is influenced. We gain trust in one another at each step and may become more likely to disclose more information, increase our time spent talking with each other, or decrease the times between connecting with one another.

2. Self-disclosure moves from impersonal to intimate information. Following the first principle, each small step leads to additional disclosure. According to Altman and Taylor's (1973) *Theory of Social Penetration,* we move from impersonal to intimate information. We might move from the exchange of names and major study areas to likes/dislikes, hometowns, and family backgrounds before discussing more personal information.

3. Self-disclosure is reciprocal. In the United States in particular, and many places in general, when you disclose something about yourself there is an expectation that the other person will also disclose something about him- or herself, usually at the same level. The **dyadic effect** is the formal term for this reciprocal process. As we've seen previously, we seek to reduce uncertainty, and this process helps facilitate understanding. But keep in mind that while there may be an expectation, you are in control of your disclosure. There are times when you might feel you have to share something, and by understanding that this expectation is part of the process, you have the choice of how you want to handle it.

4. Self-disclosure involves risk. Related to our previous principle, we recognize that by revealing information about ourselves we expose ourselves to a degree of vulnerability. Perhaps you can recall or know someone who shared something with just a best friend, only to have everyone hear about it. People are hurt when their confidence is betrayed and may think twice before sharing again. We also need to understand that the risk rejection in the process of self-disclosure is inherent, but without disclosure we have a difficult time coming to know and trust one another. By taking small steps, we are able to reciprocate and form important relationships.

5. Self-disclosure involves trust. *Trust* is the ability to place confidence in or rely on the character or truth of someone. It involves a degree of understanding and certainty, or the ability to know where someone is coming from and how you will get along with him or her. Trust is a process, not a thing. You gain it with time in a relationship, and you can lose it as well, but never lose sight that it is central to interpersonal communication and, by extension, the process that leads to interaction. If someone discloses something to you, he or she disclosed it to you and not someone else. Thus, there is an expectation of confidence. While there may be times where there is a compelling reason to disclose information, such as abuse or a suicide threat, in general it is important that people can rely on you.

Summary

In this chapter we have discussed the difference between intrapersonal and interpersonal communication. Within these contexts, we've examined self-concept and how we come to know and understand ourselves. We have also addressed what motivates us to form relationships, different theories on our interpersonal needs, and, specifically, social penetration theory as it relates to the formation of relationships through interpersonal communication. Finally, we discussed the process and five principles of self-disclosure and the importance of rhetorical sensitivity.

For More Information _____

Korzybski, A.: **http://userwww.sfsu.edu/~rsauzier/Korzybski.html**

Ting-Toomey, S.: "Cross-Cultural Face-Negotiation: An Analytical Overview" by Stella Ting-Toomey, presented on April 15, 1992, David See-Chai Lam Centre for International Communication. **http://www.cic.sfu.ca/forum/ting-too.html**

Review Questions _____

1. Factual Questions
   a. What are the levels of Maslow's hierarchy?
   b. What three areas comprise Schutz's theory of interpersonal needs?
   c. What are Knapp's stages for relational development? for relational deterioration?

2. Interpretative Questions
   a. Is it self-contradictory to say relationships are dynamic so be careful of generaliza tions in one part of the chapter, and then provide generalizations as guidelines in another?
   b. What does the term *self* mean? the term *relationship*?
   c. Can you think of an example for each of Knapp's stages?

3. Evaluative Questions
   a. Do you think interpersonal communication impact intrapersonal communication. Vice versa? Which has the greater effect? Explain.
   b. Do you think self-disclosure is natural? Is it the only way to come to know some- one? Explain your response.
   c. Do you think Maslow's hierarchy (1970) or Schutz's needs (1966) still apply to- day? Why or why not?

4. Application Questions
   a. Create a list of examples of the stages of relational development and relational deterioration. Survey an equal number of men and women, asking whether any of the stages sound familiar, and document their responses. Compare your results.
   b. Create a list of Schutz's needs, and ask people if there are any other needs that motivate people to form relationships. Do their responses fit within Schutz's three concepts, or did you create a new category?
   c. Record your self-talk in note form throughout the day. Do you notice any patterns?

References _____

Abbey, A. (1982). Sex differences in attributions of friendly behavior: Do males misperceive fe- males' friendliness? *Journal of Personality and Social Psychology, 42,* 830–838.

Altman, I., & Taylor, D. (1973). *Social penetration: The development of interpersonal relationships.* New York: St. Martin's Press.

American Foreign Service. (1997). *AFS student yearbook and the arrival orientation* (p. 71). New York: American Field Service Intercultural Programs.

Beebe, S., Beebe, S., & Redmond, M. (2002). *Interpersonal communication: Relating to others* (3rd ed.). Boston: Allyn and Bacon.

Berger, C. (1986). Response-uncertain outcome values in predicted relationships: Uncertainty re- duction theory then and now. *Human Communication Research, 13,* 34–38.

Berger, C., & Calabrese, R. (1975). Some explorations in initial interactions and beyond: Toward a developmental theory of interpersonal communication. *Human Communication Research, 1,* 98–112.

Carlson, R., Hart, R., & Eadie, W. (1979). Attitudes toward communication and the assessment of rhetorical sensitivity. *Communication Monographs, 47,* 1–22.

Cooley, C. (1922). *Human nature and the social order* (rev. ed.). New York: Scribners.

Festinger, L. (1954). A theory of social comparison processes. *Human Relationships, 7,* 117–140.

Gilligan, C. (1982). *In a different voice.* Cambridge, MA: Harvard University Press.

Gudykunst, W. B. (1994). *Ethnocentrism Scale and Instructions. Bridging differences: Effective intergroup communication* (2nd ed.; pp. 98–99). Thousand Oaks, CA: Sage.

Gudykunst, W. B. (1995). Anxiety/uncertainty management theory. In R. W. Wiseman (Ed.), *Intercultural communication theory* (pp. 8–58). Thousands Oaks, CA: Sage.

Hagel, J., & Armstrong, A. (1997). *Net gain: Expanding markets through virtual communities.* Princeton, NJ: Harvard Business School Press.

Hart, R. (1972). The rhetoric of the true believer. *Speech Monographs, 38,* 249–261.

Hesse-Biber, S. (2001). Am I thin enough yet? In P. S. Rothenberg (Ed.), *Race, class and gender in the United States* (5th ed.; pp. 527–533). New York: Worth Publishers.

Insel, P., & Jacobson, L. (1975). *What do you expect? An inquiry into self-fulfilling prophecies.* Menlo Park, CA: National Press.

Kellermann, K., & Reynolds, R. (1990). When ignorance is bliss: The role of motivation to reduce uncertainty in uncertainty reduction theory. *Human Research, 17,* 5–75.

Kessler, G. (1998). *Voices of wisdom: A multicultural philosophy reader* (3rd ed.). Belmont, CA: Wadsworth.

Korzybski, A. (1933). *Science and sanity.* Lancaster, PA: International Non-Aristotelian Library Publishing Co.

Maslow, A. (1970). *Motivation and personality* (2nd ed.; pp. 35–150). New York: Harper & Row.

Pearson, J. C., & Nelson, P. E. (1985). *Understanding and sharing: An introduction to speech communication* (3rd ed.). Dubuque, IA: William C. Brown.

Pearson, J., West, R., & Turner, L. (1998). *Gender and communication* (4th ed.). New York: McGraw-Hill.

Rosenfeld, L. (1979). Self-disclosure avoidance: Why I am afraid to tell you who I am. *Communication Monographs, 46,* 63–74.

Rosenthal, R., & Jacobson, L. (1968). *Pygmalion in the classroom.* New York: Holt, Rinehart, and Winston.

Rosnow, R., & Rosenthal, R. (1999). *Beginning behavioral research: A conceptual primer* (3rd ed.). Englewood Cliffs, NJ: Prentice Hall.

Sadker, M., & Sadker, D. (2001). Failing at fairness: How America's schools cheat girls. In P. S. Rothenberg (Ed.), *Race, class and gender in the United States* (5th ed.; pp. 556–561). New York: Worth Publishers.

Schutz, W. (1966). *The interpersonal underworld* (pp. 13–20). Palo Alto, CA: Science and Behavior Books.

Shedletsky, L. J. (1989). Meaning and mind: An intrapersonal approach to human communication. Bloomington, IN: ERIC Clearinghouse on Reading and Communication Skills. [ED 308 566]

Stokes, J., Fuehrer, A., & Childs, L. (1980). Gender differences in self-disclosure to various target persons. *Journal of Counseling Psychology, 27.*

Sunnafrank, M. (1986). Predicted outcome value during initial interactions: A reformulation of uncertainty reduction theory. *Human Communication Research, 13,* 3–33.

Sunnafrank, M. (1990). Predicted outcome value and uncertainty reduction theory: A test of competing perspectives. *Human Communication Theory, 17,* 76–150.

Woods, J. (1997). *Communication in our lives* (p. 128). Belmont, CA: Wadsworth Publishing Company.

6

Interpersonal Relationships

Chapter Objectives _____

After completing this chapter, you should be able to:

1. Identify and describe seven key characteristics of healthy interpersonal relationships.
2. Demonstrate the four functions of interpersonal relationships.
3. Identify and describe four principles of relationships.
4. Identify and provide examples for six types of relationships.
5. Identify and describe the difference between content and relationship messages.
6. Demonstrate the four myths about communication in interpersonal relationships.
7. Describe key advantages and disadvantages of interpersonal communication.
8. Describe eight skills for starting relationships.

Introductory Exercise 1 _____

Please list what is important to you. What each person values is different. What matters here is that you create your personal list mentioning what you value and what is important to you. For example, you may value your grandmother or your freedom of speech and might mention both on your list.

Introductory Exercise 2 _____

Please list five people with whom you associate or consider friends. Consider how well you know them, what kinds of conversations you have, and how you feel about yourself around them. Please list a word or words to describe the relationship.

Introductory Exercise 3 _____

Please list five people with whom you no longer associate or consider friends. Consider how well you knew them, what kinds of conversations you had, and how you felt about yourself around them. Please list a word or words to describe the relationship.

> *The relationship is the communication bridge between people.*
> —Alfred Kadushin

Relationships take many forms and are in constant change. They may range from impersonal, professional, workplace, family, friend, to intimate, and each relationship is unique. In the first exercise, you were asked to write down what is important to you. If you haven't done this yet, take a moment and use the margin. Once you've completed your list, look at what you wrote and see what relates to relationships. For many people, many if not all of what they write in this exercise directly relates to relationships. Relationships meet our needs and influence not only who we are but also who we will become. Since we can say with confidence that relationships make a significant impact on individuals, we should make every effort to understand them better.

This chapter will introduce you to the characteristics, principles, functions, and types of relationships. Within the interpersonal communication context, we will examine content and relationship messages, common misconceptions, and communication apprehension. Finally, we will discuss what is commonly referred to as the dark side of interpersonal communication, involving the constructive and destructive function of communication in relationships.

Characteristics of Healthy Interpersonal Relationships

And the day came when the risk to remain tight in a bud was more painful than the risk it took to blossom.

—Anaïs Nin

When considering the basic characteristics of relationships, it might seem natural to think about how they meet your needs. While relationships certainly meet individual needs, consider the perspective that the other person in the relationship has several expectations of you. No doubt you yourself have sat through a conversation where you asked yourself "Why should I listen?" or "What does this have to do with me?" These questions are normal and natural, but people seldom actually state these questions in so many words or say them out loud. Relationships require more than one person and more than one set of needs. By recognizing that we can meet our needs together, we can focus on the characteristics of relationships from a perspective of common ground.

1. Ethics

One central but often unspoken expectation of people is that we will be ethical. In terms of interpersonal communication, this means that we perceive one another as human beings with common interests and needs, and we do not intentionally exploit each other. Perceiving a relationship as a means to an end, and only focusing on what you get out of it, will lead you to treat people as objects. In the Tuskegee syphilis case study (found on page 60), we examined how, through language and perspective, people did inhuman things. Doctors and researchers viewed patients as only "subjects," like objects or things, and lost sight of their humanity. While not all examples are this extreme, it is a useful lesson for our everyday interactions. The best salespeople recognize that the key to success is a healthy relationship where the customers' needs are met, thereby meeting their own needs.

2. Reciprocity

Tyler (1978) discusses ethical communication and specifically indicates reciprocity as a key principle. **Reciprocity** is defined as a relationship of mutual exchange and interdependence. We've examined previously the transactional nature of interpersonal communication, and it is important to reinforce this aspect here. We exchange meaning with one another in conversation, and much like a game, it takes more than one person to play. This leads to interdependence, or the dependence of the conversational partners on one another. Inequality in the levels of dependence can negatively impact the communication and, as a result, the relationship.

Let's say you want to go to a movie, but your friend has homework and can't go out until it's finished. If you help him or her by editing a paper or finding the error in a math problem, you are helping your friend complete work and meet his or her needs. Your friend can then go to the movie with you, and you both can enjoy the evening out on the town. If, however, your friend always needs help with every assignment, and you feel like you can't just leave him or her, the balance of reciprocity has been lost. It's a process of give and take for mutual benefit, developing interdependence and strengthening the relationship. If one person is taken advantage of repeatedly, or one person is consistently dominant, that balance can be lost, which can hurt the relationship.

3. Mutuality

Mutuality means that you search for common ground and understanding with your conversational partner, establishing this space and building on it throughout the conversation. This involves examining viewpoints other than your own and taking steps to ensure that speech integrates an inclusive, accessible format rather than an ethnocentric one.

Your friend or roommate might be from a place that is very different from the place or places where you have lived. She may be used to the Chicago club scene, and you know how to line dance to country music. She may know the words to every rap song, just as you may know the lyrics to most country tunes. At first this might seem to you as very different orientations to the world. You might even not want to talk to her because you perceive that as very different from you. If you asked her what some of the rap songs are about, you would find themes of overcoming obstacles in life, dealing with loss of a loved one, and love for each other are common themes. There will still be differences, no doubt, but by finding that while your music tastes may run down different roads, the ground they cover is similar in many ways reinforces the common ground you share. We all have basic human and interpersonal needs that tie us together. Searching for this common ground can lead to conversations you didn't anticipate, and you both might learn something about each other. She might even show you the C step as you share line moves in dancing.

4. Nonjudgmentalism

Nonjudgmentalism underscores the need to be open-minded and represents an expression of one's willingness to examine diverse perspectives. Your conversational partner expects you to state the truth, as you perceive it, with supporting and clarifying information to support your position, speaking honestly. He or she also expect you to be open to his or her point of view and be able to negotiate meaning and understanding in a constructive way.

Nonjudgmentalism may include, as we saw in the previous example about rap and country music, taking the perspective that different is not inherently bad and that there is common ground to be found with each other.

5. Honesty

While this characteristic should be understood, we can see evidence of breakdowns in communication when conversational participants perceive they are not being told the whole truth. This does not mean that relationships always require frank honesty. The use of euphemisms and displays of sensitivity are key components of effective communication. The importance of approaching communication from an honest perspective where you value and respect your conversational partner is key to a healthy relationship.

Honesty directly relates to trust, a cornerstone in the foundation of a relationship. Without it, the building would fall down. Without trust, a relationship will not open and develop the possibility of mutual understanding. After you both share your insights in music and dance, you may find that gangsta rap still drives you nuts. Being honest with your roommate or friend about your feelings can let her know that it is not her that you do not want to be around, but the particular music that you dislike. Your roommate can play other music when you are in the room, and your increased understanding can build trust.

6. Respect

Respect should be present throughout a conversation, demonstrating the conversational participants' high esteem for each other. **Respect** can be defined as an act of giving and displaying particular attention to the value you associate with someone. This definition involves two key components. You need to give respect in order to earn from others, and you need to show it. Displays of respect include making time for conversation, not interrupting, and even giving appropriate eye contact during conversations.

Respect may also involve listening to your roommate's music, even asking clarifying questions to learn more about it, because you recognize it is something she values. Rolling your eyes as she explains a rap artist's motivation for writing a song may communicate contempt, and that could be taken personally, hurting her feelings. For her to understand you, and what you value, you also need to demonstrate respect for what she values.

7. Trust

Communication involves sharing, and that requires trust. **Trust** means the ability to rely on the character or truth of someone, that what you say you mean and your conversation partner knows it. Trust is a process, not a thing. It builds over time, through increased interaction and the reduction of uncertainty. It can be lost, but it can also be regained. It should be noted that it takes a long time to build trust in a relationship, and it can be lost in a much shorter amount of time. Acknowledging trust and its importance in relationships is the first step in focusing on this key characteristic.

We've discussed trust in relation to honesty, but we can also recognize that it is woven throughout all of the characteristics for a healthy relationship. It is an integral, or important, part of any relationship, from the most impersonal relationship with your local customer service representative to the most intimate with your partner or friend.

Consider these expectations when forming relationships, and you will help address many of these natural expectations of others and develop healthier relationships.

INTERCULTURAL COMMUNICATION 6.1 • *Perceptions and Difference*

Have you ever wondered what it would be like if you were born in another culture? Into a different language? With different features, race, ethnic, or gender orientation? Understanding how we form ideas of difference and how we treat one another as different is a large area of research. Understandably, it is complex and challenging. We know that self-concept is connected to communication with others, and the type and style of messages you receive (or don't receive) as you grow influence how you see yourself and what you expect you can accomplish for the rest of your life.

In the United States, people are often treated differently because of perceptions of difference each day. Regardless whether you a woman or a man, black or white, short or tall, you have no doubt been treated differently than others at some point. Understanding how that feels is an important lesson on the concept, and application, of discrimination.

In 1968, a public elementary school teacher in Riceville, Iowa, decided that, in the time of civil rights movement and an increased understanding of difference at a national level, her students lacked an awareness of discrimination first hand. In order to teach her all-white, all-Christian third graders how it felt, she divided the classroom into groups of blue-eyed children and brown-eyed children. For one day, she celebrated the success of blue-eyed children while chastising the brown-eyed children for each mistake. She instructed the "subordinate" group to wear cloth collars. Soon, the "dominant" group turned on their once friends and continued the discrimination. The following day, she celebrated the success of brown-eyed children, now freed from their collars, while treating the collared blue-eyed children with contempt. She presented messages and examples of their failures, and the now "dominant" group returned the treatment they received the day before. She observed quiz scores and performance levels fell for all children while they were in the "subordinate" group. At the end of the day she discussed the lesson with all of them, dispelling the myths of superiority.

The original case study, entitled *Eye of the Storm*, as well as a followup program, found the effects to be repeatable and the impact long-lasting. How do you think you would handle being a member of the "dominant" group? Or the "subordinate" group? How do you perceive people handling these issues every day? You can see what the original third graders thought in *A Class Divided* over fifteen years after the study.

Sources:
Eye of the Storm, produced by The Center for Humanities, Guidance Associates, 1-800-431-1242
   or go to: www.guidanceassociates.com
A Class Divided, produced by the Public Broadcasting System, 1-800-424-7963 or go to: http://
   www.pbs.org/wgbh/pages/frontline/shows/divided/ This link provides teacher's resources,
   a reading guide and video information.

Functions of Interpersonal Relationships

Relationships serve many purposes but should not be viewed as strictly in terms of their use. Across relationships, however, we can identify four key functions that help us focus on the purpose of the relationship. Through this act of identification, we can then focus on meeting one another's needs and facilitating mutually satisfying relationships.

1. Gain Information

We form and engage in relationships to gain information. This may be as simple as getting clear directions to our destination or as complex as reducing uncertainty about someone we have to come to care a great deal about. Social penetration theory, as we've previously discussed, indicates that we try to gain information about others so that we can interact with them more effectively. We want to be able to predict how they will think about ideas and situations or how they will feel about topics we consider important. We even want, at some level, to be able to predict their actions and get a sense of who they are. We often gain this information through observation or by actively engaging in conversation. The process of self-disclosure is central to our understanding.

2. Create a Context of Understanding

We also create relationships and engage in conversation to help us understand what others mean by the words they choose. We negotiate meaning through the course of conversation, and our ability to effectively understand what a person says as well as how and why he or she said it enables us to get to know him or her better.

3. Establish Identity

We come to know others through relationships, but we also come to know ourselves. Our understanding of the roles and expectations we have of each other enable us to know what needs are present and how best to meet them. We also recognize that we

COMPUTER-MEDIATED COMMUNICATION 6.1 • *Chat Rooms: Bringing People Together*

One way people connect is by setting up an "I-Seek-You" messaging program, similar to Mirabilis LTD's ICQ or America OnLine's popular Buddy List and Instant Messenger programs. It can be used as a conferencing tool by individuals (friends, family, or business associated, for example) on the Internet to chat, email, perform file transfers, play computer games, and exchange information.

Another way people connect is through an Internet Relay Chat (IRC), a chat system developed by Jarkko Oikarinen in Finland in the late 1980s. According to www.internet.com, a source for web-related information about history and current trends, IRC has become very popular as more people get connected to the Internet. The key features that contribute to the popularity are that (1) people can connect from anywhere and (2) the IRC can handle more than two conversation participants. This allows for discussions involving large groups, with each individual member receiving everyone else's comments as they contribute them to the discussion.

Source: http://isp.webopedia.com

play different roles in a relationship at different times, and our ability to perceive expectations allows us to adjust and adapt to the ever-changing nature of relationships.

4. Meet Interpersonal Needs

Schutz (1958) identified three key interpersonal needs that we discussed in Chapter 5. Our need for control, inclusion, and affection are met through relationships. We all have basic human and interpersonal needs that must be met. When needs are not met, there will predictably be an effort to meet those needs. By understanding each other's needs, we can better meet them and in turn see our own needs met.

Principles of Interpersonal Relationships

> *Everyone hears what you say. Friends listen to what you say.*
> *Best friends listen to what you don't say.*
>
> —Anonymous

1. Relationships Meet Need(s)

We've seen that relationships meet needs, and discussed Schutz's (1958) three key interpersonal needs, but Thibault and Kelley (1952) present a related view in the Social Exchange Theory that deserves consideration. This theory states that our interactions and acts of self-disclosure are based on the exchange of rewards and costs. According to this theory, people would naturally want to minimize costs and maximize rewards when considering whether to develop a relationship with someone based on the perceived possible outcomes. When the outcomes are perceived to be greater than the costs, we would be more likely to self-disclose and develop a closer relationship with that person.

On the surface this theory makes sense and is easily applicable to various situations. If we get more out of a relationship than we have to put into it, then we'd be more like to continue the relationship. That statement seems straightforward but requires us to accept the assumption that people recognize each other's point of view and needs and that people always act with full knowledge that other people will recognize their actions and reciprocate. We can readily observe that people often fail to see each other's point of view, and people sometimes act and do good things with full knowledge that no one will ever notice. Though relationships do have costs and offer rewards, and we can see that as humans we are often motivated by the promise of rewards, we shouldn't lose sight that communication interaction is not simply an exchange based on self-interest.

2. Relationships Are Universal

Regardless of language, culture, or geography, we seek to form relationships with one another. In Maslow's terms, we seek love and belonging after our basic needs for sustenance and safety are met. If we can accept that relationships are universal, then it follows that they must be important to us, and by extension that their loss would be hurtful to us. We come to know the world through interactions with others, and as we develop, we make sense of every day through conversation and introspection. When we lose someone, we go through a grieving process. Relationships are clearly important to us.

Look back at your list from Exercise 1. How many points on your list are associated with relationships? Now look at your notes from Exercise 2. What types of words did you list to describe the relationships? You may have indicated that some relationships were very important or close, while others are more impersonal. Regardless of the words you chose to describe your relationships, know that people around the word also have their own words to describe their relationships, and some might be quite similar to yours.

3. Relationships Are Confusing and Contextual

We recognize that relationships meet our needs and that we can even measure them to some extent in terms of rewards and costs, but does everyone share the same values, background, or orientation to the world? Just as each person is different, each conversation has a life of its own. Each interaction and conversation is confusing, meaning that it is a challenge to understand with any degree of accuracy what the other person means, particularly if we do not know him or her well. As we come to know the other person, we become more accurate in our interpretation of his or her meaning, and the relationship grows.

Each conversation is also dependent on context. Context involves all the psychological and physical aspects of the environment that comprise the setting or scene of the interaction. Consider the difference between dinner with your family at the kitchen table and dinner with someone special, with dim lights and candles to illuminate your faces while soothing music plays in the background, at that same kitchen table. The table stays the same, but the context is quite different.

4. Relationships Are Always Changing

While the romantic dinner setting might have been nice, it won't last forever, and even if you try to re-create it the next night, it will be different. If all the factors are the same, from the table to the lighting, then why would it be different? Because we change every day as we experience new things, think new thoughts, grow, and learn. In the same way we change, so do relationships. Each relationship also has a "life" of its own, and as the people who are part of the relationship change, the relationship transforms over time.

This is a key point because people often say "I wish we could go back to the way things were." Wanting things to stay the same may seem natural, but we would miss the point of this principle. What we often want about "the way things were" is not a time or place that no longer exists; instead, we long for the emotions and connections associated with that time or place. By focusing on those emotions and connections, we can make an effort to reconnect, and, while it will not be the same, it can help the relationship grow and develop. If you liked the times when you and a friend went out to see foreign films, but now are "just too busy with work," plan a time together to see a film. Recognize that interaction is not about the film itself, but about something you can share together.

Types of Interpersonal Relationships

1. Impersonal

In order to prepare that romantic dinner, you no doubt needed things like food and candles. When you went to the store, you may have been bumped by someone else pushing a grocery card through a small aisle. The words "excuse me" may have been the only interaction you had with that person, but it counts. After finding all your items, you probably went to the checkout line where the cashier rang up your bill by scanning each item. He or she may have greeted you with "How are you today?" or "Did you find everything you need?" and might close with "Have a nice day." This simple exchange is impersonal communication because the conversational participants to not know each other well. This can change over time, however, and if you continue to interact with the same cashier and get to know him through small talk, your relationship may resemble more of a friendship than an impersonal relationship. This relationship may transform from an impersonal one to something meaningful to the point that, when you go shopping again only to find that the cashier has been replaced by the latest automated, self-scanning machine where you check yourself out, you feel a sense of loss.

2. Professional

Professional relationships are distinct from impersonal relationships in that there is a degree of common ground. Communication might remain on topics of professional interest, but there is an implicit relationship message that acknowledges one another. Professionals often form groups and while they might not know each other well, they nonetheless interact with the common thread of their skills, talents, education, or interests to bind them together. This may take the shape of a professional association with an annual conference. This may also take the shape of a club or service organization like Rotary. At Arizona Western College, professionals in the welding industry have a group called *Soldadores Sin Fronteras*. Welders from both sides of the U.S./Mexican border come together on joint projects, and even though not everyone speaks the same language or comes from the same culture, they have a sense of common ground professionally.

3. Workplace

When we move from interactions once a year at a conference to every day, the nature and tone of conversation changes. Workplace relationships may include impersonal or professional relationships, but simply by the nature of frequent interaction, the conversation participants will come to know each other better. When we self-disclose, others will typically reciprocate and say something about themselves. Over time the knowledge about each other will accumulate and people may even come to consider co-workers as a second family.

4. Family

For most people we can safely say that you did not choose your family, but they instead chose you. If you were born or adopted into a family, the knowledge of who your family members are was something you came to know as you grew. You came to understand the concept of family, in its many forms, through your interaction with family members. Perhaps you had several brothers and sisters, or your grandmother, who surrounded you with conversation and interaction. Family communication, which may include all the categories we've discussed, is a fascinating area of study. We have the influence of significant interaction with specific individuals over normally a substantial amount of time. With all this common history, it makes interaction interesting when family members can say with certainty "remember the time you. . . ." You can also learn destructive traits at the hand of a family member, and those traits may influence your future relationships. Relationships with family members and the study of it, called family communication, is a rich area of study worth investigation.

5. Friend

Next to your parents or caregivers and your teachers, friends will make a significant impact on your life. Relationships with people to whom we are not related, though we certainly can be friends with family members, takes on increasing levels of importance the older we get. In preschool, children often parallel play, or play alone alongside one another, then slowly seek interaction. Playing well with others is an important skill we all hopefully learn as we grow, and in early elementary school friends take on particular importance. Perhaps you remember your "best friend," and how much he or she meant to you. You might not have talked about much at the time, but the interaction was important to you. In middle school and high school, friends and circles of friends become a central influence. As a person matures and gains independence, he or she can learn to negotiate this influence and develop mature friendships.

While this model of the evolution of the concept of friendship may not hold true for everyone, we can nonetheless recognize elements in it that serve us well. We can see the importance and scope of influence friends have in middle school and recognize that changing individual behaviors, like smoking, start with this in mind. We can also recognize that friendships are important, but in different ways at different stages across a lifetime. Healthy friendships often feature many of the key characteristics presented at the beginning of this chapter, and by recognizing these characteristics we can recognize a friend.

6. Intimate

The first thing that many people think of when the word intimate is used is sex. While intimate friends may be sexually involved, focusing on this aspect alone misses an important concept key to intimate relationships. **Emotional intimacy** involves the understanding and empathy formed through the expression of thoughts, feelings, and emotions over time. **Physical intimacy** involves the understanding and empathy formed through physical sharing of our bodies over time.

A common **dichotomy,** or the process of dividing a concept into two mutually exclusive or contradictory ideas, that shows up in the field of gender communication in general is that men seek emotional intimacy through physical intimacy, and women seek physical intimacy through emotional intimacy. While there is some truth in this relationship between emotional intimacy and physical intimacy, defining interaction in terms of only gender ignores the diversity of relationships we share. Whether men and women have basic traits or tendencies is a point of debate, but we can observe than not all men and women are the same. Not everyone seeks intimacy, or engages in sexual behavior, as this dichotomy would portray. Social roles also influence our relationships, and these roles and their associated behaviors are in many ways learned through social interaction. If your father was close or distant emotionally, it may set up expectations for you about how men "should be," but through interactions with others you can come to recognize this is not the only model of masculinity.

7. Nontraditional

Have you ever taken a flight and found yourself talking about very personal issues with someone whom you will never see again? Have you shared with a friend at work an issue that you would not share with your partner or family? We often form friendships that challenge the traditional notions of friendship. It can be cathartic, or involve a release of feelings or information, with someone whom we have no prior connection with and with whom we anticipate no future interaction. On an elevator, we may all observe the unwritten social code that no one talks because the time is relatively brief, but on a plane we may be more likely to self-disclose. People sometimes talk in the checkout line at a grocery store or while shopping and disclose information that may seem out of place with the normal rules of self-disclosure. There is significant research in this area involving online communication in chat rooms and bulletin boards, where people often divulge personal information to people they cannot see. This can be innocent and relatively painless, but if the "instant friend" involves a one-night stand, for example, we may open up ourselves to risks we did not anticipate. In the same way, the people you "chat" with may not be at all who you imagine them to be, or even who they represent themselves to be, and efforts to develop relationships more fully and actually meet them may involve disappointment. This category of relationships involves atypical interaction but is highly contextual. By recognizing that people sometimes ask questions one might normally consider rude in an impersonal context as an overlap of this type of relationship, we can see that people meet their need to connect in a myriad of ways. See Computer-Mediated Communication 6.1 for more information on online communication and relationships.

Content and Relationship Messages

When we interact in conversation, there are often two types of message present. **Content messages** involve the information that we share, and **relationship messages** involve the communication between us that reinforces our relationship. For example, if a teacher gives you direction on an assignment, the content comes in terms of the words and instructions. The relationship is communicated, both verbally and nonverbally, that he or she is the teacher and you are the student. This model extends across all types of relationships, from impersonal to intimate. If we focus only on the content, we may miss an important aspect of the message. Wood (1994) has conducted extensive research in this area and found that men often focus on the content while women tend to focus more on the relationship. While this tendency may not hold true in all contexts with men and women, it allows us a degree of understanding that can lead to increased sensitivity to both aspects of a message.

Misconceptions about Communication in Interpersonal Relationships

> *You may be disappointed if you fail, but you are doomed if you don't try.*
> —Beverly Sills

Now that we've examined content and relationships messages, let's take a look at four common myths about communication and how those myths impact relationships (Seiler, 1996). At first it might seem that if only we paid attention to both content and relationship messages then we would certainly have effective communication, but it is not that simple. Communication is a complex and dynamic process. These common myths may seem like common sense at first, but by examining them a bit more closely we can see how they interfere with our ability to communicate effectively.

1. Communication is a cure-all. "If we only could communicate, everything would be better," should sound familiar. People often make comments like this, reinforcing the first myth that communication can fix any problem. There are no guarantees in communication. If you have a conflict over who is going to do the dishes, you need to talk. You may find, however, that one or both of you is not ready to listen. If there is a fizzle followed by the loss of all lighting in the house, you'll need to call an electrician. You can explain the sound and point to the wall, but the electrician can't talk the wires into working better. Communication is a powerful tool, but not a magical one.

2. Quantity means quality. People who talk without reservation, use their words effectively and frequently, and seem to be at ease communicating are often perceived as friendly and outgoing. People who stumble over their words are often perceived as less friendly or knowledgeable. Both of these perceptions lead us to judgments without much information. Talking a lot is not the same as knowing a lot. You've probably heard the phrase "Don't stick your foot in your mouth," meaning you shouldn't keep talking and get yourself in trouble. There are times when each additional word or gesture only makes a situation worse, not better. Recognizing that a few choice words can carry more weight than a hundred words that miss the point is one step toward understanding the difference between quantity and quality.

3. Meanings of words are sufficient for understanding. We use words to communicate ideas and concepts to each other every day, but if you have ever told someone to meet you *here* only to find out they waited for you *there,* then you know that the words *here* and *there* are meaningless without context and understanding. We create that context and try to understand one another through the course of conversation. As we interact, we check meaning and (hopefully) learn that *here* means *here,* not *there.* What *here* and *there* mean to us is within us, and the words themselves only stand for what we want them to mean. If we fail to effectively communicate what we mean by those words, then our conversational partner will end up interpreting *here* is *there* and missing the point. We need to use concrete terms when we want to communicate specific points and enjoy the many ways we can interpret abstract terms. The term "rock" can mean a naturally occurring stone or a type of music, or even how to hold and soothe a baby. We give the word context and can generally get the idea. The word "love," however, is much harder to describe and define. People have been writing song, stories, and poems or painting pictures and trying to express their own interpretation of this word forever. The beauty of the word is its ability to mean so many things to so many people.

4. Some people have a natural ability to communicate. We are born with the motivation to learn to communicate, but that is not the same thing as being born ready as a walk-on for the latest *Look Who's Talking* film. This series of films has created comedy by giving a baby a voice, and the irony can be quite funny. However, we do not see this in the real world because we learn life one step at a time, and we learn language one word at a time. Each time we learn a word, we come to understand it in context and make connections to previous contexts, coming to grasp the many ways we use words to represent ideas and concepts. Children do this naturally, reinforcing the notion that we have a basic drive to communicate. Just as all children do not learn the same language, they also do not learn how to articulate themselves in the same way. Influences like family, language, and culture can make a significant difference in the way someone communicates verbally and nonverbally as an adult. This serves as a lesson that communication is learned and therefore can be taught. You may know someone who might say she is not a natural at public speaking. You could now respond that public speaking, like all types of communication, is a skill that can be learned and is not inborn. While you might acknowledge that some people seem to be better public speakers, or better at social engagements, you would find it quite difficult to determine where someone's nature and his or her learned behavior, or nurture, are making the difference. It is often the natural inclination combined with a lifetime of learning that makes for a successful communicator, and even a proficient communicator will recognize that there is always something new to learn. Communication is learned; therefore, we can learn new and better ways to get our point across and understanding each other effectively.

Skills for Starting Relationships

A journey of a thousand miles starts with a single step.
—Anonymous

Now that we've discussed several advantages and disadvantages associated with interpersonal relationships, a natural question might be "How do people form relationships?" Beginnings are always fragile times marked by uncertainty and vulnerability, but Beebe, Beebe, and Redmond (2002) highlight nine skills that address that question.

1. Gain information to reduce uncertainty. As much as we seek stimulation and desire new experiences, at some level we appreciate what is familiar and predictable. There are a variety of reasons for this, but the central issues are control and safety. We to feel as if we have a degree or measure of control in our environment, and if we sense we lack control, we will often take steps to regain it. We need to feel safe in order to interact freely, and knowledge about a situation, or even how we know someone will act, helps met that need. According to the Uncertainty Reduction Theory, we seek this control and predictability by gaining information and therefore reducing uncertainty (Berger & Calabrese, 1975, 1982). We can gain information passively, through observation, or actively, through interaction.

2. Provide information about yourself. Self-disclosure usually creates an expectation that the conversational participants will reciprocate. By sharing a small amount of information about ourselves, we encourage others to do the same. This helps address the central issue of uncertainty and allows the conversational participants to start with small talk. You don't have to share information about yourself right away, and you may find that talking about a subject that is distinct from you or the other person is an effective strategy. In Japan, people often start conversations about the weather instead of asking "How are you?" This strategy maintains a sense of space between the conversational participants and focuses attention on a third party, not themselves. Adults and elders in Japan can often be heard to say greetings that involve the weather like "Today is a nice day, isn't it?" or "It's getting colder, huh? We should be careful not to catch a cold." Both interactions signal interest in communication, but the second phrase moves the emphasis from the weather to how the change in the weather will affect us. This strategy of initiating conversation is often considered formal by the young people of Japan today, and while they may not use the same emphasis on the weather, the strategy is nonetheless effective. With this frame in mind, we can see how the "How are you?" question, while itself ritualized in the United States, also allows for a more personal interaction from the start. By recognizing these strategies, you can choose a more or less personal style of interaction when starting to communicate.

3. Adopt an other-oriented perspective. In the previous example, we saw an illustration of how culture can influence communication. If you found yourself next to someone from Japan, and he made a statement about the weather, you might now be better able to understand it as the initiation of small talk. If you spend time in Japan, you may find that young people and elders often speak in distinct ways, much as we see in the United States. By recognizing that people have diverse cultural backgrounds, you develop a more other-oriented perspective. This does not mean that you transform from shy to outgoing, but instead this perspective shifts the emphasis from you to the person with whom you are having a conversation. In Japan there is a saying "Even if we are familiar, we must be courteous to each other." This means that even if you live with a person and think you know him or her well, you should still be respectful and not take advantage. In the United States we often use one word to refer to something we need, such as "paper?" as a request for a piece of paper. To a person from Japan, this single word request may not follow the rules of courtesy and seem unreasonable. If you adopt an other-oriented perspective, you'll be more aware of the nonverbal cues that tell you your request was not appreciated and find better ways of communicating. Since we cannot hope to learn all the rules of every culture—and even if we tried, we would have to recognize those rules are constantly changing and contextual—we need to shift the emphasis from just ourselves to what the other person is saying and consider why and how he or she said it.

4. Observe and act on approachability cues. Approachability cues are words or gestures that indicate an openness to communicate. Eye contact is usually associated with approachability and, like many of these cues, is nonverbal communication. Smiling, sitting next to someone, turning toward him or her, and even waving all signal an openness to communicate. All learn how to pick up on the nonverbal cues that discourage communication or do not indicate approachability. Lack of eye contact, turning away, or movement to create more space between you all discourage rather than encourage communication.

5. Identify and use conversation starters. As we saw in our discussion of a common Japanese greeting, the weather can serve as safe conversation starter. While the notion of talking about the weather might seem quaint or outdated, even to Japanese youth, the strategy still hold promise. By identifying something you both can observe and making a general statement about it, you might initiate a conversation.

6. Follow initiation norms. When one person says "Hi" and someone else responds with "Hi, how are you?," followed by "Fine, thanks, and you?" and then "Good," you may recognize a certain familiarity or predictability. This sense of the familiar stems from the point that this interaction is highly ritualized, meaning we have a certain way of greeting, most people know the rules, and it is much like a game we go through over and over. Malinowski (1935) called this ritual *phatic* *communion.* Much like communion that you might receive at a Catholic church, the process involves several specific steps that are always repeated in the same order with little variation. What happens when someone intentionally or unintentionally breaks the rules of the ritual? People feel uncomfortable, less certain about the individual, and usually create some physical or psychological distance from them. Deviating from this set pattern among people who know each other well is more flexible, and they may even create their own ritual of greeting with new words or even gestures. "What's up?" may replace the words "How are you?" but the purpose and meaning remains the same. By appreciating and playing your part in the rituals of social interaction, you appear more familiar and open to conversation.

7. Present yourself in a positive way. People like to interact with people who smile, seem at ease with themselves, and display approachability cues. Argyle and Henderson (1991) offer us eight cues and ways to display those cues in a positive way and communicate approachability:

> Proximity: Move or lean closer to the person
>
> Orientation: Be in front of or beside the person
>
> Gaze: Establish eye contact
>
> Facial Expression: Smile
>
> Gestures: Nod your head, relax, and don't cross your arms
>
> Posture: Be open, arms down or apart
>
> Touch: If appropriate, touch a shoulder or arm
>
> Tone of voice: Speak clearly and demonstrate enthusiasm

8. Ask questions. Visual cues like the logo of a school on someone's sweatshirt may serve as a simple question like "Did you go to Arizona Western College?" By starting out with a simple, straightforward question, you can establish space and not be too pushy. If the conversation develops you can ask followup questions and learn more about the person. People typically love to talk about themselves and appreciate someone who listens.

9. Have reasonable expectations. You wouldn't like it if someone got too close when you didn't know him or her well or asked questions that were too personal, so return the favor and don't do that when initiating conversation. The golden rule— treat others as you'd like to be treated—serves us well on this point. By considering what you consider appropriate and prefer when getting to know someone, you can better demonstrate respect and start conversations that build into relationships.

Summary

In this chapter we started our discussion by examining seven characteristics of healthy interpersonal relationships. We supported this discussion with the four principles of interpersonal relationships and analyzed seven different types of relationships. We considered the difference between content and relationship messages and the four common misconceptions about communication in relationships. The seven skills for starting relationships offer suggestions for proactive ways for starting to build healthy relationships.

> *We all take different paths in life, but no matter where we go,*
> *we take a little of each other everywhere.*
>
> —Tim McGraw

For More Information

To learn more about strategies to improve interpersonal communication, go to the Michigan State University's website at: **http://www.couns.msu.edu/self-help/suggest.htm**

Review Questions

1. Factual Questions
    a. What is a relationship?
    b. What are the characteristics of healthy interpersonal relationships?
    c. What are the functions of interpersonal relationships?
    d. What is one way you can improve interpersonal communication?

2. Interpretative Questions
    a. From your viewpoint, how do you think that perspective influences relationships?
    b. What characteristic to you consider central to forming healthy relationships?
    c. What is meant by reciprocity?

3. Evaluative Questions
    a. To what extent do relationship help us meet our interpersonal needs?
    b. To what extent do perceptions of difference limit interpersonal communication?
    c. Who controls or regulates the development of a relationship?

4. Application Questions
    a. How do relationships change over time? Interview someone older than you and someone younger than you. See if you find common themes.
    b. How do relationships affect self-concept? Explore and research your answer, finding examples that serve can as case studies.
    c. Can people readily identify ways to improve relationships? Survey ten individuals and see what they identify and if there are common themes.

References

Argyle, M., & Henderson, M. (1991). *The anatomy of relationships.* New York: Guilford Press.
Beebe, S., Beebe, S., & Redmond, M. (2002). *Interpersonal communication: Relating to others* (3rd ed.). Boston: Allyn and Bacon.

Berger, C., & Calabrese, R. (1975). Some explorations in initial interaction and beyond: Toward a developmental theory of interpersonal communication. *Human Communication Research, 1,* 99–112.

Berger, C., & Calabrese, R. (1982). *Language and social knowledge: Uncertainty in interpersonal relations.* Baltimore, MD: Edward Arnold.

Malinowski, B. (1935). *The language and magic of gardening.* London: Allen Unwin.

Schutz, W. (1958). *Firo: A three-dimensional theory of interpersonal behavior.* New York: Holt, Rinehart, and Winston.

Seiler, W. (1996). *Communication: Foundations, skills, and applications* (3rd ed.; pp. 30–32, 283). New York: HarperCollins Publishers.

Thibault, J. W., & Kelley, H. H. (1952). *The social psychology of groups.* New York: John Wiley & Sons.

Tyler, V. (1978). Report of the working groups of the Second SCA Summer Conference on Intercultural Communication. In N. C. Assuncion-Lande (Ed.), *Ethical perspectives and critical issues in intercultural communication* (pp. 170–177). Falls Church, VA: SCA.

Wood, J. (1994). *Gendered lives: Communication, gender and culture.* Belmont, CA: Wadsworth.

Intercultural Communication

Chapter Objectives _____

After completing this chapter, you should be able to:

1. Understand the importance of intercultural communication and its role in the communication process.
2. Understand the need to study intercultural communication.
3. Demonstrate ways to guide your study of intercultural communication.
4. Identify and describe eight characteristics of intercultural communication.
5. Identify and describe three barriers to intercultural communication.
6. Demonstrate six ways to improve intercultural communication.

Introductory Exercise 1 _____

Please list all the groups you are a part of or in which you consider yourself a member. Consider your family, your job, your profession or career, and social groups.

Introductory Exercise 2 _____

From the list you created in Exercise 1, try to create a list of the different, unique, or interesting ways you communicate in each group. For example, do you use any words or terms in the course of work with other co-workers that someone from a different job might not understand?

Introductory Exercise 3 _____

Again, from the list you created in Exercise 1, try to list all the places that your groups have been or interact with and the locations of those places. For example, perhaps your family has roots in Spain and France, but your great-great-grandparents moved to Canada and later to the United States. Also consider all the places, including cities and states that you've visited or lived in. Another example might be at work, where (perhaps) you regularly communicate with offices in other states or even other countries. Note those places.

Introductory Exercise 4 _____

What do you know about the world?

1. What is the most populous country on the planet?
   A. United States
   B. India
   C. China
   D. Brazil

2. Which country has the highest population relative to consumption per person?
   A. United States
   B. England
   C. China
   D. Brazil

3. What percent of the world's population lives in an urban setting?
   A. 15%
   B. 30%
   C. 45%
   D. 60%

4. In how many years is the world's population expected to double (from currently more than 6 billion people)?
   A. 29 years
   B. 39 years
   C. 49 years
   D. 59 years

Source: Adapted from the Environmental News Network Population Quiz. To learn more, go to: http://www.enn.com/features/2000/04/04042000/popquiz_11494.asp

Cover answer key: 1-C, 2-A, 3-C, 4-C

> *The strongest bond of human sympathy outside the family relation should be one uniting working people of all nations and tongues and kindreds.*
> —Abraham Lincoln

We travel now more than ever, and the time it takes us to travel has decreased from weeks and days to hours and minutes. You have no doubt traveled to different cities, states, or even countries. Take a moment and compare your list from Exercise 3 with those of your classmates. Create a large list and see where everyone has visited or lived. If you have access to a map or globe, get it out and compare the locations and perhaps use sticky notes to mark each place. How many places are on your group list?

As you can no doubt see, as a group we have seen places far and wide. Now consider this: Does everyone communicate the same way in all these places? How many different languages are spoken in these places? How many different ways of speaking the same language are used in different places? Perhaps someone in your class has visited Montreal, Canada, and observed how French is a dominant language. Someone else may have traveled to Louisiana and heard French spoken. Still another classmate may have traveled to France and heard French yet again. Are all three types of French spoken the same, using the same words and phrases? Each dialect of French is quite distinct, and if you could bring French speakers together from these three locations, they might not even be able to understand each other. Consider why French is so widely spoken, but at the same time spoken so differently in each location. Can you think of another example? Perhaps Spanish in Puerto Rico, Mexico, and Texas?

Now pretend you could travel to each place, all expenses paid for, and imagine what you might find. An Internet search might provide information. As you began to discover information about each place, you would find that people speak in distinct ways, but also live in different ways, having distinct local customs and ways of doing common things. From the preparation of food to traditional dances, customs of dating and marriage, and times of work and celebration, different places have different cultures. Cultures and intercultural communication play an important role in determining how we see and interpret experiences in the world.

Once upon a time it was only the well-off traveler, merchant, or explorer who traveled distances who could discover new and fascinating ways of living and com-

municating. Now, many of us can expand our awareness of other cultures through travel and, if we can't travel, we can learn about places we haven't visited through the Internet, live web-cameras, and travelogues on web pages. Many researchers have long predicted our world would grow smaller, not in terms of size, but in terms of our ability to interact with each other across time and distance. Marshall McLuhan, a pioneer in the field of communication, predicted what we now know as the "global village," where information and transportation technologies have reduced the time and space required to communicate with one another (McLuhan, 1964).

With the advent of increased travel came increased interaction, the study of what we now call intercultural communication, or communication between cultures, became an important area of research and investigation. In this chapter, we will discuss intercultural communication, examine its many characteristics as they relate to interpersonal communication, and look at a few common barriers to effective communication across cultures.

Definition of Intercultural Communication

> *The most important single ingredient in the formula of success is knowing how to get along with people.*
> —Theodore Roosevelt

As you might imagine, as diverse and multifaceted as intercultural communication is, it is hard to define. Rogers and Steinfatt (1999) defined **intercultural communication** as the exchange of information between individuals who are "unalike culturally." This definition focuses on the interaction, an important part of the dynamic process of communication, but in order for us to grasp the definition, we must also understand what we mean by "culture." Klopf (1991, p. 31) states **culture** is "that part of the environment made by humans." This definition focuses on the concept that culture and language, like meaning and values, are created by us. In order to understand intercultural communication, we must come to understand ourselves and our interactions with others.

Where does culture come from? It comes from us. When we gather in groups and communities, we form culture. Coca-Cola has a different corporate culture than IBM, which has a distinct culture from Microsoft. Washington, DC has a culture different from Atlanta. Specific districts within the Washington, DC area, like Georgetown, also have distinct cultures from the larger community. You will find culture wherever people come together.

Culture is part of the community in which we live and work, and often there are many cultures, or co-cultures, that co-exist and interact. How can we recognize one cultural community from another? How do we come to understand which culture(s) we belong to? How do we become a member of our culture? Before we examine intercultural communication in more depth, let's examine ways of understanding intercultural communication.

Understanding Intercultural Communication

The more a man knows, the more he forgives.
—Confucius

Intercultural communication is one of the youngest fields within the discipline of communication, but it draws upon lessons learned from centuries of travelers from a wide cross-section of academic disciplines. You can probably recall from a history class names like Marco Polo, Captain James Cook, Christopher Columbus, or Ponce de Leon.

Each explorer investigated a part of the world already inhabited by diverse communities and civilizations. These explorers also brought back stories of fascinating new places to their own communities, sparking interest in discovery. New maps were created that, while not technically accurate as today's Global Positioning System referenced maps with the resources of a satellite network perspective, were nonetheless creative in depicting how the "new" regions and even continents were perceived. Travel diaries told stories from a personal perspective about each new place the explorer visited, and again, while not always accurate, they still captured a perspective on people, places, and customs around the time they first interacted.

This wealth of knowledge was in fact quite limited until world events and the ability to travel and communicate across distances quickly began to expand our knowledge of each other. For example, in World War II, many soldiers who had once only known their region, state, or country came into contact with people from diverse countries. One such person was Edward T. Hall. Hall worked in the U.S. Army Corp of Engineers and, as a part of his work, traveled to many countries through the war. He noticed cultures and customs and kept notes that later led him to many insights to intercultural communication. As you might expect, Hall was not the only person to study culture, but he was one of the first individuals to lay the foundation for the formal study of intercultural communication.

According to Guo-Ming Chen and William Starosta (2000), two current researchers in the field, Edward T. Hall came to share many of his insights and earned a distinct place in the field of intercultural communication. He is often considered the "father" of the field (Chen & Starosta, 2000, p. 8). His ideas provided a framework for study and sparked several other researchers' interest in investigating the field. He published *The Silent Language* in 1959, and the term "intercultural communication" came into general use. He is generally credited with eight important contributions to our understanding of intercultural communication (Chen & Starosta, 2000; Leeds-Hurwitz, 1990).

1. **Comparing cultures:** Hall focused on how people interact rather than studying the culture as a single, distinct way of living.
2. **Shift to local perspective:** Hall focused on the local level, and how culture is a practical part of everyone's lives, rather than how a whole culture, from a larger perspective interacts with other cultures.

3. **You don't have to know everything to know something:** Hall focused on cultural aspects like time, space, gestures, and voice as part of culture, stating we could learn from these individual aspects without having a complete understanding of the entire culture.
4. **There are rules we can learn:** Hall focused on the rules people use to interact, making it possible to analyze and predict behaviors and actions.
5. **Experience counts:** Hall focused on how students can learn from their own experiences and advocated personal experience as an important part of understanding intercultural communication.
6. **Differences in perspective:** Hall focused on descriptive linguistics as a model to understand intercultural communication, one the Foreign Service still uses as a base for training. The terms "etic," or studying from a general perspective and "emic," or studying from the culture's own perspective, grew out of his model.
7. **Application to international business:** Hall focused on how Foreign Service training has applications to international business, and as we continue to integrate globally, training in intercultural communication is increasingly the norm for business students.
8. **Integration of disciplines:** Hall focused on the link between culture and communication, bringing together aspects of anthropology and communication as academic disciplines.

As we can see, Hall's contribution to the birth of the formal study of intercultural communication has been significant. His focus on the use of aspects we can study and on rules and direct experience relates directly to interpersonal communication, where cultural norms are communicated between individuals. With his emphasis on a local perspective, we can see the inherent value in studying interpersonal interactions. While they may not represent the larger cultural groups, they nonetheless offer us insight into this fascinating context of communication.

We will no doubt continue to see the field expand as more people discover this fascinating area of study and perceive the practical necessity of understanding intercultural communication in their communities, where they work, and as they travel with increasing frequency. The 2000 U.S. Census for the first time allowed people to indicate their affiliation or identification with more than one racial or ethnic category, leading to the increased understanding that we do not exist as a member of a single culture but rather a community of cultures. As we continue to expand our understanding of this multifaceted area of study, we in many ways reinforce one of Hall's key perspectives, focusing on the local level of culture, to begin the process of understanding.

Characteristics of Cultures

In the following section, we will explore how we learn, share, and interact with culture. Keep in mind that culture, like language and the communication process itself, is dynamic and ever changing. We often belong to more than one community, organization, or cultural tradition, but we can recognize that each group has a common sense of history, customs, and traditions that reinforces its own identity and its place in the larger community. Within these complex systems we can still discuss eight common characteristics, which give us insight to various aspects of culture that can help us be more sensitive to intercultural communication.

Cultures Learn and Share a Common Experience of History and Tradition

A good place to start is to consider where we come to our knowledge of cultures, both those we are a part of and those cultures that we come to know through experience. When a child is born, it is not born with a sense of its culture, language, or customs. A child learns this as it grows, interacts, and becomes a member of a cultural group or a community. As a child grows, he or she comes to understand the way people interact and what is expected through a process called **socialization.** Socialization refers to the process by which a person comes to understand the cultural patterns in order to socialize or interact with other members of a community.

A **community** can be defined as a group of people who share common bonds and relationships and consider themselves a group or community. This simple definition, however, fails to capture the dynamic nature of community, changing and transforming in a process much like the communication process itself. We can say, however, that the community shares many common attributes, such as a common sense of history, values, purpose, and symbols or identity.

Rites of Initiation and Socialization into the Community

Similar examples in North American culture might include the age in which a person becomes eligible to obtain a driver's license. The ritual includes the written and driving examinations, but the license itself often symbolizes more than simply the acknowledged ability to drive. It also includes connotations of freedom and the ability to participate in activities, like driving to work or school, while parents must still drive children or older friends who have not passed the driving test. Another example North American culture might include reaching the age of 18, where a child becomes a legal adult, or age 21, where a legal adult can purchase alcohol. Can you think of examples of rituals that recognize the passing from one phase to another in your own culture? Perhaps a *quinceañera,* a celebration of a young woman's fifteenth birthday, where she is recognized by family and the Hispanic community as having reached adulthood.

Status, an important part of socialization within a culture or community, is your position or social rank in relation to others. We may discuss status in terms of what type of job you hold, what degrees you've earned, or your experience in a particular field. You may have heard of the terms blue-collar and white-collar workers. These terms refer to the shirts those people wore, which were often associated with their professions. An electrician may wear a blue shirt, but an executive would wear a white shirt, with the understanding that he or she would not have to get dirty. Beyond the color association, we can see the division into two classes, often socio-economic, of people. The shirts serve to signal status and group affiliation. Can you think of any way people show their perception of their status?

Status within a cultural group—whether it is an organization in which you work or one that shares your ethnic, racial, or linguistic heritage—is an important part of culture. Loss of status within a cultural group, or the disenfranchisement of a minority culture by a dominant culture, can significantly impact intercultural communication. For example, in the middle to late 1800s Native American tribes that signed treaties with the U.S. government were given specific rights as tribal members in exchange for their lands. Entire communities were relocated to reservations, and while the conditions were often poor, the cultural groups retained their identities as a tribe. Less than one hundred years later, the Eisenhower Administration processed legislation to terminate tribal status. This had a disastrous effect on many tribal communities, including the Menominee and Klamath tribes. President Nixon later called for a reversal of the policy in 1971, and the Commissioner of Indian Affairs "announced abandonment of the relocation policy in favor of development on or near reservations, with greater control in the hands of the Indians themselves" (Tjerandsen, 1980, p. 71).

Before we discuss communities and cultures further, please take a moment and write down a few important points about your family. Did your family come to the United States a long time ago or recently? Has your family always lived in the Americas? Has your family moved to your current location during your lifetime? Is your family close or separated geographically? What norms would you say exist within your family that people who are not a part of your family would not necessarily know? If you have the opportunity, interview a parent or grandparent and ask why he or she chose to live in his or her current location. What issues or challenges did he or she have to address? How has that affected your life?

Communities, like families, share a sense of common history. For example, the African American community has a common sense of history with elements of slavery, the civil rights movement, and overcoming historical injustices. Communities of African Americans have shared stories of past experience through written works, such as songs and poetry.

Sharing of Cultures

The transmission of culture requires communication and interaction, and the understanding that comes through socialization is one that emphasizes group expectations rather than individual ones. A person comes to understand what the group norms are in much the same way we discussed in the chapter on group communication. A person has basic needs, as Maslow and Schutz have outlined for us, and fitting into a group, or a culture, meets many of these basic needs.

One aspect of this awareness of group affiliation is the acknowledgement of others' status as nongroup members. We recognize cultures distinct from our own, and we recognize difference. Gudykunst and Kim (1997), referred to previously, offer us an insight to this dynamic process in *Communicating with Strangers*.

Cultural communities often define themselves with borders or boundaries. Have you ever seen a gated community? How about a new subdivision? How about a section of town that has its own identity, like Harlem in New York or Watts in Los Angeles? Have you ever heard of a *barrio*? Communities often form around geographic boundaries, and features like walls or fences, streets, or railroad tracks often reinforce these boundaries. Gloria Anzaldúa explores the concept of boundaries in her book *Borderlands/La Frontera* (1987). She explores the physical borderland along the Texas/U.S. southwest border with Mexico and the psychological borderlands that encompass identity, sexuality, and spirituality. In terms of the physical boundaries, she explores how a region that was once occupied by native inhabitants

INTERCULTURAL COMMUNICATION 7.1 • *Uncertainty Reduction Theory*

Have you ever met someone and been not able to figure him or her out? When we meet someone for the first time, there is a degree of uncertainty, and Berger (1979) and Berger together with Calabrese (1975) developed uncertainty reduction theory to examine the ways we come to know each other, and how we reduce uncertainty as we develop relationships.

Here are their seven axioms of uncertainty reduction:

1. There is a high level of uncertainty at first. As we get to know one another, our verbal communication increases and our uncertainty begins to decrease.
2. Following verbal communication, as nonverbal communication increases, uncertainty will continue to decrease, and we will express more nonverbal displays of affiliation, like nodding one's head to express agreement.
3. When one is experiencing high levels of uncertainty, he or she will increase information-seeking behavior, perhaps asking questions to gain more insight. As one's understanding increases, uncertainty decreases, as does the information-seeking behavior.
4. When one is experiencing high levels of uncertainty, the communication interaction is not as personal or intimate. As uncertainty is reduced, intimacy increases.
5. When one is experiencing high levels of uncertainty, communication will feature more reciprocity, or displays of respect. As uncertainty decreases, reciprocity may diminish.
6. Differences between people increase uncertainty while similarities decrease uncertainty.
7. Higher levels of uncertainty are associated with a decrease in the indication of liking the other person, while reductions in uncertainty are associated with liking the other person more.

Sources: Berger (1979); Berger & Calabrese (1975).

came to be part of Mexico and later part of the United States. Many of the inhabitants' families have lived there for generations, and she describes in detail how the intersection of cultures, languages, traditions, and borders has impacted people. She also broadens her discussion to include personal boundaries of identity and orientation, and how the turbulent history of the U.S.-Mexican border mirrors and contrasts personal turbulence.

Shared Common Values and Principles

We are by nature an organization that is unable to tolerate indifference.
We hope that by arousing awareness and a desire to understand,
we will also stir up indignation and stimulate action.
—Rony Brauman, M.D., Former President, Médecins Sans Frontières
(also known as Doctors Without Borders or MSF)

Doctors Without Borders, or MSF, was founded in 1971 by a small group of French doctors, who expressed the belief that "all people have the right to medical care and that the needs of these people supersede respect for national borders." This group delivers emergency aid to victims of armed conflict, epidemics, and natural and man-made disasters, and to others who lack healthcare due to social or geographical isolation (MSF, 2001, www.doctorswithoutborders.org).

Linked by a common sense of values and principles, medical professionals from around the world work, in many cases as volunteers, to provide emergency assistance to people in need. This community of practitioners has grown in eighteen countries, involving over 2,000 volunteers and 15,000 locally hired staff to provide medical aid in more than eighty countries.

Consider your local service organizations, such as Rotary or Kiwanis, which contribute time, energy, and resources to the community. What values do they have in common and what principles to they adhere to? Do you think the cultural norms and traditions of Doctors Without Borders is similar to other medical professionals? How might they be different?

Also consider the impact of intercultural communication on the interpersonal communication between a healthcare provider and a patient. With the increasing pressure on healthcare providers to see many patients in one day, and the increasing level of diversity between us, how might intercultural communication influence interaction? Would it be appropriate or promote effective communication to have a male physician speak to a young girl from a culture that has certain beliefs about birth control? Would it be more appropriate or effective for a female physician to have the same conversation with her?

Communication is a powerful force in all our lives, and it takes on an additional importance within the clinical setting. When you go to your healthcare provider, you want your responses to be heard and the information you provide to help lead to an effective outcome. The study of health communication is growing across the United States as we come to understand just how important effective communication in the clinical setting.

In the article "What You Don't Say Can Hurt You," Mandell (1993) discusses a case where a mother brought her children into a rural clinic when she was concerned because they had high fevers. The mother reported to the attending nurse that she had removed two ticks from one child. The physician diagnosed measles and recommended aspirin and a dark room for the children until they recovered. Four days later one child died and another was rushed to the hospital. Rocky Mountain spotted fever claimed one life, and the nurse, who failed to pass on the report of the ticks, was found liable. Listening to both verbal and nonverbal messages is key to gathering information from patients (McLean, 1996), and failure to do so can be disastrous.

In addition to individual patient/provider communication, "Health communication is concerned with the use of ethical, persuasive means to craft and deliver campaigns and implement strategies that promote good health and prevent disease" (Ratzan, 1996, p. v). You may have seen anti-smoking campaign advertisements or messages promoting a designated driver in the popular media. Compare with your friends or classmates health messages you have seen or heard or experiences communicating with healthcare providers. How did intercultural communication play a role in your previous communication with your healthcare provider?

Shared Common Purpose and Sense of Mission

For example, Doctors Without Borders has a two-part common purpose: (1) to meet the healthcare needs of those they serve and (2) to call attention to the underlying issues and challenges that contribute to those healthcare needs. Community colleges, for example, value education and have as one of their defining principles the equal access to education for everyone. Can you think of a community, group, or institution that has a common purpose? Do they have a mission statement? What does the mission statement say about the organization?

Within an interpersonal context, do people have common values in terms of their purpose or mission that stem from the culture or cultures they belong to? If you come from a culture that values the promotion of the group over the excellence of the individual, how might that influence interpersonal interaction? How about notions of modesty, dating customs, or even male and female roles in terms of what cultural expectations are present? Cultural values can be motivating influences for communication and are often expressed in interpersonal communication.

Common Symbols, Boundaries, Status, Language, and Rituals

Symbols, one way groups establish and express identity, are images, icons, and figures that represent ideas or concepts. For some groups, the symbols may involve a banner or flag, for others a logo or icon. Sometimes symbols have distinct meanings for different groups. Take, for example, the debate over the use of the Confederate flag. For some, the symbol is one that represents a shared history and common traditions. For others, it is a racist reminder of past injustice and slavery. Each group defends its right to display or call for the removal of the Confederate flag. Each group builds a common sense of community around the symbol, but from a distinct frame of reference. This debate over the use of a symbol, with the use of mass communication to share interpretations, is a fascinating from a communication perspective. The symbol itself is created from simple colors, simple patterns, and simple shapes. Its effect on communities, however, is significant and dynamic. The 1991 NAACP Confederate Flag Resolution Abhorring the Confederate Battle Flag set in motion a debate and a boycott of tourism in several states that continues in many ways today, raising issues about symbols and their appropriate use in communities. You will find several links to explore this issue further at the close of this chapter.

A similar example of how symbols serve or hinder a community can be found in school mascots. What does your school use as a mascot? How is it received? What is the role of a mascot? Historically, mascots were taken to symbolize a value, character, or prominent figure in the community it represents. Stanford University, for example, once had a Native American as its mascot. The University, however, changed its mascot to the cardinal in 1972.

What personal symbols can we link to intercultural communication that express cultural values and norms? Cultures differ in their promotion or tolerance in the expression of wealth and beauty. A person who drives an SUV in one culture might be regarded as wealthy while another might view it as ostentatious or wasteful. In a similar fashion, a person who wears revealing clothing in one culture might be regarded as daring or fashionable but less than appropriate in another. Dress can serve a symbolic function and communicate cultural identity. For women of the Muslim faith the *hijab,* a head and body covering, the *niqab,* a face covering that leaves the eyes exposed, or the *khimar,* a full face covering, communicates affiliation with a cultural group, a personal sense of identity, and displays modesty (El Guindi, 1999). In cultures that do not share this belief, this covering may be perceived as oppressive. Qur'anic verse speaks to the importance of modesty and even speaks to eye contact and gaze in interpersonal communication. In mixed company, men and women are discouraged from gaze that draws attention, and the emphasis on gaze serves a symbolic function. Eye contact also serves a symbolic function in Western culture, but gaze is expected to communicate attention and interest in communication. Given the different viewpoints in terms of dress and eye contact, how might interpersonal communication be influenced when members of these two groups communicate?

Constant, Ongoing Change

In addition to understanding that we learn, share, and acknowledge differences in cultural norms, languages, and tradition, we must also acknowledge that cultures are always changing. Look back to the introductory exercises. Are there any groups that you belonged to but do not now affiliate with? If you went back to your elementary school, would it be the same as when you were a student? Do you think the conditions that were present at the time of your grandparents or great-grandparents impacted or influenced where they chose to live or how they lived their lives? Economic, political, and social factors often influence cultures, and as a result, cultures change. Within cultures, individual members or groups of members within the large community change as well.

When Martin Luther led the Reformation in 1517, cultures changed and groups formed that still exist today. The Hutterites, the Old German Brethren, the Amish, and the Mennonites all became communities that relocated geographically in order to practice their own religions. You may have seen the film *Witness,* which featured members of the Amish culture, who have traditionally limited their use of modern technology, and as a culture, resisted the use of the telephone. At first telephones were not used, and if a telephone were used, it involved a trip to town. As times changed, so have customs. Eventually, telephones were located at the end of the street, but still not in individual's homes. Currently, some Amish families have built small "outhouses" that house a telephone on their property, but still maintain its separation from the home.

Complex Nature of Culture

We are a part of many cultures, and cultures themselves are quite complex. Each culture has its own set of norms, customs, and traditions, which as we have seen, change over time in response to or anticipation of changes in the environment of its members. Do all Muslim women wear traditional dress? Do all Amish follow the same customs in terms of technology? Just as people change in their views and beliefs over time, symbols, rituals, and the ways we express culture and cultural identity change also.

Co-Cultures and Speech Communities

There is no conversation more boring than the one where everybody agrees.
—Michel de Montaigne

Look back at introductory Exercise 1 and count how many groups you consider yourself a part of, a member in, affiliated with, or in which you are active. Are there ever times where one group you are involved with comes into contact with other groups in which you are a member or affiliated? Do your friends or fellow students ever see you at work? Do you ever interact with more than one group or community, and do the expectations and roles ever change? **Co-cultures** are groups whose beliefs, customs, or behaviors, while similar to those of the larger culture, make it distinct as its own culture. As we can see, we are often members of more than one culture.

A **speech community** is a group of people who share norms, expectations, and the use of a language or languages (Gumperz, 1971). The language may include dialects or "variations" of a language. This does not mean that everyone speaks exactly the same given the setting, scene, circumstances, and normative expectations. There is often quite a range of diversity in the use of language within distinct speech communities (Romaine, 1982). We learn language as we grow, and our individual interpretation influences how we communicate. Individual variation, or the idea that even if we were raised in the same family, house, and town, we would still speak differently from one another, is normal and can be anticipated. English in the northeast United States is quite distinct from English spoken in rural Mississippi. There are even variations, or dialects, of English in the Northeast and the closer we look, the more diverse the linguistic landscape becomes.

That does not mean that speech communities are simply a group of one person. Dialects, variations in pronunciation and word choice—even pausing and the use of silence—all vary a great deal by region and language. Within speech communities, the speakers often share expectations about how to use language and an understanding about what purposes their language serves. When we can see these patterns across a range of individuals and perceive the community of speakers, we can call it a speech community.

The way people speak not only reflects the speech communities they belong to, but who they perceive themselves to be. Displays of group affiliation are an aspect of culture and these indications of group membership are often displayed in language. Just as a tattoo of Greek letters of a fraternity might signal group affiliation, the use of specific words in certain contexts can indicate group affiliation. If you hear a group of friends say they were playing on a "pitch," you may wonder what they are talking about. The use of this specific term allows the members of that group to recognize their shared membership and helps them communicate in specific ways, in effect helping create organization for their interactions with each other. You may hear other terms like "ruck," "maul," and "in-touch," as they describe a story that resulted in a "line-out." Without knowledge of the specific terms, you may be lost. The story itself, however, will have elements that express values, perhaps of courage or perseverance, that express a connection between the individual and how the game of rugby works.

In other speech communities, similar use of language can signal common perspectives on how the world works and bring people together. In gay communities, mentioning Matthew Shepard or *The Laramie Project,* the HBO film, can be a reference to common experiences of discrimination. Members of gay communities share a similar sense of persecution. These areas of common ground, found through shared experiences that can range from celebration to persecution, can bind a group together and be expressed linguistically. The Amish share a sense of common history born out of treatment following the Reformation. African Americans share a sense of common history born out of slavery. All of these examples are expressed, reinforced, and communicated through language, words, and body language.

This sense of community created and transmitted through communication can take the form of cultural displays. Common examples in North America may include Christmas and Easter celebrations that have specific interpretations by various

Christian groups but are also celebrated in some way by the larger community. Each church, community, or even family may have a specific way of performing a ritual associated with the holidays. For example, does your family open presents together on Christmas eve or Christmas day? Does your family have any specific customs or traditions associated with the holidays? Are there certain foods that everyone always eats together on a certain day perhaps? These rituals and their performance reinforce community and illustrate specific rules of interaction.

Speech communities often overlap other categories of group membership much like co-cultures. Terms such as "culture," "heritage," "society," or "ethnicity" can all be distinct and demonstrate areas of overlap. Each category itself may involve language norms and broad patterns of language use that may or may not be used by everyone in the speech community. A good example of this concept is Black English. It is often considered a dialect of English and to better understand, simply ask yourself: Does every African American speak Black English? The answer is no, and you can see concepts of race and ethnicity are distinct from language use, though there certainly can be an overlap.

Speech communities are groups whose interpersonal interactions demonstrate relatively distinct normative expectations for language use. They often are organized along the lines of gender, ethnicity, social class, geography, and educational experience. The use of language serves to bring people together, and the norms and rules reinforce specific language use and social expectations to produce similarities within the speech community. These communities often overlap and share common characteristics, but be careful to not stereotype and overgeneralize that everyone who lives in a certain area or is part of a specific group speaks in a specific manner or dialect.

Barriers to Intercultural Communication

> *Being in the right does not depend on having a loud voice.*
> —Chinese proverb

Now that we have examined the eight characteristics of intercultural communication and learned about co-cultures, you should have a better understanding of this dynamic, multifaceted aspect of communication. To build on what we covered, we will examine three key barriers to intercultural communication: language, perception, and ethnocentrism.

1. Language

Language serves to both bring us together and help us reinforce our group status. Language can include both established languages, like Spanish or French, dialects, or even subtle in-group language styles within a larger language context. Have you ever been part of a group that has its own words or phrases that have meanings that people you do not know or that are not part of the group wouldn't know? When a group communicates in its own way, it can create a sense of belonging and reinforce your membership and place in that group.

People often tell each other stories, which often communicate a value or meaning in the culture. Perhaps you have heard the saying "The early bird gets the worm," with its underlying meaning of the one who is prepared and ready gets the reward. In North America, this saying is common and reflects a cultural value. Di-

INTERCULTURAL COMMUNICATION 7.2 • *Silence in Communication among Native Americans*

> *For a stranger entering an alien society, a knowledge of when not to speak may be as basic to the production of culturally acceptable behavior as a knowledge of what to say.*
>
> —Basso (1970, p. 303)

The importance of silence in the traditional speech of Native Americans has long been studied. Leslie Spier (1893–1961) and Edward Sapir (1884–1939) were pioneers in the study of native languages, and their work *Wishram ethnography* (1939), was a seminal work. In it they documented native speech from the Sahaptin and Wasco languages along the Columbia River gorge before the dams. It now stands as one of the few remaining documents of the languages.

Susan Philips built upon their foundation and found in her study (1983) on the Warm Springs Indian Reservation that "there is almost no interruption of one speaker by another in Warm Springs talk. . . . Rarely do two people begin to talk at the same time. The pause between the talk of two different speakers is typically longer than in Anglo conversation" (Philips, 1983, p. 58). A more recent study of intergenerational communication between Warm Springs elders and younger tribal members found that while elders retained the traditional speech style, younger tribal members spoke quicker and took much shorter pauses, making communication between generations at times difficult (McLean, 1998).

There are currently 516 treaty tribes and 46 nontreaty tribes, and where there were once hundreds of native languages, now few remain as elders age and their numbers decrease. Many Native American youth, into the late 1950s, were removed from their homes and put in dormitories at boarding schools by the Bureau of Indian Affairs. Teachers were under orders to reprimand students if they were caught speaking any tongue other than English on school premises. Tribal members today recall the loss of language—and with it cultural traditions—with profound grief.

Learn more about the importance of silence in traditional Native American speech, the loss of native languages nationwide, and what is being done to reverse the effects of boarding schools and to save endangered languages at the Cheyenne Language website: http://www.mcn.net/~wleman/langlinks.htm.

Sources: McLean (1998); Philips (1983).

verse cultures have diverse sayings that reflect differences in values, customs, and traditions.

Can you imagine what it would be like to have your language taken away from you and to be punished for speaking your language? The Bureau of Indian Affairs forced many Native American parents to send their children to dormitory schools after World War II. These boarding schools were often outside of their own communities, and English was the dominant and enforced language (McNickle, D'Arcy, & Pfrommer, 1964). Native American children were often punished for using their native languages or words, even on the playground or at recess (McLean, 1998). Many children of Spanish-speaking parents report similar stories on playgrounds and schools across the country. What would it be like if you couldn't speak the language you were brought up with, the language of your parents and community? How would you feel about yourself?

Classic texts such as Aldous Huxley's *Brave New World,* George Orwell's *1984,* and Ray Bradbury's *Fahrenheit 451* all examine the importance of language in building community, and each author explores how the intentional limitation and altering of language impacts community.

Judy Pearson and Paul Nelson (2000) and DeVito (1986) describe four key areas of language that serve to bring us together, but because they involve a specialized knowledge in some unique to the group or community, they can also create barriers to outsiders. These are often called **co-languages,** because they exist and interact with dominant language but are nonetheless distinct from it.

Argot   A secret or specialized language, usually associated with criminals. Think of police or detective television programs and the specialized language of criminals.

Jargon   A profession-specific language used by professionals. Think of how lawyers speak to one another.

Slang   A word that takes the place of a standard or traditional word in order to add an unconventional, nonstandard, humorous, or rebellious effect.Think of the word "cool" and how it is used.

In addition to language-based barriers, there are also several factors—many of which we have visited in previous chapters—that can act as barriers to effective intercultural communication.

2. The Nature of Perception

Perception, as we explored previously, is an important part of the communication process. Your cultural value system, what you value and pay attention to, will significantly affect your intercultural communication. North American culture places an emphasis on space, with an "appropriate" distance while shaking hands, for example. If a North American travels to France, Spain, or Chile, he or she will find that a much smaller sense of personal space is the norm and may receive a kiss on the cheek as a greeting. If the North American is uncomfortable, the person from France may not attribute his or her uncomfortableness to personal space, and miscommunication may result. Learning about other cultures can help you adapt in diverse settings and make you more comfortable as you enter new situations where others' perceptions are different from your own.

Role identities, which involve expected social behavior, are another aspect of intercultural communication that can act as a barrier to effective communication. How does your culture expect men and women to act and behave? How about children or elders and older citizens? The word "role" implies an expectation of how one is supposed to act and behave in certain settings and scenes, and just like in a play in a theater, each person has a culturally bound set of role expectations. Who works as a doctor, a lawyer, a nurse, or a welder? As times and cultures change, so do role identities. In business, once perceived as a profession primarily for men, women have become actively involved in the starting, developing, and facilitating growth of businesses.

Goals reflect what we value and are willing to work for and vary widely across cultures. In some cultures, the afternoon lunch and resting period is the main meal of the day followed by a time for family. In the United States, we often have a quick lunch or even a "working lunch," with the emphasis on continuing productivity with the goal of personal and organizational achievement. The difference in values—family time versus work time for example—establish themselves in how we lead our lives. To a European, accustomed to one month of vacation a year, the thought of someone from the United States on a few intense, three-day power weekends hiking, skiing, or sailing might seem stressful. To a goal-oriented North American, the power weekend may be just the rejuvenation required to get "back in the game."

We have previously discussed self-concept, and you may want to revisit the section, taking a new look at how it relates to perception and intercultural communication. In this context, **self-concept** can become a barrier to effective intercultural communication. Geert Hofstede researched the concepts of individualism versus collectivism across diverse cultures. He found the United States to be the country where people perceived things primarily from their own viewpoints and how the world relates to them as individuals capable of making their own decisions, solve their own problems, and be responsible for their own actions (Hofstede, 1982). He also found that many countries in Asia and South American to be much less individualistic, instead focusing on the needs of the family, community, or larger group.

In addition, there are two other systems that influence how we relate to the world that impact our intercultural communication. Carley Dodd (1998) discusses the degree to which cultures communicate rules explicitly or implicitly. In an explicit context, the rules are discussed before we hold a meeting, negotiate a contract, or even play a game.

In the United States, we want to make sure everyone knows the rules beforehand and get frustrated if people do not follow the rules. In other cultures from the Middle East and Latin America, the rules are more generally understood by everyone, and people from these cultures tend to be more accommodating to small differences and less concerned whether everyone plays by the same rules. Our ability to adapt to contexts that are explicit or implicit is related to our ability to tolerate the unknown (Hofstede, 1982).

In the United States, we often look to guiding principles rather than rules for every circumstance and believe that with hard work, we can achieve our goals even though we do not know the outcome. In Peru, Chile, and Argentina, however, people prefer to reduce ambiguity and uncertainty and like to know exactly what is expected and what the probable outcome will be (Samovar, Porter, & Stefani, 1998).

Individualistic Cultures: People value individual freedom and personal independence.

Collectivistic Cultures: People value the family or community over the needs of the individual.

Explicit-Rule Cultures: People discuss rules and expectations clearly to make sure the rules are known.

Implict-Rule Cultures: People are implied and known by everyone, but not always clearly stated.

Uncertainty-Accepting Cultures: People often focus on principles versus rules for every circumstance and accept that the outcome is not always known.

Uncertainty-Rejecting Cultures: People often focus on rules for every circumstance and do not like ambiguity or not knowing what the outcome will be.

When we consider whether a culture as a whole places more emphasis on the individual or the community, we must be careful to recognize that individual members of the culture may hold beliefs or customs that do not follow a cultural norm. Stereotypes, defined as a generalization about a group of people that oversimplifies their culture (Rogers & Steinfatt, 1999), can be one significant barrier to effective intercultural communication. Gordon Allport, a pioneer in the field of communication research, examined how and when we formulate or use stereotypes to characterize distinct groups or communities. He found that we tend to stereotype people and cultures with which we have little contact (Allport, 1958). How can you learn more about other people and cultures? Many colleges and universities have offices of international education that offer study-abroad programs, where you can live and learn in a culture other than your own as part of your educational experience. Not only will you benefit from first-hand experience, but you will make yourself more valuable in your chosen job or profession.

In addition, your first-hand experience will provided you with an increased understanding of prejudice. **Prejudice** involves a negative preconceived judgment or opinion that guides conduct or social behavior. Within the United States, can you make a list of people or groups that may be treated with prejudice by the majority group? Your list may include specific ethnic, racial, or cultural groups that are stereotyped in the media, but it could also include socioeconomic groups or even different regions of the United States. For example, Native Americans were long treated with prejudice in early western films. Can you imagine that groups are also treated with prejudice in other countries? In many parts of South America, indigenous people are treated poorly, and their rights as citizens are sometimes not respected. Has treatment of Native Americans changed in North America? It has also changed, and continues to change in all of the Americas, North, South, and Latin.

People who treat other with prejudice often make **assumptions** about the group or communities. As Gordon Allport illustrated for us, we often assume characteristics about groups with which we have little contact. By extension, we can sometimes **assume similarity**—that people are all basically similar—in effect denying cultural, racial, or ethnic differences. We sometimes describe the United States as a "melting pot," where individual and cultural differences blend to become a homogeneous culture. This "melting pot" often denies cultural differences. The metaphor of a "salad bowl," where communities and cultures retain their distinctive characteristics or "flavor," serves as more equitable model. In this "salad bowl," we value the differences and what they contribute to the whole.

We can also run the risk of **assuming familiarity** with cultures when we attribute characteristics of one group to everyone with connections to the larger culture. For example, people may assume that we are familiar with all Native Americans if we know one tribe in our community, forgetting the distinct differences that exist between tribes and even between Native Americans who live in urban areas versus on reservations.

With this discussion on stereotypes, prejudice, and assumptions, you may be anxious not to jump to quick conclusions. One positive way to learn about other cultures, as Edward T. Hall supports, is to learn first hand. When you travel abroad to study or work, you may at first find that you experience **culture shock,** the feeling that you are overwhelmed with the differences from the new culture in contrast to your home or native culture (Oberg, 1985). Your loss of familiar patterns of how to shop, where to go for what you need, or even how to communicate can produce anxiety and even withdrawal from the new culture. Sometimes people go home, reporting they are homesick, without acknowledging that culture shock may be an important part of the way they feel. Once you come to understand aspect of the new culture, you will feel more comfortable and be able to explore with an increase in understanding that someone who only visits for a few days cannot appreciate. You may even, upon your return to your native culture, look at it from a whole new perspective, gained by your experience abroad.

3. Ethnocentrism

Finally, your experience may help you to not view the world and its diversity of cultures in an ethnocentric way. **Ethnocentrism** means you go beyond pride in your own culture, heritage, or background and hold the "conviction that (you) know more and are better than those of different cultures" (Seiler & Beall, 2000). This belief in the superiority of one's own group can guide individual and group behavior. If you go to a new country, and people do things differently there, you would be considered ethnocentric if you consider their way the wrong way because it is not the same way you "do it back home." Groups would be considered ethnocentric if they prejudge individuals or other groups of people based on negative preconceptions.

Improving Intercultural Communication

There is nothing noble in being superior to someone else.
The true nobility is in being superior to your previous self.
—Hindu proverb

Let's now turn our attention from the lessons learned in terms of common barriers to intercultural communication to ways in which we can improve our communication with people from distinct cultures.

Seiler and Beall (2000) offer us six ways to improve our perceptions, and therefore improve our communication, particularly in intercultural communication.

1. **Become an active perceiver.** We need to actively seek out as much information as possible. As Hall supports, placing yourself in the new culture can often expand your understanding.
2. **Recognize each person's frame of reference is unique.** We all perceive the world differently, and even though you may interact with two people from the same culture, recognize that they are individuals with their own sets of experiences, values, and interests.
3. **Recognize that people, objects, and situations change.** The world is changing and so are we. Recognizing that people and cultures, like communication process itself, are dynamic and ever changing can improve your intercultural communication.
4. **Become aware of the role perceptions play in communication.** As we explored in Chapter 2, perception is an important aspect of the communication process. Understanding that our perceptions are not the only ones possible can limit ethnocentrism and improve intercultural communication.
5. **Keep an open mind.** The adage "A mind is like a parachute – it works best when open" holds true. Being open to differences can improve intercultural communication.
6. **Check your perceptions.** By learning to observe, and acknowledging our own perceptions, we can avoid assumptions, expand our understanding, and improve our ability to communicate across cultures.

Summary

In this chapter we applied much of what we have learned in previous chapters to communication across cultures. We have discussed ways to understand intercultural communication and examined several lessons learned through research, investigation, and experience that expand our understanding. There are several principles of intercultural communication that can guide us and barriers that can limit our ability to communicate effectively. Finally, we have looked at six ways we can actively improve our ability to communicate across cultures.

*The true civilization is where every man gives to every
other every right that he claims for himself.*
—Robert Ingersoll

For More Information

To learn more about Doctors Without Borders, go to: **http://www.doctorswithoutborders.
org/**

To learn more about cultural symbols, specifically the debate over the confederate flag, go
to: **http://fullcoverage.yahoo.com/fc/US/Confederate_Flag_Debate/**

Learn more about Aldous Huxley's *Brave New World,* George Orwell's *1984,* and Ray
Bradbury's *Fahrenheit 451.* Conduct key word searches on the web, using the authors' names
and titles. This will yield a diversity of information, from short summaries to in-depth
analyses.

To learn more about Gloria Anzaldúa's exploration of borders and identities, go to: **http://
www.auntlute.com/anzaldua.htm**

Review Questions

1. Factual Questions
   a. Who is generally considered the father of intercultural communication?
   b. What eight contributions did he make to the field?
   c. What is culture shock?

2. Interpretative Questions
   a. How does perception influence intercultural communication?
   b. How does our self-concept influence intercultural communication?
   c. How might the ability to tolerate uncertainty influence communication?

3. Evaluative Questions
   a. Is it possible to completely learn enough about a culture to effectively communi-
      cate across cultures? Explain your response.
   b. Is it necessary to understand a cultural completely to communicate effectively?
      Why or why not?
   c. Communication is a dynamic process. To what degree is the responsibility to learn
      communicate interculturally shared?

4. Application Questions
   a. What do people consider their culture, heritage, or background? Create a survey,
      identify a target sample size, conduct your survey and compare the results.
   b. What study abroad programs are available on your campus? Investigate the issue
      and share your findings.
   c. Research one culture or country that you would like to visit. Compare the results.

References

Anzaldúa, G. (1987). *Borderlands/La frontera.* San Francisco: Aunt Lute Books.

Allport, G. (1958). *The nature of prejudice.* Garden City, NY: Doubleday.

Basso, K. A. (1970). To give up on words: Silence in Western Apache culture. In D. Carbaugh (Ed.), *Cultural communication and intercultural contact* (pp. 301–318). Hillsdale, NJ: Lawrence Erlbaum.

Berger, C. (1979). Beyond initial interactions: Uncertainty, understanding and the development of interpersonal relationships. In H. Giles & R. St. Clair (Eds.), *Language and social psychology.* Oxford: Basil Blackwell.

Berger, C., & Calabrese, R. (1975). Some explorations in initial interactions and beyond: Toward a developmental theory of interpersonal communication. *Human Communication Research, 1,* 99–112.

Chen, G., & Starosta, W. (2000). *Foundations of intercultural communication* (pp. 8–12). Boston: Allyn and Bacon.

Condon, J., & Yousef, F. (1975). *An introduction to intercultural communication.* Indianapolis, IN: Bobbs-Merill.

DeVito, J. (1986). *The communication handbook: A dictionary.* New York: Harper & Row.

Dodd, C. (1998). *Dynamics of intercultural communication* (5th ed.). New York: McGraw-Hill.

El Guindi, F. (1999). *Veil: Modesty, privacy, and resistance.* Oxford: Berg Publisher Limited.

Gudykunst, W., & Kim, Y. (1997). *Communicating with strangers: An approach to intercultural communication.* New York: McGraw-Hill.

Gumperz, J. (1971). Social meanings in linguistic structures. In A. Dil (Ed.), *Language in social groups: Essays by John Gumperz* (pp. 247–310). Stanford, CA: Stanford University.

Hofstede, G. (1982). *Culture's consequences.* Newbury Park, CA: Sage.

Klopf, D. (1991). *Intercultural encounters: The fundamentals of intercultural communication* (2nd ed., p. 31). Englewood, CA: Morton.

Kluckhohn, F., & Strodtbeck, F. (1961). *Variations in value orientations.* Evanston, IL: Row, Peterson.

Leeds-Hurwitz, W. (1990). Notes in the history of intercultural communication: The Foreign Service Institute and the mandate for intercultural training. *Quarterly Journal of Speech, 76,* 268–281.

Mandell, M. (1993, August). What you don't say can hurt you. *American Journal of Nursing,* 15–16.

McLean, S. (1996, Summer). Communication in the clinical setting: The importance of listening. *The Journal of Multicultural Nursing and Health, 2*(3), 4–7.

McLean, S. (1998). Turn taking and the extended pause. In K. S. Sitaram & M. Prosser (Eds.), *Civic discourse: Multiculturalism, cultural diversity and global communication* (p. 224). Stamford, CT: Ablex Publishing.

McLuhan, M. (1964). *Understanding media: The extensions of man* (2nd ed.). New York: McGraw-Hill.

McNickle, D., D'Arcy, M., & Pfrommer, V. (1964). Dinexta: A community experience. In C. Tjerandsen (Ed.), *Education for citizenship: A foundation's experience* (p. 16). Santa Cruz, CA: Emil Schwarhaupt Foundation, Inc.

Oberg, K. (1985). Culture shock: Adjusting to new cultural environments. *Practicing Anthropology, 7,* 170–179.

Pearson, J., & Nelson, P. (2000). *An introduction to human communication: Understanding and sharing* (8th ed.). New York: McGraw-Hill.

Philips, S. (1983). *The invisible culture: Communication in the classroom and community on the Warm Springs Indian Reservation.* Chicago: Waveland Press.

Ratzan, S. (1996). Introduction. *The Journal of Health Communication, 1*(1), v.

Rogers, E., & Steinfatt, T. (1999). *Intercultural communication.* Prospect Heights, IL: Waveland Press.

Romaine, S. (1982). What is a speech community? In S. Romaine (Ed.), *Sociolingusitic variation in speech communities* (pp. 1–24). London: Edward Arnold.

Samovar, L., Porter, R., & Stefani, L. (1998). *Communication between cultures* (3rd ed.). Belmont, CA: Wadsworth.

Seiler, W., & Beall, M. (2000). *Communication: Making connections* (4th ed.). Boston: Allyn and Bacon.

Tjerandsen, C. (1980). *Education for citizenship: A foundation's experience* (p. 71). Santa Cruz, CA: Emil Schwarhaupt Foundation, Inc.

8

Lifecycles of Relationships

Chapter Objectives _____

After completing this chapter, you should be able to:

1. Demonstrate the five stages in conversations.
2. Identify and describe the five stages in relational development.
3. Identify and describe the five stages in relational deterioration.
4. Describe and demonstrate key features of relational dialectics.
5. Demonstrate key strategies for maintaining and improving relationships.

Introductory Exercise 1 _____

List at least five relationships that you are currently involved in. Next to each relationship list at least one word to describe it to yourself. Repeat the list, only focus on relationships you are no longer involved in, and again describe them to yourself.

Introductory Exercise 2 _____

Think of a relationship that you are currently involved in. Think back when and how it started. Write a word to describe that time. Think of the first change in the relationship, and again write a word to describe it. If the relationship has changed since that time, again think of a word to describe it. Try to characterize for yourself each step or stage where you noticed a change or something new or different about the relationship and try to put it into words.

How We Engage in Conversation

> The most important thing in communication is hearing what isn't being said.
> —Anonymous

You've had conversations all your life so this model may, at first, seem a bit too familiar. If, however, you take a step back and examine each step, you will see how the familiar actually involves many layers of meaning and detail. Our familiarity often makes us blind to the obvious, and we fail to recognize key details because we assume we know what's going on or only devote our divided attention to the conversation by also thinking about ideas that don't relate to the conversation. This process of diversion distracts our attention, and we end up relying on the familiar to get through the conversation. Look at each step and recognize its complexity as part of the dynamic process of communication. Beebe, Beebe, and Redmond (2002) offer us five key stages of conversation that are adapted here. Your efforts to focus on the points will help you pick up on new cues in the next conversation and give you greater insight into the conversational process.

1. Initiation

We have examined the word initiation from a cultural standpoint, discussing it in terms of a new beginning or a key transition to a new place, role, or identity. Here we will discuss initiation in the context of beginning or starting a conversation. In the previous chapter we covered several ways to start conversations. If you don't remember them, take a moment to look back at that section now. Being familiar with

the steps we discussed, you can see how verbal and nonverbal communication plays a central role in the initiation of conversations or interactions.

The first step or part of initiating a conversation is simply to be open to it. This can be simple, or it can be quite complex. If you are seeking information, you may be ready to listen, but if you are at the end of a long and engaging novel, with just three pages to go, you may not be ready to communicate. We discussed the role of the receiver in Chapter 1 and will underscore the importance of being ready to receive again here. If the receiver is not ready to communicate, your attempts at initiating a conversation will probably fail. Just as we discussed ways to communicate openness to conversation, pay attention to the cues others send about being open or ready to communicate. The cues or signals are often communicated nonverbally and require significant attention on your part.

The second step, once openness is present, is to start the game. In practice, the game has already begun long before you open your mouth or say your first word. Your posture, body language, dress, and attitude communicate a great deal and establish expectations for the receiver. When you say "Hi," the receiver may respond with "How are you?" and you may then go through phatic communion (Malinowski, 1935). You might talk about the weather, or engage in small talk, but think of initial words and the interplay back and forth in conversation as a delicate time. Beginnings are fragile times, and taking them for granted can impact the conversation. Your car needs to warm up its engine in order to operate properly. Most of the wear occurs in these first few minutes. Think of relationships in a similar way, where the beginnings of each conversation, when people do not know each other well, may experience friction. Friction creates heat, and while heat can be a feature of relationship, it is also a force that deserves respect. Pay attention to the cues of your conversational partner as you initiate a conversation.

2. Preview

If the conversation is initiated successfully, each conversational participant will seek the interaction and get to the point or points. While the context of the entire conversation has relevance in each of these steps, here it becomes increasingly relevant. Is this a work conversation, with the tone set by the large table, the suits and ties, and significant space between individuals? Is this an informal conversation in the hallway? Each context is quite distinct, and how you approach the preview will be different. The **preview** is an indication, either nonverbal or verbal, of what the conversation is about. The point may be a verbal business decision or a nonverbal invitation to gossip, depending on the interaction and context.

People are naturally curious and have expectations about what it is going to happen. By indicating where the conversation is going, you help meet this need for establishing expectations and encourage active listening. You may communicate your preview in your opening ritual or phatic communication (Malinowski, 1935), or may hold back and reveal your intention later. Perhaps you would say " Have you heard about _____?" or "I'd like to tell you about _____." Each of these opening statements serves the purpose of a preview. You may want to present a preview with a twist and say "If you were faced with this financial aid situation, as a college student, what would you do?" This twist involves asking the person to consider a particular perspective and helps you frame the discussion. The other person can also recognize the frame and grasp the expectations of the conversation. This technique is called **altercast** and asks the listener or receiver to respond from a specific point of view. You might also use a disclaimer to preview your central message or messages. A disclaimer might sound like "While I don't agree with this, the supervisor has announced _____." A **disclaimer** is a verbal strategy to talk about a issue while not associating yourself with it. It can serve you well by trying to establish space, but can also alert the receiver that your message is negative, and may even seem like you are "beating around the bush" or failing to get to the point.

3. Point(s)

Now that we've successfully initiated a conversation and previewed what we're going to talk about, people might feel like it is time to get down to the heart of the matter. The conversation will no doubt gravitate toward the central focus or point. The conversation is characterized by smooth flow, where there are not many awkward pauses or abrupt interruptions. DeVito (2003) characterizes this step as getting down to business and indicates the word *business* serves well because of its goal-directed connotation. Recall when we spoke of content and relationship messages and recognize that there may be many points to the conversation on many levels. One may be to exchange information, and another might be to reinforce the relationship exists and is going well. The relationship focus may be more important than the goal of communicating information.

4. Feedback

This step in the conversation is similar to the preview step. Just as you indicated what the conversation was going to be about, now people will communicate to each other what they heard and reflect back on the point(s) to indicate that the conversation is almost over. "Thanks for letting me know about _____" is a summary statement that communicates you heard what the other person said but also serves as a verbal sign that the conversation has met the goals established in the preview.

Feedback, as one of the eight essential components of communication, is inherent in the communication process and constantly present. With each turn and interaction, conversational participants provide one another feedback. In this sense, feedback is an important aspect of every interaction and an end or step in and of itself. In conversations, however, this strategic use of feedback is considered "high profile" or "highly monitored" because it is used with a specific goal in mind. Spontaneous feedback is not strategic and involves no planning. It is often interpreted as more authentic and honest, and considered "low profile." Feedback also has positive and negative dimensions. Positive feedback encourages communication, while negative feedback discourages it.

5. Closing

The final step in conversation follows the lead of the strategic feedback to signal the message was received, and the conversational participants part. This step in conversation shares a great deal with the initiation step (Knapp & Vangelisti, 2000). Just as phatic communion provides a ritual for greeting (Malinowski, 1935), it also provides a ritual for closing. People often communicate their appreciation for the conversation or reinforce future plans to meet or communicate in the closing. Both nonverbal and verbal communication play a role, and overlapping messages like "bye" accompanied by a wave are common.

People may find this disengagement from conversation challenging, particularly if the other person didn't catch the feedback cues and sometimes even if he or she did. Perhaps you find that leaving church or a similar group setting seems to take you forever, and the closing always seems to transform into an ongoing conversation. While there are no cure-all ways to end a conversation, there are several strategies that may serve you well.

Don't introduce new information in your closing. New information invites new conversations, so to successfully disengage, refrain from saying something new, even if it means you need to make a mental note and contact another person later. It gives you the option of choosing a different way to communicate, like email, that gives you more control. If another person introduces new information, make a summary statement that links the new information to the previous point and then transition to your statement of appreciation for the conversation. This will help "tie it up" and can be done with sensitivity and tact. The third suggestion to terminate a conversation that seems to have no ending is to refer to something or someone outside of the conversation. Introduce the old conversation participant to someone new. Share that you have to be at a certain place at a specific time that is rapidly approaching. Find a tactful way of diverting attention away from yourself as you excuse yourself and leave.

How We Form Relationships

There is no joy except in human relationships.
—Saint-Éxupery

We've formed relationships for most of our lives, and the process might seem natural. The assumption that it is natural is correct in that we seek relationships and interaction but is incorrect in the sense that we do it naturally. Forming relationships requires skill, and those skills can be learned.

Relationships come in all sorts of shapes and sizes. We discussed the types of relationships, from impersonal to intimate. They are part of our family life, work life, and the rest of our existence. Building on Altman and Taylor's (1973) social penetration theory, Mark Knapp, a professor at the University of Texas, outlined ten distinct stages that relationships go through as they form and dissolve. We will explore in the discussion to come the formation of a romantic relationship, but this model could just as easily be applied to a business relationship, a friendship, or even an impersonal meeting. Your formation of relationships with co-workers mirrors the formation of close relationships with partners. Feel free to associate the steps and their characteristics beyond our model to your own experiences. Also keep in mind as we discuss Knapp's stages that no two relationships are the same and many repeat or jump stages. The stages in Knapp's **model of relational development** (1978) serve to guide us through the discussion of common stages in relationships and offer insight into common characteristics that relationships share over time.

Let's say that the instructor of your communication class wants to give you a real-world opportunity to learn more about interpersonal communication. He or she decides to collaborate with the psychology instructor in an activity that will combine both classes and provides each class an opportunity to learn and apply the knowledge from each area of study.

The setting is Halloween, and your instructor outlines joint activity to focus on common areas between communication and psychology. Each class will focus on its own area of study, and each student will be responsible for partnering with a member or members from the other class in order to produce the project.

This scenario requires you to engage in the suspension of disbelief. Perhaps you have seen a James Bond film where soldiers chase him as he rapidly skis down a mountain slope, dodging bullets that come close but never hit him. The camera pulls back to reveal a large cliff and he goes right off it. He launches a small paraglider chute, floats for a moment, and the soldiers shoot at him from the edge. Then you see the helicopter. It rises up, almost underneath him, and for a moment you think the rotor blades may hit him, but he releases the parachute, falls through the rotor blades, and grasps the runners at the base of the helicopter, averting his fall into the abyss. He releases his skis and swings into the helicopter, disables the pilot, and lowers the helicopter to a nearby ski resort. The closing scene shows him walking away from the helicopter and entering the bar. In real life these events could not happen, but in the movies we enjoy the fantastic nature of the chase scene. In this scenario, you will need to suspend your own real-world relationships. You may relate your current or previous relationship to this scenario, but you will play a central role.

Your instructor announces that your classes will come together for a Halloween party. Everyone is encouraged to wear a mask or a costume to represent part of themselves. The party will be held in your student union building and will start at 8:00 P.M. As the hour approaches, you arrive near the building. You see several of your classmates but also notice people you do not know. Who do you approach first? People whom you know and who are somewhat familiar to you? Even if you don't know your classmates well, you have common ground with them in terms of the context.

As you talk about the party to come, you may notice what your speech instructor called anxiety. Anxiety itself is not a positive or negative feeling and may communicate a certain nervousness about the unknown future or what is going to happen. As you all decide to enter the building and see what refreshments are served, you will probably walk together. Will you walk as one large group? Probably not. You'll probably walk in groups of two and three, or even four and five, but you will naturally cluster together. Your sense of familiarity with each other is revealed in your choice of association and may even follow the seating pattern of the class. The people you sit next to in class are more familiar, and you will probably have had more interaction with them. You may also choose to be next to people who are similar to you, in terms of gender, race, ethnicity, or even activities outside of the class context, such as participation in an athletic team.

As you enter the student union, you may notice that people are clustered in small groups, probably along class lines, with psychology students in some groups and communication students in other groups. The common meeting area will probably be the refreshment table. Your group will no doubt see what is available and, at the same time, check out who is in the room. Costumes and masks might be a common area of comparison and conversation, and you might find yourself talking about the assignment.

When you look up from your cup, you might find that someone is watching you from across the room. You might look back, smile, and then re-enter conversation with your friends, but in the back of your mind you may be thinking about the other person and your own interest to meet that person. Let's say one member in your group recognizes a member of the psychology group and volunteers to introduce everyone. After all, you have an assignment to accomplish.

As you approach the other group, you may notice that person again establishes eye contact. Again, you exchange a smile and watch your classmate say hello to the person she knows. They might engage in a bit of small talk and then get around to introducing everyone. You naturally gravitate toward the person who has established eye contact with you and find yourself falling into a conversation. What do you talk about? You may exchange names and majors, and even say something like "So, you are taking the psychology class?" While the answer is obvious, this question serves an important purpose. It facilitates communication and expresses interest in interaction. The other person reciprocate with information about the class, the teaching style or content, or even what the psychology students are supposed to do in terms of their part of the assignment. This stage in a relationship is called **initiation,** and just like the conversational process, it involves rules of exchange like phatic communion. You may continue the conversation or find your group is leaving. You might say goodbye, indicate your appreciation for the conversation, and go on to meet other people.

As your group circulates and divides, breaking up into small groups comprised of new members, you may find yourself wondering where the other person is in the room. As you look around, you may find he is looking back at you. Again a smile might communicate acknowledgment or interest. You might even decide to go learn more about him and cross the room. As the conversation starts again, you may find that your self-talk is saying that you find this person interesting or attractive. If you could see his thoughts, you might find similar ideas. The conversation flows naturally and moves from the topics of psychology and communication, to your choice of costumes or masks, to areas and interests. You learn more about him through the process of self-disclosure, and you in turn talk more about yourself.

The conversation is engaging and you've lost track of your classmates, not really paying attention to what they are doing. The lights come on and go off, and as you look at each other and down at your watches, you realize it is almost 11:00 P.M. and time to go. You look around and see others engaged in conversation and the spaces between people starting to increase. You suggest to the other person that you should do the project together and he readily agrees. He suggests exchanging phone numbers and emails. As you finish writing yours, your classmates come up behind you and say "time to go." As you walk away, you find yourself thinking about the conversation and the new person you met.

Your classmates briefly discuss the class project and ask if you found anyone to work with on it. One classmate in particular directs that question at you with a knowing smile. You indicate that you did, and you all part for the evening.

When you wake up the next morning, what's the first thing you think of? After your basic needs, your thoughts may wander to the conversation last night. You might check to make sure you got his phone number. Knowing it is 7:00 A.M., you are not about to call him right away. You might even give some thought to when you will call. After lunch? Perhaps in the evening? You are no doubt concerned with appearing too eager and don't want to spoil what seems to be a relationship that could develop. If you could be a fly on the wall in his world, you might find the very same thoughts. Who will call first?

During the day you go to work, classes, work again, and then meet with friends. You've known your friends for varying lengths of time, but they know you well enough to see that something happened last night. You relate that you met someone but don't want to say much. You all talk about plans for the weekend, perhaps a road trip or going out to the clubs.

That evening when you are back at your apartment, you may check again to see if you have the number. You think about when to call him and decide that if you are going to get the project done by December, you need to start working on it. That means you need to focus what you are going to do, so you better call your project partner. With that rationalization in mind, you pick up the phone and find that he too was going to call you, so you are glad you called. The conversation flows almost effortlessly. Before long, you look at the time and indicate that you have work in the morning. He suggests meeting tomorrow. You go over your schedules and find a common time during the lunch break. After the conversation and on your way to bed, you may think about his words, what he means by his words, and how interesting he is to you.

The next morning comes and you think about your lunch date right away. Again you go to work, class, and then you are on your way to the student union building to meet him. You each get a tray and pay for yourselves, and the conversation flows. You talk about aspects of communication that involve psychology and determine that the perception chapter in your speech book overlaps well with the psychology material. At the same time, the conversation wanders and encompasses more than just project talk. You are getting to know each other and becoming familiar with one another. This stage in a relationship is called **experimentation.**

As the lunch hour is almost over, you are left with the decision of when to meet. He indicates that he will be on campus this weekend, and perhaps you could meet at the library. You find yourself agreeing and only later recall your plans for the road trip or clubbing. You see your friends later; they again bring up the plans for the weekend and you indicate you have an important class project to work on and will skip it this time. They can't believe that after knowing you all this time, you'll be doing your project in the library of all places long before it is actually due.

The library meeting goes well, and so does the movie that evening. The conversations come naturally, and you may even find yourself thinking that it seems like you've known this person for a long time, even though it has only been several days. You call to connect on Sunday and plan a time on Monday to meet. Soon you are meeting him more frequently and for longer periods of time. This stage in the process is called **intensifying.** If you could create a chart of your hours during the week and block out work and classes, you'd find that your leftover time increasingly involves this person. Your friends will notice this change, too, and miss your interaction. You have to choose how to spend your time, and only have so many hours in the day. This person is becoming more important to you.

The semester comes to a close and your project is completed and went well. Your instructor is impressed at the amount of time you devoted to the activity, and your grade reflects your effort and attention to detail. Your friend did well too. You plan to get together over Christmas break once or twice, and the next semester comes with a sense of anticipation.

With the excitement of the new semester and the new relationship, you may find yourself looking at things in a new way. You may give thought to all the areas you have in common and how fortunate you were to have taken a communication course. As the semester starts, you quickly learn each other's schedule and sometimes meet each other after class. You introduce your new friend to your group of friends and you all hang out together on various occasions. You also meet your friend's friends, and you seem to know more people on campus now. As the semester progresses, you both find that planning time together is a challenge, but you continue to make the time. You might even find that, when walking on campus, you might see one of his friends, who asks about him. This signals the acknowledgment of the group or community that you are recognized as part of a couple. It also signals, combined with your emphasis on integrating schedules to make time for each other, that you are in the **integrating** stage of the relationship.

Semesters come and go and so do friends, but your relationship has grown stronger over time. Graduation in nearing and you both are talking about future plans. You might even plan your next area of study or where you are going to work with him in mind. If you both decide, for example, that you want to go to graduate school, then you might choose the same state university.

At the same time you are making plans, both of your families may be asking subtle and not so subtle questions about where the relationship is going. There may be talk of living arrangements and what is acceptable. You both might be considering these issues as you make your plans. Perhaps marriage is a topic of conversation or deciding to live together. When it comes time to make the transition to the new university, you enter this new social world as a couple and a certain level of commitment to the relationship. Regardless whether you choose your apartment or walk down the aisle together, in many ways your decisions have led you to the **bonding** stage of the relationship.

Before we discuss this relationship further, let's examine the five steps that have led us to this point. The **initiation** stage is similar to the conversational process in that the goal is for the conversational participants to get to know one another. People "size each other up" and make initial judgments about each other. The conversation usually involves a relatively superficial level of interaction, and people keep their space while being careful not to alienate each other. The **experimentation** stage comes next and means that the conversational participants enjoyed the initial interactions enough to want to continue the relationship. People "try each other on" in this stage, getting to know each other in a variety of settings, introducing the other person to trusted friends, and gaining a better understanding of each other. There is not much commitment at this stage beyond setting times and places for future interaction. The **intensifying** stage is marked by an increase in the frequency of communication and a corresponding increase in the time devoted to that communication. People connect with each other more frequently and for longer periods of time. They gain a deeper understanding of one another as a result. The **integrating** stage can be characterized by an emphasis on integrating schedules and the value of the relationship. In terms of your own priority list, the relationship has moved from not very important to very important, and your time and attention reflects this stage. The **bonding** stage recognizes the relationship as a commitment and is generally recognized by families and the community. People seek to formalize the relationship through rituals like marriage or even renting/buying an apartment or house together.

Just as relationships form, they dissolve. Some impersonal relationships may never get past the initiating stage, while other relationships may see the couple celebrate seventy years together. Relationships are diverse and complex, reflecting the underlying concept that they are built through communication. Communication itself is complex and ever-changing, and it is only natural to see that relationships follow this pattern. No two relationships are identical, and no two relationships follow exactly the same patterns.

This scenario serves to illustrate the model but should be seen as only an illustration and not a forecasting of the inevitable demise of all relationships. Relationships transform over time and may experience periods where people grow apart and come back together. Recognizing key characteristics of these stages, however, places you in a position of being able to reinforce aspects of communication that promote the stage of relationship you desire. Interpersonal communication takes at least two people, and not everyone will consider the relationship at the same stage. Nonetheless, by recognizing these characteristics and the key elements of each stage, we can choose to improve, promote, maintain, or terminate our relationships.

How Relationships Come Apart

Just as people grow together, they also grow apart. Sometimes people choose to not see each other after the initiation stage, or after the experimentation phase, or the couple fails to make the transition from integrating to bonding, and the relationship comes apart. Here are Knapp's five stages of **relational deterioration** (Knapp & Vangelisti, 1996), which outline the process by which relationships disintegrate.

You may recall we left off our hypothetical scenario with the relationship going through a major transition with you both moving off to the state university. The living arrangements might involve living together and sharing costs in an apartment. Perhaps you rented a house together. You might even have gotten married before the move. Regardless which decision was made and which action taken, you are committed to the relationship and recognized by the community as a couple.

At first classes, looking for work, and all of the semester's start-up activities keep you both quite busy. Still, the relationship is young and you spend considerable time together. Your new communication department is holding an informal get-together and a faculty member indicates it is entirely appropriate to bring your partner to the party. At first he might be nervous, but as he meets people you have been talking about, you find this new step is fun. The stories about the odd professor, the challenging graduate student, and the helpful secretary take on new meaning when your partner can put a face with a name. Your peers and colleagues now associate you with someone, and your new community recognizes you as a couple.

Projects, research, classes, and work are all going well, and while you have a busy schedule, you may later feel these are the best days of your life. Your partner is also enjoying the challenge in the psychology department. Semester after semester goes by and everything goes reasonably well. You have your ups and downs like anyone and any couple, but the times you have conflicts are few, and you both work at it to move on together.

You have a role in producing a research paper that is accepted for a major conference. While at the conference, you meet someone. He listens attentively to your description of the project that led to the paper, and you just "click." Your time between sessions is filled with intriguing conversations and discussions of world travel, exotic places, and new things. It gets you thinking in a new direction and leaves you feeling hopeful for the future. You value the time you spent with your new friend and hope to see him at the conference next year.

When you get home, you discuss the conference with your partner and spend a lot of time relating your discussions of new places and expressing your desire to travel. Perhaps after your studies you'd like to work in a foreign country. Your partner meets your new interest with cool reserve. He doesn't say much, but you just know something isn't right.

Then the comments just start coming. You want to see the foreign film showing on campus. He wants to see the latest comedy showing downtown. You squeeze the toothpaste in the middle, and he rolls it up from the bottom. This is called the **differentiating** stage of a relationship. It is marked by discussions where the participants start emphasizing their individual differences instead of their similarities and common ground. Where you once placed emphasis on how much you have in common, now you start to notice some of the differences that you previously overlooked or ignored. At this point you simply acknowledge the differences and assert a bit of independence.

Your relationship is going well, but you do notice that when you bring up the issue of travel, or even exploring new places, your partner seems to want to stay at home. The comments that used to focus on the toothpaste now emphasize how you always leave a wet towel on the floor or never take out the garbage. Where the comments used to simply indicate differences, they now mark those differences and assign blame. You also start to spend less time together in joint activities. This is called the **circumscribing** or blaming stage of a relationship, where people spend less time together, and the times they spend together are farther and farther apart. The level of communication interaction decreases and takes on a negative tone.

Where conversations used to flow, now they stagnate and don't go anywhere. It seems to require more effort to communicate now, and you might not know why. You sometimes wonder why you can't have a simple conversation without its turning into a struggle or conflict. You often find yourself not wanting to talk simply to conserve your energy and prevent conflict. Your latest research paper takes more time at the office, and you seem to find solo activities that keep you busy. This is the **stagnating** stage of a relationship, where you are actively engaged in other activities. The relationship is not dynamic and requires little interaction.

Over time, this stage of a relationship can become exhausting. You find you don't want to fight, so you get up and leave early in the morning. You come home late. The other person also seems to be avoiding you in a similar, passive way. Your conversations, while possibly more frequent, are brief, awkward, and even hostile. You find communication takes considerable effort, and you're not always sure you're ready or willing to make that effort; you see that he isn't either. This is called the **avoiding** stage of a relationship, and like it sounds, it is marked by people actively avoiding each other, viewing the other as in the way. While conversations may increase, so does the level of frustration and disagreement.

At some point you have one fight too many, or perhaps you just stop talking, but you come to realize that the person you knew is no longer there, and you have changed, too. You come to a point where you want to move on, and so does he. You part, and perhaps grieve the loss of the relationship, effectively terminating the relationship. This stage, as you might suspect, is called the **terminating** stage of a relationship. People are no longer seen by others or themselves as a couple.

Hopefully, this scenario has been useful for you in illustrating the ten stages of a relationship. The processes of coming together and coming apart each feature five key steps, but relationships do not necessarily follow this model in a particular order. Each stage can be recognized by several signs, and this information enables us to see a relationship from a new perspective. Relationships can be repaired, maintained, and experience grow across a lifetime. After this brief review, we will examine several strategies to improve relationships.

Review: Coming Together

Stage 1: Initiating	People have short conversations and "size each other up," making initial judgments.
Stage 2: Experimenting	The conversational partners want to know more about each other. They share personal information, likes and dislikes, and continue to get to know each other better.
Stage 3: Intensifying	The participants recognize a desire to see each other more frequently, where the length of time together increases, and the time apart decreases. There is mutual concern.
Stage 4: Integrating	The participants recognize a relationship, and start planning their activities around those of their partner. Their friends see them as a couple, and if one is missing, people will ask about the other.
Stage 5: Bonding	The participants seek to formalize the relationship, though a public ritual like marriage, or through a joint venture like buying a house.

Review: Growing Apart

Stage 1: Differentiating	The participants start emphasizing their individual differences instead of their similarities and common ground.
Stage 2: Circumscribing (Blaming)	The participants spend less time together, and the times they spend together are farther and farther apart. Communication interaction decreases and takes on a negative tone.
Stage 3: Stagnating	The participants are actively engaged in other activities; joint activities are not dynamic and require little interaction.
Stage 4: Avoiding	The participants actively avoid each other, viewing the other as in the way. While conversations may increase, so does the level of frustration and disagreement.
Stage 5: Terminating	The participants part ways and are no longer seen by others or themselves as a couple.

Exercise

Think of different relationships you have with other people, both male and female. Can you identify elements of each stage in a real relationship?

No two relationships are the same, but many go through these stages. If a relationship goes from stage one to stage five of relational development overnight, do you think there is any possibility it may go through stages one through five of relational deterioration as quickly? Counselors often point to the importance of bonding and the need to form strong connections at each level. In addition, knowledge of these stages can help couples recognize troubles early and take a step back, possibly saving the relationship. It is important to note that a relationship can end at any stage, and that sometimes relationships never end, but instead become "polluted" as irrational conflict breaks out between relational partners as they try to hurt one another.

Relational Dialectics

> *The most important ingredient we put into any relationship*
> *is not what we say or what we do, but what we are.*
> —Stephen Covey

The work of Montgomery and Baxter (1998) offers an alternative way of looking at, and understanding, the formation and dissolution of relationships. The theory of **relational dialectics** focuses on the internal and external pressures that individuals in relationships experience. Rather than specific stages or steps, this viewpoint examines the internal and external conflicting pressures that reinforce the view that relationships are in constant state of change. This change involves both coming together, but also growing apart, often in overlapping moments or cycles, as people come to know one another.

Have you ever been in a relationship where you came to know someone well, and because of the close relationship you've developed, you could almost predict what he or she might say or do? And then he or she did or said something you didn't expect, or hurt your feelings, and you ended up not feeling as close or connected? After more communication and time, you may regain a new understanding of that person, at the same time he or she learns about you, and the relationship grows deeper. This example illustrates the push (coming together) and pull (growing apart) that, according to the theory, we all experience in interpersonal relationships. This natural state of change is often described in waves or cycles, with things going well until a shift or change occurs, again redirecting the relationship. This inherent tension is called **dialectical tension.**

The theory of relational dialectics goes on to outline how, as people grow closer to each other, they also experience more conflict that will come up and pull them apart. If you are on your first date with someone, you may be much more likely to attribute her behavior (and your own) to nervousness or a lack of understanding because everything is new. Time passes and you come to know each other better, but this familiarity may breed contempt or conflict. Let's say she is talking about really wanting to get in shape and later suggests going out for ice cream. If you don't know each other, it may not be a source of conflict, but when you get to know someone well, you see all her inconsistencies (and your own), leading to internal and possibly external conflict.

Internal Dialectical Tensions

Montgomery and Baxter (1998) offer six main areas of tension and clearly divide them into two groups: internal and external dialectical tensions. These are inherent contradictions that are often at odds with each other in an internal level within the relationship. Let's examine three internal dialectical tensions and how they influence interpersonal relationships.

Connectedness and Separateness.   It is natural to seek a feeling of connection and devote time and energy to a relationship you find rewarding and fulfilling. As people seek connection with each other, they also influence each other and may adopt each other's ideas, values, or viewpoints. Too much time together, however, can come to blur the lines between individuals, and in effect weaken the relationship to the point it cannot last. Individuals need to spend time alone, exploring their own interests independently, to reinforce their own individual identities. Interdependence in a relationship can be a healthy attribute, but if it changes to dependence, it can become destructive.

Let's say you are involved with a relationship, and your partner wants to spend every waking moment (and possibly all nonwaking moments as well) with you. At first this attention, time, and energy may be exciting as you learn about each other, but over time it may become too intense, too predictable or routine, or simply too close for comfort. This raises the question of how can you communicate with her that you value the relationship, you believe you can keep close and connected, but both of you also need to have some time on your own. You may fear that she will perceive this as a threat to the relationship, fear rejection, and reject you so prevent herself from getting hurt, hurting both of you in the process. If you both came to an understanding that spending time alone can enhance a relationship, and that it is natural and normal to spend time alone or apart and therefore not a threat to you losing each other, then taking about making changes in the relationship may be easier. Sometime couples turn to counseling and the independent third party, the counselor, can raise this point for discussion and help the couple communicate about this important issue. This tension between the degree of connectedness and separateness is one of three key relational dialectics.

Certainty and Uncertainty.   People want to feel safe around one another, and one way they do that is to watch, listen, and predict how each other will react to situations and stimuli. This sense of certainty or predictability brings a measure of assurance in the relationship that leads to trust and a feeling of connectedness. Without a level of predictability, people tend to feel on guard and watchful rather than free to explore the relationship. This does not mean, however, that the key to a successful relationship is to be predictable. Have you ever done something for a long time that later became boring and mundane? Relationships that are completely predictable can also follow this pattern. Without the uncertainty associated with the spice, variety, and novelty or new experiences through spontaneous interaction in new and exciting ways, the relationship will fall into the trap of being completely predictable.

Go back to the example of the relationship where you spent all your time together. Perhaps you walked to each class together, saw each other after work every day, saw movies, visited friends, and went out to eat together. Over time, the movies may seem a lot alike, and all the restaurants may taste the same. Even your time together has lost some of its flavor. The antidote is to do something new and bring in a little more uncertainty to the relationship, but how much, when, and what type of "new and different" activity may prove to be a challenge. We like predictability, even if we grow a bit bored, because we feel safe and have a sense of trust. We risk losing that when we explore new ideas, places, or activities. This is where the tension of certainty/uncertainty plays a role in interpersonal relationships. There may never be a perfect mix because, as we previously discussed, the relationship is always changing. Finding a balance is elusive and leads to tensions that can lead to conflict, again bringing people together or pulling them apart.

Openness and Closedness.   What happens when someone says something about him- or herself in a relationship? There is often an understood requirement of reciprocity where you are supposed to also reveal or share something about yourself on a similar level. This self-disclosure allows a relationship to grow and increases certainty and predictability, leading to a sense of connection and trust. It can also feel uncomfortable. You may not have wanted to know that particular fact or story about his past, and now that he has gone ahead and said it out loud, he is looking at you for a response. This pressure to self-disclose can create tension and illustrates the relationship between our desire to be transparent with each other, not holding anything back, with our need for privacy, and not sharing everything about ourselves. This struggle, like our two previous areas that create tension in interpersonal relationships, is a natural one and there is no one right answer. Relationships are always changing. We need to share to come to know each other better, but we want to be able to choose when, how, and why we share or choose not to share. Since everyone has different levels of comfort with these two issues, tension in the relationship will result. This point in the theory reinforces the idea that the path to intimacy is not a straight line or a series of logical, predictable steps, but instead a balance between "push" and "pull" tensions across several key dynamics or relational dialectics.

External Dialectical Tensions

Problems that arise between the couple and the community are called external dialectical tensions. This includes expectations of how the couple is supposed to behave, where and when they are supposed to be together (or not be together), and all the social norms and customs that are associated with the formation of relationships. We'll now examine three key areas of tension that involve the couple's relationship to the community.

Inclusion–Seclusion.   William Schutz (1956) discussed inclusion as one of three basic interpersonal needs. Abraham Maslow (1970) also discussed a similar theme in the need for "love and belonging" as part of the hierarchy of human needs. In the theory of relational dialectics, we see again the importance of the need to belong, to be loved, and to be included. Here, however, the emphasis is on the inherent tension between this need and the need for seclusion.

In the previous example, your relationship was presented with several tensions between two distinct but related interpersonal needs. Here, that theme is continued with an emphasis on external dialectical tension, or a more public level that involves more than just two people in a relationship. Let's say you got a promotion. Congratulations are in order, and you might want to celebrate. The validation you feel for hard work well recognized makes you feel like you belong, secure in your place and role in the company. This promotion means you might be more visible to your co-workers and may have to spend more time on new assignments with greater responsibility. As you tell your partner the good news, you feel a tinge of regret. You recognize that you can't accept this new responsibility and have everything else in your life stay the same. Change is an ever-present part of a relationship, and you recognize that you may not be able to spend as much time with your partner as you once did. You may have to travel for work, or be gone on some weekends, and this will create some time apart and distance between you. You feel the pull of not wanting to accept this new change, preferring to maintain your relationship, but there is the push of the new assignment in the back of your mind. This tension is between inclusion, or being part of the group or team, and seclusion, or time alone or in your interpersonal relationship. There are no easy answers and again it is all about balance and change.

Conventionality and Uniqueness.   You are ready to take that new assignment, but plan on trying to negotiate the frequency of your travel time away from home. You stand in front of the mirror and get ready for work. The tie-dye shirt in the closet is fun and colorful, but may not fit in very well at the office. Your choice of a suit or outfit to some degree is based on external expectations of what you should look like in your role or job. This conventionality is all about fitting in, and you learn conventions, or acceptable ways of presenting information, including information about yourself, as you grow up. What do you wear to a job interview? To a rock concert or club? Are they the same? You know the difference and society, through its members, reinforces norms and standards on dress, behavior, and even speech. Do you talk the same at the club as you do at work or school? What is acceptable in one place may be unacceptable or inappropriate in another. Your need to fit in is in tension with your need to be you as an individual. You want to express how you perceive yourself, and a tie-dye shirt might say to the world that you think today is going to be wonderful day. The only problem is that your boss might not see it that way. There is inherent tension between your need to fit it in and your need to be unique.

Revelation and Concealment.   The final area of external tension involves your need to share information and feelings, which might be quite intimate and help you form a close relationship with your partner, and the need for you as a couple to be recognized in the larger community. You choose to share with each other, but then comes the dilemma of what you tell others about you as a couple. At first it might seem like there is no obligation, or tension, to reveal anything. No one needs to know unless you want them to, or so it might seem. When you start spending a lot of time with your new friend and the relationship develops into something more, your friends are going to be curious. You are going to feel this pressure, and so is your partner. There are advantages to "going public" with the relationship, from the way people treat you to even "married filing jointly" for taxes. These advantages are put in check by the potential loss of privacy. People might try to meddle in the relationship. There will be questions from family and friends, and it just starts to get complicated. This tension between you as part of a relationship and the community's recognizing you as a couple is not a step-by-step path. It is complicated, and the push and pull of this dynamic places stress on the relationship.

To summarize the basics of the theory of relational dialectics, the first thing to keep in mind is that change is a constant state, and the relationship is always to some degree in flux. Rather than looking at a relationship as a series of steps leading toward a set goal, this theory highlights the inherent contradictions that involve a couple on both internal and external levels. The couple places pressure on themselves as they try to balance competing needs, and the community also places pressure on the couple, again over competing needs. This creates tensions over contradictions that are not easily resolved.

Through these six relational dialectics we can see three themes emerge. Integration is balanced against separation both on internal and external levels. The need for stability versus the need for change crosses both levels, as does the drive to express yourself as an individual and as a couple versus the need for privacy. This table summarizes the main points.

	Integration/ Separation	*Stability/ Change*	*Expression/ Privacy*
Internal contradiction	*Connection/ Autonomy* Need to be part of relationship versus need for individuality	*Predictability/ Novelty* Need for intimacy and predictability versus need for novelty and change	*Openness/ Closedness* Need for self-disclosure versus need for privacy
External contradiction	*Inclusion/ Seclusion* Need to belong versus need for privacy	*Conventionality/ Uniqueness* Need for the familiar versus need for unique identity	*Revelation/ Concealment* Need for acknowledgement of the relationship versus need for confidentiality

Key Strategies for Maintaining and Improving Relationships

> *People are lonely because they build walls instead of bridges.*
> —Joseph F. Newton

Let's say that we can, for the sake of argument, go back in time in our scenario. We will explore several key strategies that offer ways to maintain and improve the relationship. Not all strategies are equally effective, and not all effective strategies are equally effective at the same time. You need to be sensitive to the verbal and nonverbal cues in order to adapt. One underlying assumption in this section is that you want to improve the relationship. Beebe, Beebe, and Redmond (2002) together with Knapp and Vangelisti (2000) offer us several strategies that have been adapted here. Use you communication skills to consider ways not discussed that may be effective and share them with your classmates.

1. Honor Each Other with Respect. The first strategy to maintain or improve a relationship provides a foundation for all other strategies that follow. Regardless whether the relationship is work, family, or even intimate, it is important to always communicate how you value the relationship to the person or people involved. This relationship message should always accompany the content messages you communicate. The goal is that there should be no moment when your communication places the relationship in question. This means that while you may argue, fight, or get frustrated with each other, your conflict is about a point, idea, or issue, but not about your relationship. By threatening the relationship, you play a dangerous card in a losing game. People grow defensive, lose trust, and the process of growing apart, from differentiating to blaming, will follow. By communicating that you value the relationship, your message is that day-to-day struggles do not threaten your relationship. It is healthy to communicate independence and acknowledge differences, but displays of respect for the relationship and emphasis on relationship messages provide a strong foundation to build a healthy relationship.

2. Communicate Attraction. In the scenario, what was the cue that the other person wanted to learn more about you? Gaze and eye contact were probably your first clue. You might have noticed the physical distance between you became smaller as you got to know one another, one of you might have leaned forward, or perhaps it was as simple as a smile. By communicating attraction, we demonstrate our familiarity with each other and communicate relationship messages. If, on the first lunch date, you accidentally bumped the other person in the cafeteria line, there might have been an awkward sense of invading someone's space. But over time, that same type of bump or touch can take on new meaning and lose the sense of awkwardness.

Verbally, we communicate attraction by reinforcing the relationship through language. "We" communicates attraction, while "I" communicates independence. Both terms are fine, but remember words are contextual and there may be some contexts where you want to communicate the relationship. In the scenario, if you are talking with someone at the informal communication department office party and your partner joins the conversation, a proper introduction and indication of your relationship may reaffirm the relationship and make your partner feel important. In that same scenario, where your partner is from another department, if you did not introduce him or provide an indication of relationship, he may feel slighted. By respecting each other and using both nonverbal and verbal messages that communicate attraction, you can reaffirm the relationship.

3. Be Open and Self-Disclose Appropriately. We have discussed the process of self-disclosure and will see its importance again here. When you came to know each other in the scenario, the process involved self-disclosure. That required time, effort, and a certain attitude of openness to sharing. When you came home from the conference in the scenario, excited about the possibility of travel, the conversation with your partner was not completely open. Perhaps you or he did not discuss feelings and thoughts, but there was miscommunication. Perhaps he interpreted traveling as your wanting to "spread your wings" and leave him. Perhaps he didn't want to travel and had different ideas. We won't know because it wasn't discussed. Be open to how others might interpret your messages and try to communicate your own openness to their points of view. Use open-ended questions to draw out other people and actively listen when they choose to respond. You'll learn more about where they are coming from and improve your relationships.

4. Express Emotions. Emotions will express themselves eventually, but it is up to you to choose when and how they will be expressed. Emotions will come through in your voice, your body language, even your sense of timing and space as you communicate. By holding emotions back for a long time, they can come through in many ways you did not anticipate. Emotions linked to stress can lead to more than a few healthcare issues, including heart disease, high blood pressure, ulcers, and the list could continue. People who report satisfaction in relationships and people to talk to often live better (Levenson, Cartensen, & Gottman, 1994) and possibly even longer than people who do not. In our scenario, your discussion on traveling and enthusiasm over meeting someone who caused you to think in a new way created emotions, both for you and your partner. You didn't talk of these emotions much, but they nonetheless came out in day-to-day conversations and started a cycle that continued. Expressing emotions is important in a relationship and so is a sense of timing. Make time for their expression in your relationship.

5. Commitment and Commitment Talk. Commitment in the context of a relationship involves a choice, and that means you *want to,* not *have to* or *ought to,* be involved. This sense of wanting to be involved can come through in your verbal and nonverbal messages. Commitment talk can involve the retelling of a story together to a third person or group, reinforcing how you both overcame a challenge together. It can be talk about a common future together, focusing on the rewards you gain by being together and those you will earn together. By identifying with the relationship, you can also reinforce commitment talk. The "we" orientation comes through in your content and relationship messages. You may also discuss topics that illustrate that the alternative to being together is less attractive. "I'd hate to be dating again" might be said while discussing a friend and her new acquaintance. It also involves choosing the relationship over other activities such as hobbies, sports, or even work.

Another strategy for developing the relationship is to recognize your personal idioms (Knapp & Vangelisti, 2000). **Personal idioms** are the unique words, phrases, or ways of saying things that only people in the relationship understand. For example, let's say you had a negative boss named Greg who always forgot things, had a vengeful or mean streak, and really frustrated you. If told your partner about him and later referred to a new supervisor's actions on a particular day as "just like Greg's," then only your partner would get the inside reference. This inside knowledge reinforces the relationship and builds a "library" of common references. Your personal idioms may also involve expressions of affection or nicknames that you call each other. Perhaps you have a favorite restaurant, maybe even have "your" table, or know each other's favorite food or drink. You may have developed roles and responsibilities that are understood between you, such as who is going to cook and who will take out the garbage. Special songs, places, or words all represent understood references that reinforce the relationship. By investing time and energy in the relationship, you are communicating you are committed through your actions and words.

6. Monitor Your Perceptions. You can choose how you react to situations and stimuli. Stephen Covey, the author of *Seven Habits for Highly Effective People* (1989), uses the term *proactive* to mean accepting responsibility for your actions and choosing how you respond. Reactive means responding to a situation or stimuli, but possibly not planning where your response will leave you. In the case of a hot stove, your spinal cord gets the message that your hand is near a heat source and sends the message to pull your hand away quickly. The message doesn't even reach your brain by the time you respond. In the case of a game of pool or billards, when you hit one ball, it may bounce off the sides of the table or even other balls on the table and then come to rest in a specific spot. A good player plans each shot to leave the ball in an advantageous position for him- or herself or in a less advantageous one for his or her opponent. This requires planning and a proactive response.

Covey (1989) articulates this well when he states the word *responsibility* is comprised of two words, "response" and "ability." You have the ability to respond and if you consider the impact of your communication and how it will affect your partner. In the case of our scenario, when you choose to share your new goals of travel, considering how this will be perceived by your partner will help you communicate more effectively. It also means monitoring your own perceptions and asking questions to confirm that your perceptions are accurate. As we discussed in the perception and listening chapter, you perceptions are influenced by many things but you have the ability to question and respond. See Case Study 8.1 for a list of his seven habits and see how they relate to the strategies for maintaining and improving relationships.

CASE STUDY 8.1 • *Developing Healthy Relationships*

Relationships come in all shapes and sizes, from short term to long term, from imper-sonal to intimate. Forming, maintaining, and developing healthy relationships is a chal-lenge, and a useful guide that applies across this range is available in Stephen Covey's book and related materials, entitled *The Seven Habits for Highly Effective People* (1989). This book is often referred to in business and professional circles and also has a lot to offer in interpersonal contexts beyond business. Here is a brief summary of the seven habits (Covey, 1989).

1. **Be proactive.** Focus on you ability to respond instead of react to situations.
2. **Begin with the end in mind.** What do you want in your relationships and what steps are necessary to make it a reality?
3. **Put first things first.** Focus your time and attention on what matters and your priorities.
4. **Think win/win.** In a healthy relationship, there is no loser.
5. **Seek first to understand, then to be understood.** Understanding is key to ef-fective communication.
6. **Synergize.** Cooperation can increase understanding.
7. **Sharpen the saw.** Take time to renew yourself and your relationships.

Consider how each of the habits relate to interpersonal communication. Increase your understanding by learning more about the habits at: http://www.franklincovey.com/

Source: Covey (1989).

7. Listen Actively and Respond Confirmingly. Listening skills are key to your perceptions. In the scenario, you learned a lot about your partner in the early stages of the relationship but that information reduces over time. You may be more certain of his or her likes and dislikes and even develop personal idioms, which allow you to listen less and still feel like you know what he or she is saying or feeling. Since we all change over time, recognize that your partner too will change. While some infor-mation may stay the same, some will change, and you need to listen for his or her thoughts and feelings in order to understand new attitudes and behaviors. When you understand, respond confirmingly, communicating your understanding to your part-ner and reinforcing your commitment. By putting down the newspaper, turning off the television, or turning down the music, you send a message that you want to actively listen to the other person and value what he or she has to say.

8. Socially Decenter and Adapt. As we have discussed previously, becoming other-oriented means you actively consider what someone says and why he or she says it, trying to see things from the other's perspective. Decentering involves this process of becoming other-, or partner-oriented, and shifts the emphasis from just your needs, wants, or desires, to the other person's or the goals of the relationship. Adapting your messages, in terms of word choice, timing, and your choices, can help reinforce the message that your partner is important to you.

9. Be Tolerant, Supportive, and Show Restraint. Not everything will go as planned, and goals may be delayed as life's circumstances change. If the relationship is important to you, however, you need to be tolerant, supportive, and show restraint. Perhaps your partner has had a bad day and his or her bad mood affects your interaction. Tolerance recognizes you also have had similar days, and you have sense of give and take, of sharing, in the relationship. If your partner's paper was not accepted to be presented at a conference, but yours was, be supportive of his or her point of view and offer assistance when it's appropriate. Problem solving, such as finding a different place to present his or her paper, might help, but your partner may just want you to listen and express support. Refrain from reacting to his or her words and sense of disappointment, even if hurtful things were said, with the knowledge that he or she wouldn't normally express him- or herself in that way. Later, when the opportunity presents itself or you make time to share, you can talk about how you felt when he or she said words that hurt you.

10. Manage Conflict Cooperatively. Conflict is part of relationships, and people do not always see or express things in the same way, even after years of developing the relationship. Keep in mind the first point—expressions that you value the relationship need to be present even when you have a conflict—will help you manage conflict cooperatively. You may also consider timing and choose to not argue in front of others or at the end of a challenging day. Managing conflict does not mean avoiding it all together. Conflict can present an opportunity to gain a new understanding and strengthen the relationship. There is common suggestion of never going to bed angry with each other, which holds truth on this point. Choosing to wait to discuss a point of issue does not mean ignoring it, and managing conflict effectively requires communication. Making time for a discussion without the distractions of friends, work, or family can help you do this.

Summary

In this chapter on the lifecycles of interpersonal relationships, we have examined five steps in how we engage in conversations. We have seen how these steps mirror the stages of relational formation and deterioration. The process of how we come together involves five stages and we have seen though our scenario examples of key characteristics of each stage. The process of how we grow apart also involves five stages, and by recognizing their characteristics we can maintain and improve our relationships. We discussed ten strategies to maintain and improve relationships and examined how each can relate to our scenario. We closed this chapter with a brief introduction of conflicts in relationships, and in the next chapter we will examine this issue in depth.

People don't care how much you know, until they know how much you care.
—Anonymous

For More Information

To see more about *The Seven Habits for Highly Effective People* (1989), go to: **http://www.franklincovey.com/**

The Corporation for Public Broadcasting offers teaching resources on the discussion of living longer, including the importance of communication interaction, as well as ways to expand our discussion that can be adapted for classroom use. Go to: **http://www.pbs.org/stealingtime/resources/lesson1.htm**

Review Questions

1. Factual Questions
   a. What is a strategy for starting a relationship?
   b. What is one stage in relational development?
   c. What is one stage in relational deterioration?
   d. What is one way you can improve and maintain a relationship?

2. Interpretative Questions
   a. From your viewpoint, how do you think knowledge of relational development can influence relationships?
   b. From your perspective, what strategy is effective for starting relationship?
   c. Can you think of an additional way to improve and maintain a relationship that is not listed?

3. Evaluative Questions
   a. To what extent do we influence the beginning of a relationship?
   b. To what extent do we influence the maintenance and improvement of a relationship?
   c. Who controls or regulates the development of a relationship?

4. Application Questions
   a. What factors influence changes in relationships over time? Interview someone older than you and someone younger than you. See if you find common themes.
   b. When relationships terminate, do they follow the model? Explore and research your answer, finding examples that serve can as case studies.
   c. Do people perceive they are in the same stage at the same time? Survey ten individuals, see what they identify, and relate their responses to the models of relational development and deterioration.

References

Altman, I., & Taylor, D. (1973). *Social penetration: The development of interpersonal relationships.* New York: St. Martins Press.

Baxter, L. A. (1988). A dialectical perspective on communication strategies in relationship development. In S. W. Duck (Ed.), *Handbook of personal relationships* (pp. 257–273). Chichester, UK: John Wiley.

Beebe, S., Beebe, S., & Redmond, M. (2002). *Interpersonal communication: Relating to others* (3rd ed.). Boston: Allyn and Bacon.

Covey, S. (1989). *The seven habits for highly effective people.* New York: Simon & Schuster.

DeVito, J. (2003). *Messages: Building interpersonal communication skills* (5th ed.). Boston: Allyn and Bacon.

Knapp, M. (1978). *Social intercourse: From greeting to goodbye* (pp. 3–28). Boston: Allyn and Bacon.

Knapp, M., & Vangelisti, A. (1996). *Interpersonal communication and human relationships* (3rd ed.; pp. 34–40). Boston: Allyn and Bacon.

Knapp, M., & Vangelisti, A. (2000). *Interpersonal communication and relationships* (4th ed.). Boston: Allyn and Bacon.

Levenson, R. W., Cartensen, L. L., & Gottman, J. M. (1994). The influence of age and gender on affect, physiology, and their interrelations: A study of long-term marriages. *Journal of Personality and Social Psychology, 67,* 56–68.

Malinowski, B. (1935). *The language and magic of gardening.* London: Allen and Unwin.

Maslow, A. (1970). *Motivation and personality* (2nd ed.; pp. 35–150). New York: Harper & Row.

Montgomery, B. M., & Baxter, L. A. (1998). Dialogism and relational dialectics. In B. M. Montgomery & L. A. Baxter (Eds.), *Dialectical approaches to studying personal relationships* (pp. 155–183). Hillsdale, NJ: Lawrence Erlbaum.

Shutz, W. (1966). *The interpersonal underworld* (pp. 13–20). Palo Alto, CA: Science and Behavior Books.

9

Interpersonal Communication and Conflict

Chapter Objectives

After completing this chapter, you should be able to:

1. Identify and describe eight principles of interpersonal conflict.
2. Identify and describe three stages in the process of interpersonal conflict.
3. Identify and describe three strategies to resolve interpersonal conflict.
4. Identify and describe the dark side of relationships and three main criteria.
5. Identify and describe ten methods for managing conflict resolution.
6. Identify and describe five ways to improve interpersonal communication.

Introductory Exercise 1

Please consider conflicts you have had in the last week. List several and see if you can find a word to describe what each conflict was all about.

Introductory Exercise 2

When was the last time you had a miscommunication? Did it result in conflict? How did it make you feel, and how do you think it made the other person feel? Please write three words to describe how you felt and how you think the other person may have felt. Without getting into too much detail, see if your words match those of your classmates. We often find common themes in conflict even though we come from different perspectives.

> *We are never so likely to settle a question rightly as when we discuss it freely.*
> —Thomas Babington

We have all experienced conflict in our relationships at some point. We can recognize the stress and pain that may come with conflict. We can also recognize the joy of overcoming a challenge and resolving the conflict. This range of experiences and emotions underscores the idea that conflict exists in all relationships. How we manage conflict makes a significant impact on the relationship, and how we manage it over time influences how our relationships grow or dissolve. Recognizing the importance and universal nature of conflict in relationships, we will build on our previous discussion with the principles of interpersonal conflict, examine the process and a number of conflict management styles, and examine ways to manage, resolve, and improve interpersonal conflict.

Principles of Interpersonal Conflict

Interpersonal conflict is different for everyone, but we can focus on elements of the experience that we have in common. This common ground lays the foundation for our understanding by highlighting several principles of interpersonal conflict. Hocker and Wilmot (1991) offer us several principles that have been adapted to offer additional insight into the nature of conflicts between people.

1. Conflict is universal. Every relationship involves conflict. **Conflict** is the physical or mental struggle that comes from the perception of opposing or incompatible demands, desires, wants, or needs. This definition allows us to see that conflict can be both physical and mental. We also see that individual perception is a key point in understanding interpersonal struggles. It also involves what we perceive we have to do, want to do, or need.

Conflict can be expressed in many ways. Your choice of words, or your silence, may communicate your opposition to something. It can be subtle or overt. It can be brief and quickly resolved or linger and resurface again and again. Conflict is a part of every interpersonal relationship at one time or another.

2. Conflict is associated with incompatible goals. Please look back at your responses to Exercise 1. What were your conflicts with others about? Money? Time? Insensitivity? All of these points may be involved, or you may express other ideas. What does not change is the idea that the words you wrote refer to goals, and conflict is often associated with the perception of incompatible goals.

One way to consider this principle is to think about how long it takes you earn your money and what you choose to spend it on. Perhaps you are working your way through school, and one way you spend your money is on your education. Your choice reinforces the idea that, to you, education is important. Do you know anyone, or have you known anyone in the past, who chose not to continue his or her formal education? This person may have spent his or her time and money on other goals, illustrating a difference between you. If you find your education is challenged by a work schedule, another's behavior, or the idea that this other person does not share your goal, conflict may result. This offers us a clue to how to resolve conflicts: Recognize what the other person's goals are and how to meet both sets of goals at the same time. It is not always possible, but this strategy does provide us with a starting point we will explore later in this chapter.

3. Conflict is associated with scarce resources. You bring home a paycheck and so does your partner or spouse. He or she wants to buy the latest video game system and needs your help. You need to buy textbooks and know they will take most of the money that will remain after the bills are paid. The conflict that results has everything to do with scarce resources. Your partner may argue that if you just wait until next month to buy the books, then the problem is solved. You may say the same idea to wait applies to the video game system. There are only enough resources for one choice at this time.

Go back to our discussion of interpersonal relationships and refer to Maslow (1970) and Schutz's (1966) ideas about the priorities for people. You know that we all need food, water, and air to survive and seek shelter next. Your paycheck and your partner's will cover your basic needs this month. Your needs for belonging, self-esteem, and even self-actualization may be met in some ways met through education, both in learning and in social interaction with your classmates. Your partner may have a group of friends who are into video games and wants to be the person to have the latest system, meeting in some way the need to belong to a peer group. Schutz (1966) might also offer that the need of inclusion in the relationship as well as the relationships at school or the video game group are involved, as well as affection and control. All these factors relate to the scare resources that are often associated with interpersonal conflict.

4. Conflict is associated with interference. Your friend might perceive that you are interfering with his or her desire to get the new video game system, and you might perceive interference in your educational goals. You need to do well in your classes and know that not getting behind is important. You need the books to keep up. Your partner might perceive the need for the system to keep up with friends. This aspect of the conflict reinforces the principle that conflict is associated with the perception that the other person or persons are interfering with your progress toward your goals.

Interference can take the form of using scarce resources in ways you don't want, but it can also take other forms. Perhaps your partner's friends come over all the time, eat all your food, and stay up late playing their loud music and video games. You might like a good time and the interaction with them, but might perceive that they are taking up valuable resources in terms of your food budget or your study and sleep time, interfering with your ability to focus on your homework.

5. Conflict is not a sign of a poor relationship. People often assume that conflict is a sign of a poor relationship. If we know that all relationships have conflict at one point or another, then this logic would indicate that all relationships are bad. Relationships can be the most rewarding experiences of our lives, but don't lose sight that conflict is a part of the process. Beebe, Beebe, and Redmond (2002, p. 242) indicate that "disagreements do not necessarily signal that the relationship is on the rocks." Constant bickering and fighting can indicate there are more serious issues that have not been resolved, but so can the awkward silence and pointedly polite conversations of people who were once quite relaxed with each other. Healthy relationships express disagreement and negotiate conflict successfully. Conflict can even play in the construction and development of the relationship, and the struggle or challenge that people overcome can actually bring them closer together.

6. Conflict cannot be avoided. Perhaps you've thought if you just leave the problem alone for a while, it will naturally resolve itself. The other person will eventually come around to your way of thinking or see how your point is reasonable. Perhaps this worked for you once, or maybe you learned this strategy from your parents. The problem with this view is that if we know that conflict will arise in every relationship, then avoiding all conflict loses the opportunity to resolve this issue and move on. The conflict will come up again and can build over time. The nature of our ability to perceive our world reinforces the idea that we all see things differently, and it naturally follows that we won't see everything eye to eye. Conflict provides an opportunity to understand each other better, and by trying to avoid it, we lose this opportunity. This allows conflict to grow and resurface later in ways that may be even more challenging to the relationship. It is also important to consider that confrontation is not necessarily the opposite of avoidance. We don't have to confront each other instead of avoiding each other. Communication provides the process to share and understand what we mean by what we say and how we feel about an issue, priority, or goal. Use your good communication skills to address, rather than confront or avoid, interpersonal conflict.

7. Conflict cannot always be resolved. You still need your books and your partner still wants the new video game system. You can't have both and have to make a choice, which underscores the idea that conflicts cannot always be resolved. You can listen and even tell your partner what you heard him or her say, communicating your understanding of his or her point of view, but the essential elements of the conflict will remain unresolved. You may have to make the choice that is best for you, agreeing to disagree for now, but indicating next month or later that the video game system can be a mutual savings goal.

8. Conflict is not always bad. There are countless self-help books on the market that promise the elimination of conflict between people if only they would follow certain steps. While some of these books may have good ideas, the tenet that we can eliminate all conflict is false. As long as we remain individuals, with different languages, cultures, thoughts, hopes, and dreams, we will naturally have differences. The idea that we should eliminate conflict often comes from the idea of conflict as bad or undesirable, thus we should get rid of it. Conflict can be a valuable opportunity for learning and coming to understand each other. If the group goes along with the first idea and no one indicates the idea doesn't match the goals, relies on unproven technology, or is not feasible, then the group falls victim to groupthink (Janis, 1983). This can simply waste time or become quite serious. The role of the critic in this communication context is important. The critic not only points out flaws in the original plan, but also offers new ideas and provides an opportunity for other people to reflect and add additional insight, possibly improving on the original plan. Be careful not to view conflict as strictly bad or in a negative way. It can offer good outcomes in unexpected ways, provide new discussions, and even lead to a positive negotiation between the conversational participants.

Process of Interpersonal Conflict

Now that we have examined eight principles of interpersonal conflict, let's examine three key stages in the process. Each stage plays an important role in the overall process, but can be distinguished from the others by key characteristics. Your ability to recognize these characteristics will help you determine where the conflict currently is and enable you to help the conflict be resolved.

1. Before the Conflict

People often think with both their heads and their hearts. This is another way of saying people use both logic and emotion to make decisions, plan activities, and interact with each other. When we are in the midst of an interpersonal conflict, we may not think clearly and base our perceptions and resulting responses on our emotions. This makes it challenging to understand each other or find a way to negotiate

CASE STUDY 9.1 • *Patient/Provider Communication*

The last time you went to see your healthcare provider, did you perceive that your concerns were heard? In a time when healthcare providers are under pressure to see a large volume of patients in a short time frame, your answer might be "no." Consider the complexity of interpersonal communication, factor in the diverse backgrounds of patients and providers, and you can observe how challenging the medical office visit has become.

Patients come from diverse language and cultural backgrounds, and so do healthcare providers. Intercultural communication involves communication across cultures and is a significant issue in the context of healthcare. Is it appropriate for a young male healthcare provider to educate a young female on the appropriate use of birth control? Do her Hispanic background and her cultural values play a role in listening and comprehension of the material? What if language is an issue (McLean, 1996)?

Healthcare is not an exact science, and the medium of communication plays a significant role in the gathering and distribution of information. The cultural or linguistic background of the patient or provider may play a role in facilitating understanding or become an obstacle to effective communication.

Increasingly, nurse practioners, physician's assistants, and related healthcare providers are meeting the growing need in an age of assembly-line medicine. Many have additional training in communication and, more importantly, may have more time to devote to each patient and tailor the information gathering and education to individual needs (Guglielmo, 2001). Medical schools are even changing their curriculum to add emphasis on patient/provider communication and even intercultural communication as part of training (Pust & Moher, 1992).

Focus on your communication skills, take a list of symptoms with you to your next visit, and recognize your role as your own healthcare advocate.

Sources: Guglielmo (2001); McLean (1996); Pust & Moher (1992).

the conflict. It stands to reason, then, that if we could use our head to think clearly before we engage in conflict with each other, we might be the better for it.

Since we are not actively engaged in the interpersonal conflict, we can do a bit of thinking about the challenge that lies ahead. One good place to start is to consider the prior conditions that lead to the issue. Looking back at the principles of interpersonal conflict, do you see any that relate to the conflict? Knowing that the conflict involves the allocation of scarce resources might mean that one constructive step might be to take another look at the budget. If your money is funding video games rentals, thus taking up resources, by identifying this area and deciding together to save the rental money for the new video game system, the conditions that lead to the conflict may change or disappear.

Another good point to start, since we are thinking clearly, it to try to summarize the point of conflict clearly. By writing down our thoughts and feelings, we can go back to them and have a better insight into out own perceptions. By writing down what the main point of difference is in several words, we can see clearly the issue and then focus on ways to resolve it.

A key issue central to all conflicts is your attitude. How you approach conflict can directly influence the interaction. Your partner or spouse will respond to your attitude, and if it is one of aggression and anger, then defensiveness may be a natural result. Communicating from a defensive stance changes the nature of the communication and, by extension, the interpersonal conflict. By maintaining an open attitude, you may reinforce trust and facilitate better communication, leading to a resolution through mutual understanding. Another way of considering your attitude is to think about how your attitude impacts the communication climate.

In order to create healthy, long-lived relationships we need to learn how to manage conflict in a positive way. One way to do this is to consider the kind of climate, defensive or supportive, that we create when we communicate. A **defensive climate** is characterized by a threatening one another's interpersonal needs. When one person shows indifference to another, inclusion and affection are sacrificed. When someone attempts to impose his or her will on another, the issue of control will divide rather than bring them together. A **supportive climate,** however, focuses on the task or problems to be solved instead of the judgments of others. It is also characterized by spontaneous, honest, and open communication, in which people ask each other's opinions and actively listen to responses.

While competition may be present in some conversations, conversation is not by definition a competition. In the game of chess, the goal is dominate your opponent and win. In interpersonal communication, one of the goals may be persuasion, but it also involves content messages, relational messages, and is far more dynamic. Biologists once thought the notion of "only the strong survive" as an indisputable idea. Modern biologists are now coming to consider the importance of cooperation as a strategy for survival in nature and note that many species cooperate to succeed. For example, dolphins will come to the aid of one who has been injured, defend one another, switch roles in feeding if needed, and develop life-long relationships with one another (Mann & Smuts, 1999). In conversations, we need to cultivate a supportive climate, focusing on assessing our own observations and interpretations, our emotional responses, and our intentional and/or unintentional requests for information or interaction rather than on activities and behaviors that contribute to a defensive climate.

Our own awareness of our frustration and what we feel, in combination with an understanding of the point of difference, the degree to which the principles relate to the conflict, and how our attitude is influencing are important aspects of conflict. By taking account of the issues that relate to our conflict and how we influence the conflict through our attitude, we can take positive steps to resolve the issue.

2. During the Conflict

Sometimes people perceive that conflict just happens, and then they want to find a way to solve it. As we saw previously, lots of issues contribute to why we perceive conflict in the first place. We've now arrived at a point where the conflict has begun and each partner is expressing himself or herself. Both may try to articulate their thoughts and feelings, or why they see things the way they do, and they hope the other person is listening. This leads us to our first strategy in conflict: listening. If you want to, go back to the section of this book and review active and empathic listening to refresh your memory. Active listening involves choosing to listen and demonstrating that you are listening in your body language, posture, and even nodding your head. You may engage in paraphrasing, or saying back to someone what you perceive he or she said to demonstrate your active listening and to confirm that you got it right. You might also consider not only the other person's words, but the motivation as well, trying to see things from the other perspective. You may incorporate your interpretation of his or her motivations in your paraphrasing and show that you care about where the other person is coming from. Stephen Covey says this best when he states, "seek first to understand, then to be understood (Covey, 1989, p. 235). So many conflicts involve a "he said/she said" misunderstanding, where the conversational participants may use the same words, but those words have different meanings to each other. By first trying to understand what the other person means, you can better respond and share your point of view. It can also encourage reciprocity, or the sharing of speaking and active listening, in your partner.

While engaged in conflict, it is important to consider the climate of the discussion. Is the communication interaction between you involving strategies that are constructive for the relationship, meaning that you are gaining understanding and building the relationship? If not, then consider whether the strategies you and your partner are using are destructive, destroying the ability to understand, share, or effectively communicate.

Constructive strategies involve the use of good listening skills and paraphrasing your responses to indicate your interpretation of their meaning. How many conversations have you been a part of that when you finished your point, the other person responded to a minor detail and proceeded to go off in a new direction, leaving you wondering if he or she got your point? This person may have tuned into an internal monologue right after hearing this detail and have been preparing his or her response the whole time you were talking. This is not an effective strategy for effective communication: It is only an exchange of monologues and little understanding. Communication is the process of understanding and sharing meaning, and by definition, if we bypass each other or fail to listen because we are too busy listening to ourselves as we prepare our response, then we fail to communicate. Show your partner that you are listening and choose to not prepare your response while he or she is talking. You will learn more about what the other person is trying to communicate and your response may communicate your own concerns more effectively.

Another effective strategy is to stick to the point of the discussion. We discussed the importance of clarifying for ourselves what the conflict is all about before trying to communicate or resolve the issue. If you bring up related issues from the past or confuse your central message, miscommunication can occur, which can also give rise to defensiveness in your partner.

When we feel attacked, our most primitive instincts can overwhelm us and cloud clear thinking. Our "fight-or-flight" response is an effective adaptation to a hostile world, but it can actually undermine effective communication. The associated increase in adrenaline, pulse rate, and feelings of anxiety and fear can confuse our thoughts. This response can move us from a climate where we want to understand each other to one where our focus is to protect ourselves. When we become defensive, it directly impacts how and what we listen to. Recognizing the signs of defensiveness is a positive step in conflict. You can choose to take a time out and agree to communicate when you both have clearer heads. You may also consider agreeing to both go back and consider issues that relate to your conflict, clarify your point(s), and make time to talk with out distractions.

Defensiveness can lead to destructive strategies for handling conflict. If one partner uses profanity in response to a point, it may communicate defensiveness and also give rise to defensiveness. A good rule to avoid becoming defensive in an interpersonal conflict is to have the understanding prior to the conflict that certain words, like profanity, are not allowed. Words can hurt, and by agreeing that some words can serve as triggers for powerful emotions, you can try to keep the conflict from hurting each other.

Another type of destructive strategy is the avoidance of conflict. One partner may withdraw while another seeks interaction, and they may reverse roles later on in the conflict. This cycle can repeat endlessly, and this does not constructively resolve the conflict. Make time to talk and be ready to communicate when the time arrives. It is ok to take a time out when you recognize defensiveness in your partner or yourself, but if it becomes an avoidance strategy, then it will become destructive. Seeking professional counseling can help guide the discussion with a fresh perspective that is not part of the conflict.

Knapp and Vangelisti (1996) note that during conflict between couples exchanges that express dissatisfaction with their relationship are far more predictable than those of satisfied couples. Criticism gets criticism in return, and disagreements result. Satisfied couples provide a range of responses that cannot be easily categorized, but the value of the relationship and trust in its permanence comes through. Gottman (1979, 1982) indicates that dissatisfied couples engage more cross-complaining, or turn-taking that involves one complaint after another without paraphrasing, seeking understanding, or steps toward resolution. Conversely, satisfied couples often indicated the validity of their partner's complaint. This sends the message that the complaint was heard and has value, and the couple may seek solutions to resolve the complaint.

Dissatisfied couples also spent time arguing about how they were arguing instead of getting to the point of conflict. This may involve questioning whether the partner is paying attention or listening or complaining about the response ("don't get so emotional"). Satisfied couples were more likely to focus on the message and the motivation and again communicate respect for the interaction. Finally, dissatisfied couples often got caught up in the arguing and frequently got off topic or brought new topics into the conflict. Satisfied couples generally got back to the point and original issue of disagreement and were more likely to acknowledge when they got off track.

3. After the Conflict

By now you have shared your thoughts at least once and so has your partner, and you both have started to focus on ways to resolve the conflict. The conflict is in many ways over, because you both have moved from why you disagree to what you are going to do about it. This stage can come quickly or slowly and take a few key decisions or a long time. In the example of the textbooks and the video game system, you and your partner might decide on using the money on textbooks now, saving rental costs, and planning on a system purchase in a month. In the case of a divorce, the steps involved to resolve the conflict may take considerable time and effort.

It's important to recognize that the point when the conflicting stops and the resolving starts is not a clear stage, and it may be a challenge to identify. One way to recognize that the conflict has moved toward resolution is that the conversational participants have moved from exchanging viewpoints and issues to discussing solutions. Another is to recognize when people go over the points involved to reach a resolution, reiterating key points and ensuring understanding and everyone's responsibilities.

From this point, the resolution transitions to followup, where people share with each other their experiences during the conflict. This might not happen right away. People sometimes need time to reflect and think before sharing how they felt or what they learned during the conflict. People may open up and share their experiences, and sharing may arise naturally when another situation comes up. One person then states the resolution to the other again, in effect as a reminder. If the issue was renting video games, and the agreement was no rentals and saving the money to get the new system, then the renting of "just one video" would bring up the conflict again. It may be quickly resolved or give rise to the larger conflict again. People often reassure one another that they care about each other after a conflict. Often called reassurance rituals, people express their affection and their value of the relationship in verbal and nonverbal ways, like kissing or making up.

One important idea to consider when thinking about resolution is "Who wins?" Conflict is often framed in terms of a winner and a loser, and in formal athletic competition this idea may serve well. In the arena of interpersonal communication, however, no one wins if there is a loser. Stephen Covey (1989) again says it well when he emphasizes the importance of thinking "win/win," where both partners benefit from the resolution. If you enter a conflict with the idea that it is not just about your winning, it will help your attitude and the overall communication climate. If both people perceive that they benefit from the mutual decision, it helps reinforce the idea of "saving face." As we saw in the chapter on intercultural communication, face-saving strategies are important in many cultures. Face saving involves strategies where a person retains his or her dignity, integrity, and sense of worth in a public or private communication interaction. Even though the person's comments may have been challenged, the person is worthy of your respect and deserves it. By saying "You are right on when you say _____, but I think we should consider _____," you acknowledge the other person. By making sure you consider ways where he or she can also feel a sense of benefit and respect after a conflict, you effectively use a face-saving strategy.

We recognize that conflict is part of communication interaction. We also acknowledge the importance of understanding key stages and using constructive strategies to negotiate resolution. We can also see how resolution involves mutual understanding and benefit, and we have learned the importance of face-saving strategies. Now we'll examine three conflict-management styles and their relative strengths and weaknesses.

Conflict Management Styles

Just like we can clearly recognize formal and informal conversational styles, we can also identify key characteristics of conflict management styles (Beebe et al., 2002) to better understand and adapt our responses to effectively facilitate a positive resolution.

1. Nonconfrontational

One approach people use to handle or negotiate conflict is to simply avoid it. As we discussed previously, conflict is part of communication and will resurface again. However, that doesn't stop people from backing off or avoiding interaction to postpone, delay, or avoid the conflict altogether. One nonconfrontational approach involves agreeing with or placating the person with whom someone has a conflict, for example, saying "Sure, that sounds fine—do what you think is best," in effect, choosing to not respond to the conflict. This does not mean, however, that the other person understands your point, agrees, or will even support you as you form the solution. Placation as a strategy involves communicating agreement when there has been little or no dialogue to achieve agreement.

Another strategy for avoidance involves changing the subject. When one person brings up the issues that relate to conflict, the distracter will move the conversation to a new topic or use a diversion to get out of the confrontation. Related to this strategy for avoidance is the "calm, cool, and collected" pose where nothing bothers you; the conflict or drama seems to not mean a thing to you because you give no reaction. Other people might take on a professional, aloof tone and attitude, repress their frustration or anger, and delay or deny their response. People using this strategy generally communicate little empathy and involvement in the conversation.

Physically or psychologically withdrawing from the conflict—for example, taking a step back to create more space or even leaving the room—is another avoidance strategy. Someone might also express psychological withdrawal with a reluctance to establish eye contact or a verbal message intimating no involvement.

The final avoidance strategy is submission. When someone submits, he or she gives in to the request or demands. A good example involves several recent death penalty cases. Judges nationwide are taking a closer look at prisoners convicted and sentenced to death and the degree to which their confessions were coerced. By using interrogation-style tactics, including sleep deprivation, lack of access to counsel (a lawyer), or repeated threats, people have been known to sign a confession just to stop the abuse when in fact they were innocent. False confessions have been discovered after DNA evidence clears the convicted prisoner. This type of submission violates several constitutional rights; as a consequence, cases where overt coercion is found are often overturned (Johnson, 2003).

2. Confrontational

Confrontational conflict management styles all feature the tendency to confront rather than avoid or cooperate to resolve conflict. This emphasis on confrontation can also be expressed in terms of control. We all need to feel a sense of control in our lives, and Schutz (1966) reaffirms this as one of our basic interpersonal needs. Where does control of ourselves end and the control of others begin? With strategies like intimidation, people attempt to exercise control over each other through the use of a physical or psychological threat or warning. They may anticipate that the fear response will be submission or avoidance—and by default, they win. Returning to our previous discussions, you can easily see how the focus on winning is flawed, and the person on the "losing" end of the conflict loses face. This is no recipe for a resolution, but instead reinforces the idea that conflicts that are not well resolved today will rise again tomorrow. People who engage in a controlling behavior strategy to resolve conflict are typically ego-centered, instead of focused on the needs of others or mutual needs. They may use blaming or scapegoating to confront the problem. With blaming strategy, the confrontational conversation partner assigns blame to someone other than himself or herself or simply denies personal responsibility. Scapegoating is essentially the same thing: An attempt is made to hang the whole conflict onto someone else.

What do you do when someone is confrontational or verbally aggressive? The easy answer is to avoid contact. In reality, it is not always that simple. You can recognize that being verbally aggressive is linked to control issues, and you might consider why the person is saying that particular thing. Does the person sense a lack of control? Is he or she frustrated not to be "in the loop" for information, leading to feelings of slight or hurt because he or she was not included? By considered what motivates someone to communicate in a certain way, you open yourself up to seeing things from the other perspective. This can give you insight into how and why someone communicates and enable you to better predict, and possibly avoid, confrontations. Also recognize that the only person you can truly change is yourself. Stop trying to change someone else and find other ways to communicate. Email provides a comfortable distance that face-to-face communication does not. Changing your choice of channels for communication may prove an effective strategy.

3. Cooperative

Some people choose to view conflict as a challenge and focus on solving the problem. This approach is quite different from avoidance, wishing the problem would go away, or confrontation, which in many ways has more to do with control that the conflict itself. A cooperative approach focuses on the problem—and not the person as the problem. As we discussed previously, Stephen Covey (1989) frames this viewpoint as a "win/win" approach, where the emphasis is on mutual benefit.

In formal argumentation, an ad hominem fallacy confuses the messenger and the message. The speaker confronts the other speaker as the conflict or problem, confusing the real issue or problem, which is separate from the messenger. In this cooperative approach to conflict management, there is clear emphasis on the difference between people and problems. People are not the problem in and of themselves, and the problems exist separate from people. This allows a professional distance and personal detachment and encourages people to be less ego-involved in the problem and its solution. Personal preferences or biases are left out of the discussion, as are personal attacks or blaming. In addition, this approach incorporates an emphasis on mutual benefit, the possibility of more than one solution, and a fact orientation. These characteristics can encourage a free exchange of ideas and more than one effective solution that benefits everyone.

The Dark Side of Interpersonal Communication

In order for us to understand how people communicate effectively with each other, we need to also study what happens when they do not. We are going to examine what is often called the "dark side of communication" (Spitzberg & Cupach, 1998). From social interaction to close relationships, we can see that conversations are sometimes difficult, problematic, challenging, distressing, and even disruptive. How people cope with challenging communication and conflict in their daily lives is the general focus of research in this area. Examples of areas of current study include fatal attractions, jealousy and envy, misunderstanding, gossip, conflict, codependence, sexual coercion, stalking, relationship termination, unrequited love, and mental health problems in relationships. Particular research on negative interactions during courtship, including physical aggression and sexual exploitation, has been conducted by Sally Lloyd and Beth Emery (1999).

Lloyd and Emery (1999) tell the story of Lisa (a pseudonym), a Marine who went on a camping trip with fellow Marines and was raped. When she returned to base, she filed charges against the perpetrator, only find herself charged with slander and defamation of character. She was told not never speak of the incident again. Five years later she turned down a marriage proposal and was beaten, raped, and stabbed repeatedly. She escaped and filed charges, only to see them dropped. Her assailant only spent 20 days in jail. Because of harassment in her workplace over the assault, she had to move and start over. Her marriage years later also involved physical and verbal abuse and ended in divorce. The accumulation of abuse has left her physically and psychological impacted to the point that she can hardly walk and has a hard time trusting other people and forming relationships.

While her experience may sound extreme, there is an increase in the research about and awareness of abuse in relationships that tends to indicate a much greater impact on relationships than previously thought. There is growing research into the impact of jealousy and violence in relationships, for example, to support the assertion that it is not "just" a problem of people who lack education or are in particular socioeconomic classes. This impacts relationships across all categories of race, ethnicity, culture, and social class. Interpersonal violence, the experience of battered wives and husbands, and elder abuse were once issues that people preferred to ignore or deny. Research into this area is bringing the extent and impact of these issue to light and scrutiny.

James Makepeace (1981; cited in Lloyd & Emery, 1999) found, for example, that 21 percent of college students have experienced or perpetrated an act of physical aggression in the context of a dating relationship. His findings have led others to study the area and the issues of aggression, personality, attitudes, and behaviors associated with what is often called courtship aggression.

The three main points that frame "the dark side" provide us with a context for discussion (Spitzberg & Cupach, 1998) and address the central question "What is the dark side?"

1. The dark side refers to things we cannot see. While words and gestures are part of courtship aggression, someone who has experienced it may report a point of view in terms of feeling and emotions. We know that feeling and emotions can be challenging to express, because they lie within the individual who experiences them. We can observe the interaction that leads to these feelings and emotions, but the impact on the individual is often misunderstood or ignored, intentionally or unintentionally, due to ignorance.

2. Actions are not always what they seem. Spitzberg (1998) offers the example of honesty as an action that we value in a relationship, but notes that self-disclosure early in a relationship can lead to exploitation. We can readily observe that complete honesty is not always appropriate or even called for, and sharing without trust and understanding built over time in a relationship can be destructive. We can see in this example how the characteristics of healthy communication can each be turned into negative or destructive forces in a relationship. We may display respect for someone only to be taken advantage of, or have our sense of ethics transformed into duty and obligation and tolerate behavior that we would not normally permit.

3. Unethical, unpleasant, or dysfunctional encounters may be productive. In the course of relationships we may encounter events that at first appear to be negative but in the long term have positive outcomes. This may as straightforward as ending a relationship that allows you to start over and move on. At first it will be unpleasant, but if you both move on, then the new relationships to come may prove positive. Spitzberg (1998) offers the example of an employer releasing well-thought-of employees, leading to uncertainty in the workplace. This may appear unpleasant, but the remaining employees may be more productive in an effort to ensure the same outcome does not happen to them. While this example may provoke debate, it nonetheless reinforces the notion that from encounters that appear negative or destructive, good things can result. In an article in the *Innovative Leader,*

Spitzberg (1998) provides an insightful discussion of myths of effective communication associated with interpersonal communication. A link to the article is provided in the "For More Information" section of this chapter.

Obsessive relational intrusion (ORI) is defined as the repetitive unwanted pursuit and invasion of one's sense of physical or symbolic privacy by an acquaintance desiring and/or presuming an intimate relationship (Spitzberg & Cupach, 1998). ORI occurs when someone pursues a relationship that another person does not want to have and involves behaviors that attempt to see if the rejection is real. In its mildest form, it may involved repeated unwanted attempts to interact. In more extreme forms, it involves stalking, physical abuse, or even killing.

Advantages and Disadvantages of Interpersonal Communication

After our discussion on the dark side of interpersonal communication, you may question the nature of relationships. Relationships themselves, like communication, are neither good nor bad independent of context. Relationships can and do have positive and negative outcomes, but as we have examined, they are universally a part of the human experience. In light of our previous discussion, let's examine several advantages and disadvantages that DeVito (2003) offers us about relationships.

Advantages

1. To not be alone. One distinct advantage to interpersonal relationships is that they require more than one person. Being alone and being comfortable with being alone is important. It enables us to be self-reliant and independent. In a country that often values independence over dependence, the hero that is "our only hope" to save the day is a theme across mass media production. He or she uses ingenuity and skill to overcome insurmountable odds. We even celebrate the underdog, supporting the person who might not make it to the goal line but fought for every inch. In Darwinian evolution we see the central notion that "only the strong survive," but modern biologists are increasingly adding that it is not only the strong, but also the cooperative, that survive. We can readily observe how cooperative behavior among animals as well as humans has enabled populations to survive and thrive.

Building on this point of cooperation, interpersonal relationships require sharing that can benefit the individual in profound ways. We learn language from one another as we grow, and we learn to express ourselves. We find our place and learn about expectations through interaction. We meet our basic interpersonal needs through communication with others, not by being alone.

2. Meet the need for stimulation. The phrase "there is nothing to do" has no doubt been said by almost everyone, in every language and culture, at least once. Interpersonal relationships meet our innate need for stimulation and help us grow.

For example, children might find "nothing to do" once the television, computer, or video games are turned off, but will soon find that life without batteries is not so bad. They will use their imaginations to create games and occupy their time together, and possibly be the better for it. In the same way, adults find conversation stimulating and find creative ways to occupy their time. If you look at a magazine rack, you will no doubt see countless magazines devoted to hobbyists in a wide range activities. Some of these activities may involve more or less social interaction, but all will involve the sharing of information in some form. We are naturally curious creatures and often find the interaction with each other to be enlightening.

3. To learn about yourself. Through the experiences of others we learn about ourselves, our likes and dislikes, but also our beliefs and values. Let's say you enjoy art and a friend invites you to a car show. Perhaps you are not into cars, but prefer the company of this friend and decide to go. While walking through the car show and observing all the chrome and paint, your first thought might be along the lines of "How can people devote so much time and money to their cars?" Through conversation with your friend and even meeting an owner or two, you may come to see that the cars in some ways are works of art. In the same way you enjoy artistic expression, so do the owners at the car show. Their expression may be different from yours, but the motivation and appreciation of expression is in the same vein. You may learn something about yourself and how you have something in common with people that you once thought were quite different from you.

4. To learn about others. At that car show, you may have learned to see the key differences between model years of Chevrolets® built in the 1950s. This information in and of itself may fall into your personal category of "useless trivia," but you may also learn through the conversations that many car owners are devoted to recycling and see the restoration of these cars as a legitimate response to the consumeristic, disposable trends in our culture. In your own life you may value recycling and might even make decisions about what to buy based on issues such as packaging and reuse of materials. You will have learned something about yourself that you have in common with them, but at the same time you will have learned something about them that influences how you perceive your environment. The next time you see a large SUV with plastic sheeting from the belt line down, you may give thought to the words of the car owners you met stating that many new automobiles are disposable and built with little thought of practical reuse in mind.

3. Enhance your self-esteem. Your sense of self-worth, much like your self-concept, comes primarily through interaction with others. This, of course, means you need to interact with other people, and relationships provide that opportunity, but it also underscores the importance of those relationships on how you see yourself. Your expectations of what you can accomplish require self-motivation, but to a large extent they are influenced by what other people have expected from you in the past. Look back at Chapter 2 and the discussion on self-concept. You see the classic study where teachers were told what to expect from their students, irrespective of their actual abilities or test scores, and the students consistently met, for the good or for the bad, their teachers' expectations of them. Your self-esteem can be enhanced or diminished by your relationships.

Disadvantages

1. **Pressure to self-disclose.** One important disadvantage that DeVito (2003) discusses is the pressure to reveal yourself and expose your vulnerability through self-disclosure. We naturally move from superficial to intimate information about ourselves across the lifecycle of a relationship, but how, when, and why we choose to share information is an important area to consider. Have you ever had someone say something to you about himself or herself that you really did not want to know, and that self-disclosure was followed by an awkward silence that was supposed to be filled by your response? Self-disclosure can be one strategy to develop a relationship with a person, but that sentiment may not be shared. Perhaps you like to keep work and home environments relatively separate. You try not to bring home work or even stories about issues at work, preferring to leave it at the office. In the same way you do not as a general rule discuss your home life at work. If a co-worker spends considerable time talking about his or her family, there may be an unspoken expectation that you will do the same.

2. **One person's behavior influences another's.** In the same way that one person's choice to self-disclose often encourages others to also self-disclose, one person's behavior influences another's. If someone is upset or happy, his or her moods can prove contagious. Being in close physical proximity, combined with frequent interaction, can lead to people's often transferring or sharing their attitudes and even behavior with one another. Parents may express concern over who their teenagers hang out with for this very reason. People who you choose to associate with may engage in behaviors that you might not agree with and lead to trouble. This concept can also work to your advantage. Imagine that you have to work in a group project for a class and know there is a test coming up. If you choose to hang out with the person who is doing well in the class, you may come to understand his or her perspective on the material, which may in turn positively impact your study habits. We can learn things from each other, for the good or the bad.

3. **Sharing of time, energy, and possibly resources.** Relationships may take up your time, energy, and maybe even your money. You may have a relationship with someone who calls you frequently or always emails you between the times you actually see each other. At first it might feel good to feel needed or important, but over time you may feel drained by this frequent interaction. You may find that after you hang out with this person, you feel drained and your energy levels are low. You may also know people who make you feel energetic and not drained at all. Money may become an issue if you can't afford to do the things your friend wants to do.

Your friend might not have much money and always ask you to pay for things, creating a sense of imbalance. There are costs associated with relationships as well as rewards.

4. Loss of other relationships. Relationships may cost you more than time, energy, and money. When you devote time to one thing, you necessarily take the time away from something else. Perhaps you and a circle of friends have been together for a long time. You meet someone new whom you are attracted to and start spending considerable time with that person. Your friends will notice your absence and even excuse it at first, but over time, as your relationship with your partner is growing, the relationships you once had with these friends may diminish.

5. Openness to risk of physical and psychological harm. Finally, being part of a relationship makes you vulnerable to physical and psychological harm. Courtship aggression is a serious issue, but a more subtle issue, such as jealousy, may also take its toll. Jealousy can lead to efforts to control behavior, and the perpetrator may become even become aggressive or violent. Taking small steps in self-disclosure can help people learn more about one another, but recognize that close physical proximity and frequent contact associated with relationships carries certain risks.

Methods for Managing Conflict

> *You cannot shake hands with a clenched fist.*
> —Indira Gandhi

We have examined the principles, processes, and strategies associated with interpersonal conflict. Each section provides a valuable foundation for our next discussion. How you handle conflict day to day makes a significant difference in how you feel about yourself and others. Let's examine ten ways to manage conflict that may offer new tips and ways to handle conflicts on a daily basis. We'll draw on the work of communication researcher Joseph DeVito (2003) and adapt it for our use.

1. Avoidance

Avoiding the conflict may involve changing the subject or leaving the room. As we have discussed previously, this method for conflict management has several issues associated with it. If you avoid a problem or conflict, it will resurface again. It may grow and change, and the problem can become worse. The reluctance to communicate can send the message that you do not value or respect the other person and impact how he or she perceives the relationship. While both these are valid points, there are also positive aspects of this strategy. One positive attribute is it gains time to think and explore solutions. If a child is confronted by another child on the playground, running away may be a better alternative than fighting. The issues that have contributed to the conflict will still exist and will need to be addressed, but at least there will the opportunity for intervention and mediation. In that same fashion, you may not be ready to communicate. Your emotions may be running high, or you might be focused on the task at hand. By side-stepping the conflict for the moment, your delay tactic has gained you time. Recognize that the conflict needs to be addressed, but timing is important. As we have discussed, repeated use of this strategy can make the conflict worse. It is important to recognize the negative and positive aspects of this method.

2. Active Fighting

> *Violence is the language of the unheard.*
> —Martin Luther King, Jr.

Fighting can be physical or psychological and can employ fists or words. Dr. King says it well in the quote above that people often come into violent conflict when they perceive they cannot communicate. This involves both speaking and listening. People may lack the ability to articulate their feelings and resort to physical violence in order to express their emotions or thoughts. People also may perceive that they have not been listened to, that their views do not count, or that they are powerless to change the situation. Actively fighting involves hurling hurtful words or even physical contact to inflict pain and suffering on each other. There are many reasons why people may resort to violence to communicate, but the result is always damaging. People, relationships, even communities are negatively impacted when people actively fight.

At one time students would resolve some of their conflicts "behind the haystack or out behind the gym." Their fights involved fists, and students were sometimes hospitalized. In our modern era, weapons are increasingly a factor in conflicts between students and young people. Events like the school shootings at Columbine underscore the importance of communication before tragedy occurs. It also reinforces how serious violent conflict can become. Counseling and teaching students on how to effectively handle interpersonal conflict is more important than ever before.

In a study by Marshall and Rose (1987), over 50 percent of both single and married couples indicated they had personally experienced physical violence. When the researchers included threats of violence in their analysis, the percentages grew to over 60 percent for singles and 70 percent for married couples. In related studies, 11 percent of children were found to be the victims of physical abuse by a parent (Straus, Gelles, & Steinmetz, 1980), and over 47 percent of surveyed college students reported experience with a violence in a dating relationship (Marshall & Rose, 1987).

Not all fighting is physical. A person might be argumentative or give the impression that he or she prefers to confront and challenge others' ideas. This seems to be associated with stimulation and may even be considered in some ways a game, like a debate. People who tend to be argumentative become even more argumentative when they come up against someone like themselves (Rancer & Infante, 1985).

Their actions may, however, involve verbal aggressiveness, or the tendency to attack in conversation with the intention of causing hurt (Infante & Wigley, 1986). An attitude of nonnegotiation and a persistent hammering on a point can be considered fighting. Hurling insults and profanity and engaging in personal attacks verbally can inflict wounds and seriously damage a relationship. The key difference between argumentative and aggressive behavior is the focus of the speaker. An argumentative speaker debates the points under consideration, while the aggressive speaker attacks the other speaker verbally. Actively fighting may be a method for resolving conflict, but regardless whether you are throwing fists or hurtful words, the effects are damaging.

3. Defensiveness/Supportiveness

Gibb (1961) examined methods of conflict management in terms of defensive and supportive communication interactions. A defensive orientation involves talk that involves control, evaluation, and judgments. As we discussed previously, when the emphasis is on controlling each other, the conflict becomes personal. People respond with defensiveness, and this negatively impacts their ability to listen and respond to the conflict in constructive ways. Evaluation means you assert a value statement and associate it with the person, not the message or issue at hand. Passing judgment inhibits discussion and the free exchange of ideas, leading to blaming and assessments of responsibility.

A supportive orientation focuses on the points or issues within the conflict and not the persons themselves. When people are free to examine these issues without fear of evaluation of judgment, and don't feel they are being controlled, conversations can then focus on constructive ways to address the central issues.

4. Face-Detracting and Face-Saving Strategies

When we talk about face-detracting messages or statements in the context of conflict, it means statements or positions that take away from the respect, integrity, or credibility of a person. Conversely, face-saving strategies involve ways to examine issues of debate without attacking the person. When people feel attacked, they become defensive, and it changes the climate of conversation. Donohue and Kolt (1992) discuss these strategies and ways we express them and their outcomes. Verbal attacks focus on the ego or reputation of a person and relate to verbal aggressiveness. By shifting the emphasis from a battle of wills and personalities to the points within an issue, we provide each other with space to retain face. In cultures that promote the community over the individual, often called collectivist cultures, this dimension can take on particular importance. In Japan, a culture recognized for its emphasis on the community, humiliation is perceived as a great insult. In individualistic cultures, like we see in the United States, humiliation is viewed as negative but to a lesser degree. Forgiveness and redemption are promoted as face-restoration strategies. By recognizing the importance of not confusing the message with the messenger and by providing space to discuss ideas without it becoming personal, we create a more supportive climate for conflict resolution.

5. Empathy

Look back at our chapter on listening and see how empathic listening relates to interpersonal conflict. By considering not only someone's words but why they were said, we place ourselves in position to better understand that person's position and points. This method of managing conflict can be effective and allows the participants greater insight into each other's approach and interpretation of the issue. Conversely, blaming implies a lack of empathy and discourages mutual understanding.

6. Gunnysacking and Your Backpack

Bach and Wyden (1968) discuss the concept of *gunnysacking* in terms of an imaginary bag in which problems, grievances, and unresolved conflicts are stored over time. Another way to view it is in terms of a backpack. You probably have some type of backpack to carry books and materials for classes, but imagine you have a backpack with you at all times. Every time you have a conflict that goes unresolved, you add a stone to the backpack. Some stones are small, representing small grievances. Others are large, representing larger problems and issues. Over time your backpack becomes heavy, and the load is unbearable. At the point where you can no longer bear the load, you unload the contents in the course of a conflict. In may be a small stone that is the proverbial "straw that broke the camel's back," but it provokes open conflict. The other person can't see your backpack or its contents and perceives the stone or conflict of the moment as a relatively small issue, while you unload all the contents and overwhelm the other person. When someone unloads his or her backpack or gunnysack all at once, it can confuse an individual issue to the point that the conflict spirals out of control. Rather than allow each stone to accumulate weight, it is important to address each issue in the moment and choose not to add it to your backpack. By handling each issue, a relationship can grow from each challenge and you will experience less stress. Bottling up your frustrations is an ineffective way of handling conflict and can actually impact your physical health. In diseases ranging from heart disease to diabetes and asthma, stress is a relevant factor. Alleviating stress as it occurs will help you prevent your backpack from growing out of proportion. This may involve conversations at the time you experience conflict, but also take the form of exercise and other physical activities that allow you to release stress.

7. Fair Fighting

After our discussion on fighting, there may be a tendency to view fighting in negative terms. Conflicts do not always follow predictable patterns and can extend into the arena of fighting. In order to keep conflicts constructive, it is important to communicate what you consider to be fair and appropriate. Unloading your backpack all at once may not be fair, and you may decide with your partner to refrain from letting issues accumulate. You may also decide to refrain from using profanity and personal attacks, and you may also decide to reinforce the importance of empathy. You may discuss ways you become defensive and decide to provide a supportive climate for conflict resolution. This may involve making time to discuss issues without interference or distractions like children, work, or related demands on your time and attention. See Case Study 9.1 to learn more about fighting fairly.

8. Emotion Management

One constructive way to manage interpersonal conflict is to be aware of your emotions. If you are tired at the end of a long, frustrating day, a challenge or conflict at home might not get all the attention it deserves, and you may not be ready to talk. You may have heard "never speak or make decisions in anger." This saying reinforces the idea that clear thinking is not generally associated with our emotions running high. Take time to clear your thoughts and make time to address the conflict when you know you are ready. Also consider an empathetic approach, as well as where your partner or spouse is emotionally and whether he or she too could use a break.

9. Information Evaluation

Conflicts are often based on misunderstanding of information, and you may not have all the facts. By jumping to conclusions, you can make the conflict appear as more of a challenge that it may be in reality. Clearly identify the relevant issues that contribute to the conflict and see if there are assumptions that have not been checked. The use of "I" statements can also be appropriate when addressing assumptions. "I understand that _____" can be used to allow others to inform you that you may not have all the information; this does not involve blaming or judgments that create defensiveness. "I" messages or "I" statements are a way to talk about a problem or conflict without accusing or threatening someone. To learn more, go to the link featured in the "For More Information" section of this chapter.

Call on your effective listening skills to gather information to check against what you already know. These steps can help you manage the information as it relates to your conflict and help you focus constructively on the key issues.

10. Problem Management

This method of conflict management involves taking a step back from personal involvement and going through a structured process to determine the best solution (Beebe et al., 2002). One effective way to facilitate this method is to use a piece of paper and first address the question "what is the problem." Try to **define the problem** in your own words from what you know. You can share this with your partner and see if he or she sees things differently. Once you arrive at a common definition, you both can constructively **analyze the problem.** Your analysis of the problem from this vantage point will keep the focus on the problem and not each other. Break the problem down into its main components or parts. What can you control or influence, and what is beyond your control? Focus your attention on areas you can control, where you can make a difference. Once you have analyzed the problem, focus on **determining your goals.** This is another way of asking, "What is the best outcome for both of us?" The more concrete you make your goals, the easier it will be to verify that you've accomplished them and know you are making progress. Try to

CASE STUDY 9.1 · *Fair Fighting*

Think of a relationship you care about and respond to the questions below. One (1) is the lowest level of agreement and five (5) is the highest.

Personal Assessment

It takes a long time to get over a fight.	1	2	3	4	5
Fights get personal.	1	2	3	4	5
I've forgotten what we fight about.	1	2	3	4	5
One or both of us uses foul or abusive words.	1	2	3	4	5
I want to prove my point.	1	2	3	4	5
My partner never listens to me.	1	2	3	4	5
My partner brings up past issues.	1	2	3	4	5
I sometimes blame my partner.	1	2	3	4	5

If your score is: 1–10 The relationship may be static, but overall you fight fair.

11–20 One or both of you make mistakes, but together you can improve ability to discuss points of conflict.

21–30 One or both of you make mistakes and may well hurt each other and the relationships. Seek ways to fight fair and not harm.

31–40 You both should take time out to cool off, and then seek guidance from a professional.

While this self-assessment is not meant to diagnose your relationship, it is intended to raise issues about how to conflict with your partner in ways that will not harm your relationship or each other. George Back and Peter Wyden (1973) state that verbal conflict can actually benefit a relationship, providing the couple follows positive guidelines. Here are a few suggestions (Stewart, 1998):

- Listen to each other. Take turns talking. Wait a few more seconds before speaking to make sure your partner has finished.
- Do not mind read or second guess each other.
- Stick to the subject. Don't bring up old issues.
- Show respect and empathy. Crossed arms show you are defensive, not open.
- Avoid arguing over details. Stick to the main points.
- Work it out; don't quit. Cancel other plans and complete your conversation.
- Choose a time when you will not be distracted (by family or work, for example).
- Show the other person that you really heard what he or she said.
- Remain calm. Don't engage in blaming, name calling, threatening, foul language, or sarcasm. These decrease intimacy and increase hostility.

Forgive and accept each other. Once you are finished, make up and move on together.

use objective criteria or descriptions of specific actions to take in order to be able to mutually recognize each step. Part of this process may involve identifying more than one goal. This can be a productive strategy because you explore more than one solution or outcome and, as a consequence, more than one way to resolve the conflict. Once you are confident in your analysis and range of goal options, it is time to **select the best solution.** The best solution may not be your favorite option or goal, but it should be one you can both agree benefits you both and can be achieved.

Family Communication and Conflict

Now that we have examined the principles, process, strategies, and methods for conflict management and resolution, we'll focus on improving interpersonal communication. We need to remember that every interpersonal relationship experiences conflict at one time or another. **Conflict** is an expressed struggle between at least two interdependent individuals who perceive (1) incompatible goals, (2) scarce resources, and (3) interference from the other party in achieving their goals (Hocker & Wilmot, 1991). People may avoid each other, blame each other, or even perceive they have something to lose. None of these activities leads to effectively managing conflict. By providing a supportive climate for discussions, and using many of the methods of conflict management we've discussed, we can look to improved communication.

What is a family? You may answer that you know it when you see it, and you might be right. Two parents, two kids, and a two-car garage? That may not be the family experience for many people in the United States today. Families may contain parents, step-parents, grandmothers and grandfathers, and siblings related in a variety of ways. Still, there are common elements that bind family members together, elements that can at times produce conflict. Families often share physical space, are related in some way, and meet individual and group needs. They can be intergenerational, involving more than just parents and children, or a traditional "nuclear" family. Families do not exist only to support children. Families rise out of our motivation to meet our interpersonal needs through human interaction, and common ties—including birth, death, adoption, marriage, divorce, and separation—contribute to our overall understanding of the family dynamic as it changes over time.

How Is Family Conflict Different from Other Forms of Conflict?

Family conflict is distinct in several ways. Since family communication often involves people you have an established connection to, whether you want to or not, it simply can't be as easily avoided. You can change your friends, even where you live, but your family members will stay family. People are often more direct in family conflict, stating the conflict in verbal and nonverbal ways that people who lack an extended history or significant time together might communicate in a more subtle way. You always hurt the ones you love, the saying goes, and who better to know what buttons to push or how to hurt you than family? By the same token, who better to know how to help you, rally around in times of need, or support you but family? The issue of extended history, and anticipated future, can also impact family communication. People in family groups often share a common history and can see continued involvement into the future. This contributes to the inherent expectation that you'll be more tolerant with your family members and forgive them when, if the family member was a friend or an acquaintance, you might cut off all communication.

What Leads to Family Conflict?

Two primary factors contribute to family conflict. The first, power, underlies our basic human need to control our environment, and by extension, other people who reside in our environment. Who does the dishes? Who is supposed to take the trash out? Responsibilities, gender expectations, and differing values lead to power struggles within families. Family members may conflict with each other over money, ideas, and activities, and even each other's lifestyle. In your family, what types of power struggles have you observed?

The second factor that often contributes to family conflict are roles, including norms and expectations. These relate to power in that "who does what when and why" is a common area of conflict, but roles also involve expectations of multiple roles. Mom is a mother and may be a wife, a daughter, and an employee. Each role and its accompanying set of expectations is internally and externally influenced and reinforced, often with competing values and ideas. Problems at work may influence family conflict, and the reverse can occur. What kinds of expectation do you perceive your primary family members have for each other? For you? Make a list of descriptive terms and share them with a classmate.

Improving Interpersonal Communication

While there is no recipe for a perfect relationship, and we know that relationships are not static but rather dynamic systems that change over time, we still recognize how important relationships are to each other. The need for healthy relationships is universal, and here are a few strategies to help you improve yours. Canary and Stafford (1992) provide a useful framework for our discussion on improving relationships, and they identify five maintenance strategies that have proved successful in long-term relationships (Tubbs & Moss, 1994, p. 189).

1. Positivity. Be positive. The degree to which you can keep positive, about things in general and specifically the relationship, has a connection to the way your relationship will proceed. If you start thinking in negative terms, differentiating between your likes and your partner's likes, you start to build a wall between you, one brick at a time. You may not even notice the wall as each of you builds it, but one day you may not be able to see eye to eye, and it will take considerable effort to dismantle that wall, brick by brick.

2. Openness. Be open. Try new things together. See a movie, read the same book, or go camping together. Find some way to build common memories, a sense of shared history and common purpose, together. Part of openness is honesty. Be honest with the other person about your needs, and listen with empathy when he or she discloses personal information. Try to see things from your partner's perspective. Remember what you learned in Chapter 2, how our perspective makes a difference on how we act and react. Understand your partner's actions from what he or she perceived to be the situation, not just from your own point of view.

3. Assurances. Value each other. Remind your partner what she means to you. Give her a hug, tell her why you think she is great, or write her a letter. Do little somethings that convey clearly the message that you value the person as a friend or partner. Have you ever noticed the joy older couples have as they tell a joint story of something that once happened to them, even if they correct each other's version? Tell a story and include your partner. People like to be reminded and assured that the relationship is on solid ground.

4. Networks. Keep connected. Call each other during the day. Write letters. Email. Bring him to the office and let him meet the people you talk about all the time. Form relationships with other people together. Make an effort to build common networks and clear channels of communication.

5. Task sharing. One way to improve the communication is through action. If your partner typically cooks, and you know that today was a hard day for him and that cooking tonight is perceived as one more thing to do, pick up the spatula and get to work. Your partner will appreciate your taking the initiative, and he may take the time while you are cooking to relax, allowing for better communication later on.

This idea can extend to helping your partner find more time for what she likes to do. Let's say your partner likes to garden, but the laundry pile is near the ceiling and the sink is full of dishes. Before she gets home, get the laundry sorted and do the dishes. When she gets home, hand her the gloves and trowel, and get back to the laundry. By using the principle of giving through your actions, you may meet your own needs through an improved relationship.

Summary

In this chapter we discussed interpersonal conflict in terms of the eight basic principles. We then discussed the process of conflict in three stages and used this understanding to reinforce the importance of managing conflict effectively. We discussed three strategies to resolve conflict, comparing their relative strengths and weaknesses. The dark side of interpersonal communication was defined and discussed. We then examined ten ways to manage conflict and offered tips and ways to handle conflicts on a daily basis, and we explored the issue of family conflict. Finally, we identified five strategies that provide a useful framework for a discussion on improving relationships.

> *Feelings of worth can flourish only in an atmosphere where individual differences are appreciated, mistakes are tolerated, communication is open, and rules are flexible—the kind of atmosphere that is found in a nurturing family.*
> —Virginia Satir

For More Information

To learn more about violence in relationships, go to: **www.cdc.gov/ncipc/dvp/dvvp.htm** and **www.igc.apc.org/fund/index.html**

To learn more about the work of Brian Spitzberg and "The Dark Side of Interpersonal Communication," go to the National Communication Association's website at: **http://www.natcom.org/research/Profiles/Spitzberg.html**

To learn more about "I" messages or "I" statements, go to: **http://www.colorado.edu/conflict/peace/treatment/istate.htm**

Review Questions

1. Factual Questions
    a. What is one principle of interpersonal conflict?
    b. What is one stage in the process of conflict?
    c. What is one way to manage conflict?
    d. What is one way you can improve interpersonal communication?

2. Interpretative Questions
    a. How does the perception of scarcity influence interpersonal conflict?
    b. From your perspective, what strategy is effective for managing conflict?
    c. Is it ever acceptable or appropriate to avoid conflict? Explain.

3. Evaluative Questions
    a. To what extent do we influence the climate of a conflict?
    b. How do conflicts form?
    c. What happens when they are resolved to mutual satisfaction?

4. Application Questions
    a. What factors influence conflict in relationships? Interview one couple each, take notes, share with classmates, and see if you find common themes.
    b. When relationships terminate after a conflict, what happens? Interview one person each, take notes, share with classmates, and see if you find anything in common between each case.
    c. Do all people perceive conflict as bad? Survey ten individuals, see what they think, and relate their responses to the text.

References

Bach, G., & Wyden, P. (1968). *The intimacy enemy.* New York: Avon.

Bach, G., & Wyden, P. (1973). *The intimate enemy: How to fight fair in love and marriage.* New York: Avon.

Beebe, S., Beebe, S., & Redmond, M. (2002). *Interpersonal communication: Relating to others.* Boston: Allyn and Bacon.

Canary, D., & Stafford, L. (Eds.). (1992). *Communication and relational maintenance.* New York: Academic Press.

Covey, S. (1989). *The seven habits for highly effective people.* New York: Simon and Schuster.

DeVito, J. (2003). *Messages: Building interpersonal skills* (5th ed.). Boston: Allyn and Bacon.

Donohue, W., & Kolt, R. (1992). *Managing interpersonal conflict.* Thousand Oaks, CA: Sage.

Gibb, J. (1961). Defensive and supportive communication. *Journal of Communication, 11,* 141–148.

Gottman, J. (1979). *Marital interaction.* New York: Academic Press.

Gottman, J. (1982). Emotional responsiveness in marital conversations. *Journal of Communication, 32,* 180–220.

Guglielmo, W. (2001, November 5). Above and beyond just doctoring. *Newsweek,* 72.

Hocker, J., & Wilmot, W. (1991). *Interpersonal conflict.* Dubuque, IA: William C. Brown.

Infante, D., & Wigley, C. (1986). Verbal aggressiveness: An interpersonal model and measure. *Communication Monographs, 53,* 61–69.

Janis, I. (1983). *Groupthink: Psychological studies of policy decision and fiascoes* (2nd ed.). Boston: Houghton, Mifflin.

Johnson, D. (2003, January 20). A leap of faith. *Newsweek,* p. 34.

Knapp, M., & Vangelisti, A. (1996). *Interpersonal communcation and human relationships* (3rd ed.; pp. 34–40). Boston: Allyn and Bacon.

Lloyd, S., & Emery, B. (1999). *The dark side of courtship: Physical and sexual aggression* (Sage Series on Close Relationships). Newbury Park, CA: Sage.

Mann, J., & Smuts, B. (1999). Behavioral development in wild bottlenose dolphin newborns. *Behaviour, 136,* 526–566.

Marshall, L., & Rose, P. (1987). Gender, stress and violence in the adult relationships of a sample of college students. *Journal of Social and Personal Relationships, 4,* 299–316.

Maslow, A. (1970). *Motivation and personality* (2nd ed.). New York: Harper and Row.

McLean, S. (1996). Communication in the clinical setting: The importance of listening. *The Journal of Multicultural Nursing and Health, 2,* 4–7.

Pust, R. E., & Moher, S. P. (1992, February). A core curriculum for international health: Evaluating ten years' experience at the University of Arizona. *Academic Medicine, 67,* 90–94.

Rancer, A., & Infante, D. (1985). Relations between motivation to argue and the argumentativeness of adversaries. *Communication Quarterly, 33,* 209–218.

Schutz, W. (1966). *The interpersonal underworld.* Palo Alto, CA: Science and Behavior Books.

Spitzberg, B. (1998). Myths of effective communication. *Innovative Leader, 7*(7), 349.

Spitzberg, B., & Cupach, W. (Eds.). (1998). *The dark side of close relationships.* Mahwah, NJ: Lawrence Erlbaum Associates.

Stewart, J. (Ed.). (1998). *Bridges, not walls: A book about interpersonal communication* (7th ed.). Dubuque, IA: McGraw-Hill.

Straus, R., Gelles, R., & Steinmetz, S. (1980). *Behind closed doors.* New York: Doubleday.

Tubbs, S., & Moss, S. (1999). *Human communication* (8th ed.). Dubuque, IA: McGraw-Hill.

10

Professional and Crisis Communication

Chapter Objectives

After completing this chapter, you should be able to:

1. Understand the importance of communication in the work environment.
2. Identify strategies to search for employment.
3. Identify and describe the interview process and the types of interviews.
4. Describe key qualities employers seek in applicants.
5. Identify and describe communication in meetings.
6. Demonstrate the importance of a good attitude in a crisis situation.
7. Identify and demonstrate three ways an emergency response professional communicates during a crisis.
8. Identify and describe the role of a central place to communicate during a crisis.
9. Identify and describe the role and importance of a crisis communication plan.
10. Demonstrate five ways to express yourself effectively.

Introductory Exercise 1

Have you ever considered how we use communication in the workplace? Is communication important to our success? Is it something we just do, or is it a skill that can be learned? Take these three questions and your responses and ask yourself how communication is used where you work. Take your notes and compare them with those of other people in your class.

Introductory Exercise 2

Interview a friend who has a job or a fellow co-worker, asking specific questions about the types of communication skills he or she uses on the job. Compare his or her responses to the information you gathered for Exercise 1. What did you find?

We are what we repeatedly do. Excellence, therefore, is not an act but a habit.
—Aristotle

What was the common theme in the first introductory exercise? If you said communication is the key to success, you got it right! Employers around the world consistently include good communication skills in their list of top requirements for most, if not all, positions. Why is communication the key to success at work? Work is all about relationships with co-workers, supervisors, clients and customers, suppliers and producers.

In this chapter, we will discuss communication in the work environment, including interviewing, interpersonal interaction, and listening skills, as well as the diverse ways you will communicate as part of employment. We'll also examine crisis communication and the importance of clear and concise communication in the emergency environment. Apply what you've learned from experience and your understanding of material from previous chapters to these areas and you will see how important communication is in your work environment.

Communicating what you want to say is a difficult task, and people who can do this well are often rewarded. In business, the ability to communicate effectively is highly prized. A 1997 survey of executives who work for Fortune 500 companies indicated they want workers who know how to speak, listen, and think effectively; who work well with people from diverse backgrounds; and who can make good decisions on their own and in groups (Seiler & Beall, 2000).

Exercise

Ask someone not in your class:
1. When was the last time he or she had miscommunication with someone at work?
2. Describe what happened.

Compare your notes with other students in the next class session.

Have you ever had a miscommunication happen at work? With someone you cared about? Perhaps an email that got the facts across but offended the person it was sent to caused friction or interrupting someone in a meeting took his or her turn away, so he or she didn't get to share the information he or she prepared. Failure to have face-to-face communication, with all the nonverbal signals present, or neglecting to respect each other while competing for attention can often contribute to miscommunication. Your knowledge of the communication process and how to pay attention to all the communication cues can help prevent miscommunication.

Consider this: If you work at a job for 40 hours a week, take a two-week vacation each year, and have a 25-year career, you've worked 50,000 hours. This example fails to account for the many anticipated job changes you will make in your lifetime, all the retraining you will do to increase your knowledge and improve your skills, all the overtime you may work, and any delay in the anticipated retirement age. Work, like communication, is a dynamic process that changes as the need for skills and services change, shifts as markets move, and evolves as knowledge and technology develop.

To illustrate the importance of communication in work environments, a 1997 survey of Fortune 500 company executives indicated employers want all employees to know how to communicate, get along well with others, be sensitive to differences in cultural perspectives, and make good decisions as individuals and in groups (American Council on Education, 1997; Seiler & Beall, 2000).

> Effective communicators in the workplace, according to a number of surveys, can explain ideas clearly, can give good directions, can be good listeners, can work well with others, can deal sensitively with people of diverse backgrounds and cultures, and can represent their companies well in small group and large group settings. Personnel directors have described their needs in prospective employers as follows:

> Send me people who know how to speak, listen, and think, and I'll do the rest. I can train people in their specific job responsibilities, as long as they listen well, know how to think, and can express themselves well. (Seiler & Beall, 2000, p. 7)

Given the importance of the job interview, do you think good communication skills are key? In fact, in related research, oral communication skills were identified as the number one factor, ahead of self-motivation, problem solving, decision making, leadership, work experience, and appearance (Maes, Weldy, & Icenogle, 1997). "In a survey of 480 companies and public organizations, communication abilities were ranked first among personal qualities of college graduates sought by employers" (*The Wall Street Journal*, 1998). According to the National Association of Colleges and Employers (www.naceweb.org/) fall 2003 survey, the top ten qualities employers seek are:

1. Communication skills (verbal and written)
2. Honesty/integrity
3. Teamwork skills
4. Interpersonal skills
5. Strong work ethic
6. Motivation/initiative
7. Flexibility/adaptability
8. Analytical skills
9. Computer skills
10. Organizational skills

You can see from this variety of sources that communication skills are key to your success in the work environment, whether you run your own business or work for an employer. Interpersonal skills are specifically identified in the NACE study as one of the key skills employers seek. Conduct a web search on Google® (www. google.com) or Altavista® (www.altavista.com) with key words like "employer survey communication skills" and see the extensive information that relates to this point. Work relationships involve the same set of knowledge and skills we have discussed in previous chapters.

We'll now discuss a common area of interest: interviewing. This engages your communication skills in your pursuit of employment that will lead to a relationship between you, your employer, customers and clients, and co-workers.

Interviewing

Preparing for an Interview

For many people, the job interview is an experience they do not look forward to, fearing that they will make a mistake. Draw from the lessons learned to date in terms of interpersonal communication and apply them to this context. What are effective strategies to start a conversation? What are key characteristics of a healthy interpersonal relationship? Look back at previous chapters to refresh your memory if needed and apply those lessons to the challenge of interviewing.

We'll examine constructive steps you can take before, during, and after your interview to help you be more aware of the process and your role. Have you ever taken a test you were not prepared for? How about a test over material you didn't have in class? How well did you perform? Now let's reverse the situation. Have you ever taken a test you were very prepared for, one where you knew the content and the material, and were ready to take? Now how did you perform? Most people do reasonably well when they have clear objectives, know what is expected of them, and have time and the opportunity to prepare and perform.

A job interview is both a test and a performance. It is a test of your knowledge and skills, and performance much like a speech. You hear questions and try to respond while making sure you reference your skills, work experience, and appropriateness for the job. Wouldn't it be advantageous if you had the questions before the interview? In many cases, you actually do have the same or similar questions.

What Do You Know Already?

Chances are you already know a lot more than you think you do about the job you would like to have, people who work in that field, and possible interview questions. Most of all, you know what you like and your preferences can help you find a good job fit. If you aren't sure, take a look at Case Study 10.1 for information and links about personality and preference tests available on line to get you started.

First, let's look at who you know, and then we'll examine what you know. You may have heard the saying "It is not what you know, but who you know," and there is some truth in it. One researcher contacted 280 people in Boston who had taken a new job in the last year. He discovered the majority found their jobs through people they knew, but were not close to, like former college friends, colleagues, and friends of the family (Granovetter, 1973). Another researcher also found similar results and noted that associates and people we are less familiar with, but nonetheless in some way connected to, often know valuable information that can assist us in finding new jobs (Rogers, 1983). Give some thought to people you have known and stayed in contact with. Perhaps there are parents of a friend you played with as a child who will remember you. You may never know where the connection may assist you in your research, but getting the word out concerning what you are looking for means you enlist the help of several other sets of eyes and ears, and the more people helping you the better.

Now let's examine what you know. No doubt you have given serious consideration to what you want to do for a job or profession. You liked something about the

CASE STUDY 10.1 • *Know Your Personality*

If you had to indicate what type of dog you'd be, would it be an empathic collie, a glamorous poodle, a trustworthy St. Bernard, or even a playful pug?

Knowing yourself is an important part of effective communication, and there are several ways to get to know your "style" better. One personality test is called the Myers-Briggs Type Indicator. It involves four different scales of personality characteristics, and a combination of the four indicates your styles of communication, reasoning, and processing information. According to the test, you are either:

- Extraverted or Introverted
- Sensing or Intuitive
- Thinking or Feeling
- Judging or Perceiving

The combination of these tendencies contributes to an overall personality type. Carl Jung, a pioneer in the field of psychology, would indicate that they reflect a combination of your genetic predispositions and your earliest environmental influences.

While dynamic people do not generally fit well in static boxes or categories, the analysis can be beneficial. Many people train for a field only to discover too late that they don't like it, don't feel satisfied, or want to pursue a career in a different field. Some of the online tests are comical and fun, while others involve a more serious analysis of your personality and preferences. See the links below for a range of popular websites.

> *Popular links:*
> **www.colorquiz.com**
> **www.emode.com**
> **www.enneagraminstitute.com**
> **www.ivillage.com**
> **www.knowyourtype.com**
> **www.queendom.com**
> **www.rateyourself.com**
> **www.thespark.com**

Sources: Hamilton (2002); Kroeger & Thuesen (1988).

field or area, and hopefully your curiosity led you to explore it. Perhaps you have examined related fields, talked to people who currently work or have worked in the past in the area you are considering, examined the employment advertisements to get an idea of basic and desired qualifications, and perhaps even had an internship in your desired work environment. The accumulation of knowledge from your research and experience is what you know about the job right now. If you have missed any of these steps, it may be in your best interest to spend more time on background research, getting to know more in general terms about what you want to do or where you would like to work. Many college campuses offer employment counseling for students, with tests to help reveal your strengths and weaknesses, interests and goals. Your investment in thoroughly researching your chosen profession or job is an investment in yourself, and considering you may work over 50,000 hours in the job or a series of jobs, it is worth the effort.

From the information you have gathered—either through interviews with people in the field, from books about your field, from discussions with your professors or colleagues, and your research on basic and desired job qualifications—you can create a list that briefly summarizes what you know so far. Take a moment to write down simple words to reflect what you've gathered to date. You may want to consider keeping a journal, both as you complete this exercise and as you research your chosen job or profession.

What Do You Need to Know?

Once you have completed the list, re-examine it to see if there are any patterns. You may have lots of friends who work in the industry, and you may have even had an internship, but your background research into the field may be lacking. What is the turnover rate in the industry? What are the future prospects for the business? Are you preparing to become a VCR repairperson when the rest of the world is going digital? Looking at the big picture from a variety of sources will help you know more about your subject, so you can better adapt the information for yourself and to your audience, your future interviewer or employer. Perhaps you have done your homework and know about the growth and future in the industry, but you don't know anyone who actually works in the field. Look at your list to see where you are lacking information, and then go try to fill in that gap. Do you know anyone who knows someone who does the job you want to do? Perhaps as part of this course you could interview an employer in your area of interest, stating you are not actively seeking employment but rather researching the field. Again, consider keeping a journal to keep your information organized and accessible and to show yourself what you have learned as your research progresses.

Making Contact

Once you have thoroughly investigated your field of interest and are confident that you want to work in the area, you need to identify potential employers you want to work for. You'll want to consider factors like location, potential for growth within the company, and the degree to which your skill set matches what the company needs. If you want to work overseas, look for employers who send their employees abroad rather than hiring people within the country. If you want to reach a certain position, but know you lack experience, look for a job that will use some of your skills while allowing for growth and promotion to your goal.

You've Got the Invitation to Interview!

First of all, congratulations are in order. The invitation to interview means you already passed a series of tests. You have been found to have the basic qualifications, and now the company wants to learn more about you. It is now time to consider who is going to interview you and what they want to learn from you.

If you have the opportunity, see if you can learn who is going to interview you. Will it be one individual or a group? Will it be a human resources professional or the supervisor who has hiring authority? Will it be a panel of people who work with the position? Audience analysis, or a clear understanding of your audience and its characteristics, is key to being prepared. The degree to which you can analyze your audience will help you better prepare, adapt, and feel more comfortable with the interview process.

If you do not have the opportunity to learn who will be interviewing you, make some educated guesses and consider various scenarios. What can you learn about the company in general? How about the specific departments that interact with the position? Who is the supervisor for the position? Pretend you have interviews with each person, from a human resources professional to the boss. What information would each one like to know when considering you for the position from each particular frame of reference? What has led the company to offer the job in the first place? What skills or services does the position involve, and what employer needs have to be met by this position? Answering these questions and others you come up with will help you focus your pre-interview preparation.

As you can see in Case Study 10.2, you are already familiar with many interview questions. It may seem difficult to answer all the questions in preparation for the interview, but consider how the questions are similar. The questions have common themes that you can categorize into groups. Through practice, you can learn how to hear the interview question and recall how it is similar to a question you have prepared for, allowing you to adapt your response to the new question with the benefit of preparation. You will also want to examine these questions and categories, preparing and practicing responses for twice as many questions as you are likely to be asked. The better prepared you are, the more equipped you are to adapt to new questions in the interview process.

Now let's examine a popular, but difficult question: "Tell me about yourself." This is not an invitation to tell your life story, but rather an opportunity to state a little about your background and experience and how you came to acquire skills and knowledge central to the job. Try to include references to the basic qualifications

CASE STUDY 10.2 • *Common Interview Questions*

1. Tell me about yourself.
2. Have you ever done this type of work before?
3. Why should we hire you?
4. What are your greatest strengths? your weaknesses?
5. Give me an example of a time when you worked under pressure.
6. Why did you leave your last job?
7. How has your education prepared you for this position?
8. Why do you want to work here?
9. What are your long-range goals?
10. Do you have any questions?

There are also many resources available online that discuss common interview questions.

CareerBuilder.com offers a comprehensive site, with questions, guidance, and tips at: **http://www.careerbuilder.com/gh_int_htg_questions.html**

Victory University of Wellington, New Zealand, offers both questions and guidelines for responses at: **http://www.vuw.ac.nz/st_services/careers/common.htm**

To learn more about job interview process, as well as job opportunities in Canada, go to: **http://jobsearchcanada.about.com/aboutcanada/jobsearchcanada/ library/weekly/aa123099c.htm**

and information about how your experience also relates to the desired qualifications. Employers typically focus on five key areas. Consider them when preparing for your interview: educational background, work experience, knowledge of the company or organization, the specific job tasks, and your own career goals (Adler & Elmholst, 1999).

Your first interview may be a **telephone interview,** and it is important to understand the purpose of this type of interview as well as the medium in which you will be communicating. Telephone interviews are often used as a low-cost way of screening candidates who have met the required qualifications to get a sense of the person through a series of questions. Since the purpose is to screen, some candidates will be eliminated from the list, while others move forward in the process. You'll want to be by the phone before the actual interview and be prepared, with your research on the company readily available in an easy-to-read format. You don't want to be hunting for information during the interview. You may want to make friends and family aware of the interview to prevent them from calling during your scheduled interview time. The employer will have a set schedule and will have brought people together specifically for this time with you.

Once the phone rings, typically the human resources professional will confirm you are ready and then introduce each person in the interview. Respond with a short hello and write down each person's name. If there is an opening after the round of introductions, thank them for the opportunity to speak with them today. They will then ask you a series of questions, with some time at the end should you have any questions. Keep in mind there is a set time for this interview, so keep your answers short and to the point, usually less than two minutes. Use your words effectively, underscoring your experience and how it applies to each question with connection to the stated (or unstated) needs of the employer. Brief examples can help capture interest and make you memorable, but be careful not to get carried away. After you have completed their questions, and if there is time remaining, you may have the opportunity to ask a question of your own. Perhaps you are interested in management style, or want to know examples of projects the person selected may be involved with. Here is your opportunity to research the potential employer further. Leave questions of salary for later in the process.

Keep in mind that you are communicating over the telephone, and your voice is the channel for your messages. The interviewers lack the nonverbal cues present in face-to-face interactions, and your attention to the pauses, and when they are ready for you to answer, is important. Try not to overlap or interrupt, as the interruption may be accentuated simply because of the medium. Be enthusiastic, and it will carry through to your voice, encouraging people to listen. Before you leave the telephone interview, thank the interviewers for their time. Once you have finished, promptly write a thank-you note to go out in the mail the same day. This simple act can reinforce your interest and help reinforce a positive perception of you as a potential employee.

The next type of interview may be a **personal interview.** A personal interview will feature verbal and nonverbal components, and you will want to consider both aspects as you prepare. How you **dress** is important. Professional dress is usually expected, and you will generally want to dress one level above what you believe the employer expects in during the normal course of business. If tan slacks and a button-down, collared shirt are the standard, a well-fitting suit or dress may work well. Prepare your clothes ahead of time, and have an alternate outfit should you need to change, spill something on your clothes, or otherwise find yourself needing a quick change of clothes.

Make sure you have time to be at the right place at the right time. Walking in the door, you should already **know the company or organization** from prior research. You should familiarize yourself with the company, getting a feel for the pace and the employees. Introduce yourself to the receptionist. Be courteous to everyone you meet. Employers have been known to consult secretaries about potential candidates, and should you come to work for the company, they will be able to assist your settling into your new role. You should also **know the job,** having a good idea of specific tasks and functions prior to interview. Interviewing someone in the company or a similar company who works in a related position during your research phase can help you understand the position and give you a more insightful perspective. Always **consider the employer's needs** and how you can, through a combination of your education, training, and experience, meet those needs. The position was created for a reason, and your understanding of the job will help you prepare and be confident when your interview takes place.

When the interview starts, much like in the telephone interview, be attentive to cues from the employer. A brief hello, firm handshake, and take your assigned seat. Taking notes while maintaining positive eye contact with each person present for the interview can communicate your interest and listening skills.

Be honest in your responses, drawing from your actual experience. You may remember the story of Pinocchio, where each lie makes his nose grow longer. Your employer may not catch your exaggeration, but your nonverbal communication may give you away. Regardless, you want to present yourself honestly and sincerely. Your goal is to obtain a job where you want to work, not one where your false impression of yourself sets up unreasonable expectations or one you grow to dislike months later only to have to start the search all over.

Be positive in your responses, discussing challenges and ways you solved problems in a positive way, demonstrating respect for people you have worked with in the past. If you are negative about a previous employer, this is not the place to demonstrate your feelings. Your employer is considering how well you would represent them, and negative communication will not serve you well.

Be brief in your responses, usually under two minutes, allowing for discussion and followup questions as you get to know each other. Keep in mind that brief should not be too short, where the response fails to answer the question. Instead, consider the content and your key examples, but watch out for getting off track or wandering in your response.

In addition, **incorporate "because"** into your response with a concrete example. If the interview question is "How do you handle deadlines?," an effective response is "I believe I am very good at working under a deadline because when I wrote for my college newspaper, I learned how to start promptly on an assignment and how to budget enough lead time to so that I always had my submission in on time." The "because" clause gives the interviewer more vivid detail to remember, encourages active listening, and builds credibility through the effective use of evidence.

Finally, consider what you want to learn from the interviewer(s). What do you want to know about the company, possible opportunities for growth, or work abroad? Leave questions for salary until the interviewers decide to interview you again or offer the job.

Other Types of Interviews

In addition to the job interview, there are two other types of interviews. The first is the **information-gathering interview.** The purpose of this interview format is to gain information and insight into an area or subject. The person you are interviewing can offer a unique perspective, information, or referrals to new sources of information for you to explore. You can't get answers to the question "what is it like to work for Company X" from a book or an Internet site the way you can from an employee. More than one interview can broaden your base of information and give you a wider perspective.

The second type of interview is the **performance appraisal interview.** Once you have accepted the position and have time on the job, you should anticipate periodic evaluations of your performance and productivity. The purpose of this interview format is to establish and strengthen a relationship between the employer and the employee, inform the employee of how he or she is doing, discuss what has been accomplished, and set goals for future performance. You will know from specific job duties what the position involves, and taking notes while you work about projects completed and goals reached can help you prepare for the performance appraisal interview. Be aware of the specific duties your job description calls for and keep notes so when it comes time for your interview, you are prepared and can take advantage of the opportunity to showcase your accomplishments.

Effective Communication in the Work Environment

> *I know that you believe that you understood what you think I said, but I am not sure you realize that what you heard is not what I meant.*
> —Robert McCloskey, State Department spokesman

Interpersonal Interaction

We previously examined language and communication and common barriers to effective communication. Now let's apply this knowledge to the work context. We'll start with using language that reduces possible misunderstandings. Specific, concrete terms are much less open to possible misinterpretation than abstract terms. Using terms that can be easily understood the first time will help decrease misunderstandings. For example, if you send an order out for 100 units to be sent to Miami University, make sure you write "Miami University in Ohio" or the shipper might send it to Florida. Simpler terms are also preferred over more complex ones. As we saw in the discussion of jargon and doublespeak, words that abstract a concept can result in misunderstandings.

In the year 2050, demographers predict one out of every two Americans in the United States will be black, Hispanic, or Asian American (Kikoski & Kikoski, 1996). Between now and then, the workplace will continue to become more culturally diverse. Clichés, or often-used phrases, and trigger words can lead to problems and misunderstandings. Not everyone will have the same cultural background as you or be familiar with your favorite clichés. Saying "You're such an early bird," or making a reference to the "early bird gets the worm" cliché, may be misinterpreted by someone who is not familiar with the saying. Trigger words can cause an emotional response in some listeners who have strong emotional associations with them. For example, referring to the ability to manage money with a reference to

Jews is both racist and offensive. Find concrete terms to describe the idea you are trying to communicate, or simply say "You certainly handle the money well in this organization."

Avoid using terms that have an **inherent language-based bias.** Gender-specific language, which fails to include a large percentage of the workforce, may inhibit the listener's desire to accept your information. Choose words like "law enforcement officer" as opposed to "policeman," to avoid a gender bias. Can you think of an example when abstract language or language-biased terms led to confusion or misunderstanding in the workplace or school environments?

Sexual harassment refers to a hostile work environment where sex is an issue in the course of completing job functions. The Civil Rights Act of 1964 and the many court cases that have followed focus on two types of sexual harassment. The first is *quid pro quo,* or "this for that," in which sexual favors are directly or indirectly attached to employment, such as promotions. The second, *hostile work environment,* refers to both verbal and nonverbal behaviors in the work environment that intimidate, offend, or are hostile. Avoid terms that are not appropriate and treat everyone with respect in your verbal and nonverbal communication.

Listening skills are also related to work communication, and lack of attention to them can lead to problems. Here are six barriers to effective listening that may impact workplace communication:

1. **Physical Barriers.** Hearing for some can be a challenge. It may involve the vocal range of your voice combined with the selective hearing loss in that range by a co-worker. Modern hearing aids are increasingly effective in tailoring the amplified range to match the specific hearing loss of the individual.
2. **Psychological Barriers.** You may be preoccupied, which may impact your ability to concentrate on the speaker. You may not listen unless you think the information directly benefits you. You may not want to reveal your lack of knowledge in a certain area. By focusing on the speaker and actively listening,

COMPUTER-MEDIATED COMMUNICATION 10.1 • *Sexual Harassment*

Sexual harassment is a serious issue, and one that you will want to investigate. Here are a few online sources:

The U.S. Equal Employment Opportunity Commission offers a comprehensive summary of facts involving sexual harassment at: **http://www.eeoc.gov/facts/fs-sex.html**

The University of North Carolina–Greensboro offers a site that provides a wealth of links at: **http://library.uncg.edu/depts/docs/us/harass.html**

You can also test your knowledge and learn more through *Business Week*'s interactive test at: **http://www.businessweek.com/1997/41/b3548040.htm**

finding value in the information regardless of its direct benefit to you, and be open to asking clarifying questions, you can improve your listening skills.

3. **Sociocultural Barriers.** If someone speaks with an accent, you may focus on the accent and not on the content, creating psychological noise. Psychological noise, differences in need for context, differences in values, and cultural values of silence all impact the listening process. Being aware of these differences can be the first step to improving your ability to actively listen.

4. **Assumptions.** Predicting is an important skill in the communication process, but assuming you know what someone is going to say may influence your ability to hear the whole message. Effective communication requires interaction, and the responsibility lies with both sender and receiver.

5. **Environmental Barriers.** Noise, interference, and even too much information at once can all be present in your work environment. By taking the time to have a conversation in a quieter setting, you may be able to listen better, get more of the message, and communicate more effectively.

Praise and criticism are inherent in the work environment. You may hear your boss congratulate a team on reaching its goal or your supervisor asking you to work harder in a specific area. How praise and criticism are presented make a significant impact on their effectiveness and the degree to which they positively or negatively contribute to the work environment. Praise should be sincere and should follow several guidelines that reinforce its effectiveness. Make sure you offer **praise for specific tasks, performance, or activities** rather than vague generalities. For example, you might say "Your extra effort in working with that client made the difference!" rather than "You work well with clients." Your praise will acknowledge the job well done and reinforce what you consider a job well done. **Incremental praise** at the completion of steps in progress toward a goal instead of just the completion of the project will both acknowledge incremental accomplishments and motivate employees as they work towards the next step in the process. For example, you might hold a staff party during the lunch hour to honor the completion of an important goal, and then toward the end of the lunch, lead a meeting that covers the next goal. **Criticism** should come in the form of a constructive goal, with a clear definition of an area to be improved with suggestions to address the issue. Be careful not to allow criticism to become negative, as this can arouse feelings of defensiveness, impact the ability to effectively listen, and fail to constructively address the issue. Finally, **relay praise** from third parties such as customers or clients. "I want you to know the clients on this project told me directly how happy they are with your handling of their project" carries more weight than your just stating your own satisfaction with the employee's progress.

Teams and Groups

Group communication is a dynamic process that involves leadership, purpose, and interactions distinct from interpersonal communication. As we've discussed previously, your ability to understand group communication will contribute to a positive group climate that draws on everyone's talents and expertise.

Here are five ways to promote effective communication in groups and teams:

1. **Recognize Goals.** The group should set clear goals and objectives, with ways to measure progress. Recognize that you and others have personal goals, but that your group goals should come first.

2. **Establish Positive Group Norms.** Each group will create norms, but focusing on this task and establishing positive norms from the beginning can help everyone feel more comfortable and contribute to a creative environment.

3. **Focus on Cohesiveness.** Group members need to feel committed to the group and need to want to stay a part of it. Shared values, common goals, recognition of progress, and interdependence all contribute to cohesiveness.

4. **Avoid Groupthink.** While conflict may be uncomfortable at times, it is more desirable than all group members agreeing to tasks and ideas for the sake of group harmony.

5. **Establish a Creative Environment.** Brainstorming, mapping, and engaging group discussions where individual members are allowed to share freely creates a more creative environment and discourages groupthink. (Janis, 1983)

Meetings

Meetings are part of the work environment and, like working in teams, require an understanding of the purpose of the meeting, what the group hopes to accomplish, and your role in the meeting. Here is a brief summary of the four common types of meetings you may encounter:

1. **Sharing Information or Knowledge.** Everyone brings a different skill set and level of experience to the group, and the sharing of information or knowledge is an important task. Be prepared when you gather, have your information organized, and use your active listening skills.

2. **Problem Solving.** Problems are part of the work environment. Coming together to brainstorm solutions, or to delegate further information gathering to use to solve the problem, is key to effective problem solving. Bring your insight to the problem, use your active listening skills to gather insight from others, and record specific steps to solve the problem.

3. **Decision Making.** Like problem solving, decision making is an important activity on the job. Employees may use information gathered after a problem-solving meeting to decide where to buy a product or service, develop a new product to meet a need in the marketplace, or set new group goals.

4. **Social Meetings.** Relationships in the workplace are important to an interactive, dynamic work environment. Getting to know your co-workers while discussing a problem or possible decisions may also be a goal of meetings.

As we discussed in verbal communication, turn-taking (Sacks, Schegloff, & Jefferson, 1974) is an important part of discussions. Be open to listening to others, giving them the time and space to complete their ideas or sentences, and take turns with the goal clearly in mind. Side discussions can be productive, but you are gathered to learn from and benefit each other in your job functions and ultimately the company or organization. Keep side discussion to a minimum and focus on effective listening habits. Finally, consider the cultural environment in which you work. As we have seen, silence is an important part of conversation in many cultures, and your ability to actively listen and adapt to distinct turn-taking styles will influence your ability to effectively participate in meetings.

Virtual Meetings

We increasingly meet or gather in virtual space, either via a teleconference, video-conferences, or, increasingly, online conferences. New technology and adaptations of existing technology allow us to connect in new and innovative ways without having to travel extensively, holding down costs while often allowing us to exchange information more effectively.

Teleconferences allow more than two people to have a discussion over the telephone. Job interviews—particularly information-gathering interviews—allow the company or organization to get to know the job candidate briefly without the expense of travel. This allows the committee or supervisor the ability to screen a larger number of candidates before selecting a few for face-to-face interviews. Intraorganization teleconferences may involve all of the types of meetings we have examined, but again require less travel. Preparation and organization are still key to effective teleconferences. In this format for gathering, remember there are no visual cues, and the channel of voice and sound carries the messages. This can allow you to focus on the words, but it also means turn-taking skills are important. Interference, such as background noise or the speaker's proximity to the microphone, may influence the quality of the sound.

Videoconferences allow a group to gather in an interactive television environment. Now you have both visual and vocal channels, allowing for a more lifelike meeting. Job interviews may also incorporate this meeting strategy, and with the proliferation of sites such as Kinko's, the possibility you may participate in this type of meeting is increasing. Like teleconferences, turn-taking skills are key, but you also add the dimension of dress and presentation, much like a speech, to establish your credibility. Videoconferences can bring together people in remote locations and allow for interaction that until recently was only feasible in a teleconference format.

Online conferences use the Internet and a private chat room or bulletin board to exchange information. Messages can be typed and read in real time, allowing for dynamic interaction with a large number of people. Turn-taking skills again are important, and the ability to follow the thread of the discussion cannot be underestimated. Like in a teleconference setting, this format allows for only one channel, the written word, to convey your thoughts and ideas. Placing emphasis on concrete, specific terms can assist you in getting your message across in an online discussion.

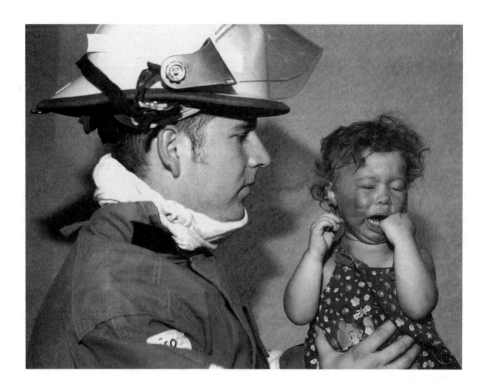

In addition, with the integration of visual images over high speed and large bandwidth lines connecting people, a hybrid videoconference is possible, with the added capability of sharing files or attaching documents.

Crisis Communication

> *A loud voice cannot compete with a clear voice, even if it's a whisper.*
> —B. N. Kaufman

Emergencies and crisis situations happen daily around the world. People are trained to respond to these situations, but they are still people. Accidents and miscommunication can and do occur. There is significant research to support the assertion that when an emergency occurs, people often do not get the information they need for the purpose of taking appropriate action (Auf Der Heide, 1989; Mallet, Vaught, & Brnich, 1999). In this section we will focus on ways an emergency response professional can focus on effective communication, ways a supervisor can focus on communication and priorities, and the importance of a crisis communication plan. Across each of these areas we will draw on previous lessons from prior chapters and come to see what an important role effective interpersonal communication has in the response and resolution of crisis situations.

What do the following cases have in common?

- A boy survived a brain tumor operation only to be killed by a flying oxygen container inadvertently left in the MRI (Magnetic Resonance Imaging) room that was attracted to the high-powered magnet (Laliberte, 2003).
- A child was brought to the emergency room by her mother who mentioned to the nurse that she removed a tick. The nurse failed to report the tick. The child was sent home with fever medication, but returned later and died. Rocky Mountain Spotted Fever claimed the life of the child (Mandell, 1993; McLean, 1996).

Each of these cases involve miscommunication at an interpersonal level that had serious consequences. Each of these cases also involve tragedy that will be investigated, and reported by, the media. In this section we will discuss the importance of effective interpersonal communication in emergency and crisis situations. Later we will examine a process to communicate with others once the event is over. Overall, the goal of effective communication in a crisis situation is to (Mallet et al., 1999):

1. Reduce confusion
2. Increase confidence in decisions
3. Stop incorrect rumors
4. Improve the likelihood of success

A Good and Professional Attitude

The first prerequisite for participating as a law enforcement official, firefighter, or emergency response professional is a good and professional attitude. People will look to you for reassurance and, more importantly, to see if you are ready to make a difference. Your calm voice and body language will communicate that you are ready to help and will create a sense of trust. One often overlooked factor in communication is how your presence as a representative of the public trust can make a significant impact on those around you. People will respond with fear and anxiety, but they will respond to your calm presence and, with your effective communication skills, calm themselves to a degree. Their response will help resolve the situation and make it safer for everyone, including yourself.

Interpersonal Communication and the Emergency Response Professional

As a professional you will communicate on three levels. The first involves information and protocol in accordance with your duty as a professional. You will be given instructions, and it is critical that they are communicated by you in the same way, even in the same words, as they were presented. You are probably familiar with the game "rumors," where one person tells the story to the next person and by the time it goes around the circle it has changed significantly. In an emergency or crisis situation, you do not want to lose message fidelity, or the integrity of the message, as you pass along information or instructions.

The next level involves information that originates with you. You are told by a fire victim that there is another person in the house. You will need to communicate this information clearly to your supervisor. You will need to do this right away and use as few words as possible. In emergency communication it is important to convey all of the meaning and say as little as possible. Brevity and clarity are your key goals. Brevity means you need to keep it brief, reducing the possibility that long phrases or explanations will be misinterpreted or passed along incorrectly. Clarity means you need to keep it clear so there are no misunderstandings. This is not the time for you to include opinion or attitude, and valuable time can be lost if someone focuses on your attitude or an opinionated remark instead of the main point. Demonstrate good listening skills and make sure you acknowledge communication and seek acknowledgment from others. Communication in emergency situations requires you to be precise, and while eloquence may be fine for an after dinner speech, it is not required for effective emergency communication. Refrain from verbal fillers like "ahh" and "umm" that both confuse and distract from the clear message and impact your credibility. Finally, keep your good attitude and calm voice in check at all times. People involved in an emergency will experience a range of emotions but will look to you for stability and clear-headed thinking.

You may recall that in Chapter 1 we focused on the eight basic components of communication. Each component is important in effective communication, and interference can become a particular challenge in an emergency situation. Interference can involve physical noise, but also may involve psychological noise. You may be experiencing thoughts or emotions that focus your attention on your internal monologue. It is important to think, but it is equally important to quiet your mind and focus on the information that surrounds you. The first place to look for interference is within, and then focus on the task at hand.

Physical noise may prevent clear and effective communication, and you will need to focus on strategies to get your message across. One that is routinely utilized is spelling key codes or words when physical noise prevents dialogue. You will need to speak quickly and accurately to convey exact information. This requires that you speak distinctly at all times. If you know that the information you announce is to be written, pace your speech with brief pauses to allow others to follow along. If you have to announce the information, then people need to hear what you are communicating and understand it clearly. Repeat yourself in exactly the same way you said it the first time to allow anyone who missed a letter or word to fill in the gap or understand your message. Standard International Telecommunication Union (ITU) phonetics are often used to spell words when it is noisy or clear communication is compromised. They are also used in various professional settings, from law enforcement to aviation. ITU phonetics were chosen so that each word sounds completely different from all other words in the code. Here is a brief summary of the ITU phonetic alphabet:

A - alfa (AL-fa)	N - november (no-VEM-ber)
B - bravo (BRAH-voh)	O - oscar (OSS-cah)
C - charlie (CHAR-lee)	P - papa (PAH-PAH)
D - delta (DELL-tah)	Q - quebec (kay-BECK)
E - echo (ECK-oh)	R - romeo (ROW-me-oh)
F - foxtrot (FOKS-trot)	S - sierra (SEE-air-rah)
G - golf (GOLF)	T - tango (TANG-go)
H - hotel (HOH-tell)	U - uniform (YOU-ni-form)
I - india (IN-dee-ah)	V - victor (VIK-tor)
J - juliet (JU-lee-ett)	W - whiskey (WISS-key)
K - kilo (KEY-loh)	X - x-ray (ECKS-ray)
L - lima (LEE-mah)	Y - yankee (YANG-key)
M - mike (MIKE)	Z - zulu (ZOO-loo)

In terms of numbers, it is standard protocol to pronounce numbers as each individual number. The number 70 is pronounced "seven zero," not "seventy." The goal is clarity—you want to make sure your number is understood the first time without confusion. Combination numbers require you use the same protocol. The number 205 is pronounced "two zero five," not "two hundred five" or "two *oh* five." In the same way you need to speak clearly and check for acknowledgment of your message when communicating words and phrases.

The third level of interpersonal communication you will use while handling an emergency as a professional will involve emotions and body language as you maintain an awareness of your surroundings. You may experience a tendency to focus on clear verbal communication and the steps required to solve a problem, but ignoring important nonverbal cues can actually increase the risks of everyone involved, victims and professionals. Look back at the nonverbal communication chapter. The principles and suggestions for improved understanding of body language and nonverbal cues are particularly important when people are under stress. People may not respond in rational, predictable ways and may lack the presence of mind to articulate themselves clearly. Use guiding questions based on your observations to gain information and establish dialogue if it is appropriate. Consider people involved in the on-site emergency as key sources of information and be alert to cues that may provide valuable information.

In addition to the practical aspect of gaining valuable information, make sure you pay attention to people's emotional states as expressed by their nonverbal communication. Physiological cues like tremors, dilated pupils, or elevated pulse rate may indicate a variety of medical conditions that require attention. People may even say they are fine when in fact they are not. Look for incongruities between their words and actions and seek additional help. Shock is a common condition for victims, and it can have serious consequences. Also consider the age of the person

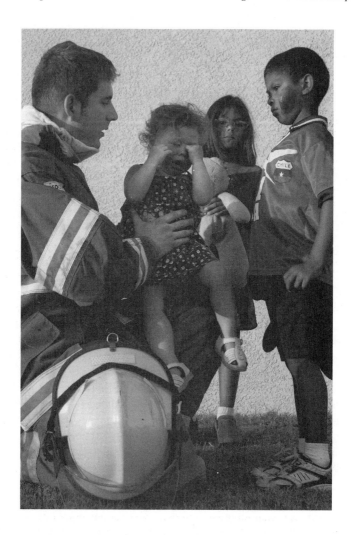

when communicating with him or her. Providing assurance for an adult might require a calm professional demeanor from you, but a teddy bear for a small child might meet an important need for security. Many law enforcement agencies have taken to carrying a teddy bear as part of their standard "response kit" for this reason.

Developing Your Own Crisis Communication Plan

Emergency and crisis situations may involve fire and floods, but they might just as well involve a robbery, the arrest of a key company official, or the recall of one of your products. How you handle it can make a significant difference. A crisis communication plan is simply a way of organizing information into responsibilities and lines of communication prior to an event. With a plan in place, each person knows his or her role, and responsibilities and effectiveness can be enhanced for a swift response. This section will introduce what happens when companies fail to adequately plan for a crisis, key information you need to assess, working with a designated spokesperson, creating a media message center, and practicing prepared and unprepared responses to common questions.

What do the makers of Tylenol® pain-relieving medicine, Ford® automobiles, Firestone® tires, and INTEL® microprocessors all have in common? Each had a crisis situation that challenged the company significantly and cost them millions, even billions of dollars. In the case of Tylenol, cyanide was found in capsules, and a public scare ensued. The parent company, Johnson & Johnson®, at first indicated the situation was under control, but the common perception and the message via mass media was alarming (Foster, 1983). Eventually, Johnson & Johnson pulled every bottle off store shelves and spent years regaining its credibility. Ford was sued by several Explorer owners for injuries as a result of rollover accidents that were attributed to design and Firestone tires. Ford asserted its automobiles were well designed and blamed Firestone. Firestone refuted the charge and blamed Ford. Both lost market share, credibility, and millions of dollars in recall costs and plummeting sales (Greenwald, 2001). In 1994 INTEL microprocessors were found by a mathematics professor to have an anomaly that produced an inaccurate calculation. INTEL released a report acknowledging the error but indicated that only an advanced math professor would ever find the error to be an issue, and the common user would not perceive a problem. The problem arose, however, in the credibility of the company's product and widespread discussion of whether the chip could add 2+2 (Patrick & Alsop, 2001). This perception influenced consumer response and INTEL, like Ford, Firestone, and Johnson & Johnson, paid a high cost for misunderstanding and miscommunication.

Each of the cases features information, the release of information, and to some degree a control of that release. The central question is who is managing the information? If you do not have a clear crisis communication plan, the answer might be the media or even a government subcommittee. Every organization experiences crisis, and it is important to prepare in advance for action. Interpersonal communication plays a central role in the management and distribution of information, and the first place to start when developing a crisis communication plan is to determine who communicates what and when.

A crisis communication team includes people who can decide what actions to take, people who can carry out those actions, and people who offer expertise or education in the relevant areas. Let's say that your company has a serious water leak that crosses your production floor, an area that is exposed to chemicals used in the manufacture of your product. A representative of company administration may be the indicated decision maker, but make sure you have a person who can speak to the media as well as company representatives in the areas that cover the use of chemicals and distribution of water included on the team. The word *team* should be understood to mean a group effort, as crisis situations often call on the experience and contributions of many people. When creating a crisis communication team, focus on a list that has everyone's name, work and home contact information, and relevant area of expertise and responsibilities. Keep the list in an accessible location.

Information Needed during an Emergency

According to Mallet and colleagues (1999), it is important to focus on key types of information during an emergency. As a supervisor, emergency response professional, or company employee, you may be required to assess the situation and outline key priorities. Mallet and colleagues (1999) offer us the following questions to guide the assessment and prioritization of information:

- What is happening?
- Is anyone in danger?
- How big is the problem?
- Who reported the problem?
- Where is the problem?
- Has a response started?
- What resources are on-scene?
- Who is responding so far?
- Is everyone's location known?

These questions help you quickly focus on the basics of who, what, and where of the crisis situation. You will be receiving information from the moment you know a crisis has occurred, but without a framework or communication plan to guide you, valuable information may be lost.

Focusing on Your Message

People will want to know what happened and will find out information about the crisis. Lack of information breeds rumors, and that can make a bad situation worse. Once you have addressed the central questions above, you need to prepare your position. People will want to know what happened and why. In the same way an emergency response professional needs to focus on a clear and concise message, so too does the designated spokesperson. The spokesperson should be designated prior to an actual emergency. The designated spokesperson should be comfortable in front of a microphone, a camera, and media lights and be able to stay calm while under pressure.

The spokesperson for your company will focus on communicating the information to employees and the media. Interpersonal skills will be key as he or she effectively coordinates the distribution of information and prepares it to share with the responding media. It is important to note that the designated spokesperson needs to be clear and straightforward to communicate trust in the information he or she communicates. One of the best ways to do this to be truthful. You will need to communicate complete information right away, and communicate its authenticity, in order to minimize negative outcomes. Perception of lying or withholding information encourages rumor, and as we saw in the case of INTEL, for example, the costs associated for that loss of trust are high.

When the spokesperson focuses on the "why" of his or her message, he or she should consider how best to communicate in simple terms. Possible points to consider include human and/or clerical error; unauthorized procedures; inadequate supervision, quality control, or standard operating procedures. Each of these terms helps pinpoint the "why" of the crisis, and while they do not cover every possible reason for an accident, they should nonetheless serve as a guide to focus clearly on an important part of the message.

Creating a Place to Communicate

Just as we have seen in our discussion of interpersonal relationships, making time and creating space is critical for effective communication. In a crisis situation, people may be moving all over the scene but lack any central focus for information. This lack of centralization means there may be critical information, like pieces to a puzzle, that never gets put together. Part of your communication crisis plan should focus on where you will meet to coordinate communication and activities. For your own house in case of a fire, you might meet in the front yard. For an organization, a building or office might serve a central place for communication. From this central meeting place, your designated spokesperson can gather information and prepare responses to anticipated questions. Again, the media and public will want to know information and reliable information is preferable to speculation.

Handling Requests for Information

When an emergency happens, members of media will want to interview people who speak for the organization, and people who don't. Official responses help clarify the situation for the public, but the unofficial interview can make the tragedy personal and attract attention. Management of information and safety are key concerns when handling a crisis. Your organization may set a policy that members of the media must be escorted at all times. This policy may be supported by issues of private property and liability that exist. You may also want to use this policy to channel the flow of information and protect your employees' privacy. People may be injured and not want to talk to the camera. Regardless of the policy your crisis communication team decides on, it will need to plan the flow of information. The designated spokesperson may not only be articulate and good on camera, but he or she might also be good at handling challenging questions from members of the media. Rather than have unreliable interviews with everyone involved with the emergency, you may prefer to indicate that the designated spokesperson is the key point for current information. Enable that person to have access to the place you indicated as your central coordination place and allow that professional to prepare and respond to inquiries.

Now that we can see how important a designated spokesperson can be in an emergency situation, let's consider effective ways to handle requests for information. Using the previous guideline questions, you can anticipate questions that require information in an emergency. You can also anticipate that journalists and media representatives will focus on these key areas of information:

- Who
- What
- Where
- When
- Why
- How

Preparing your responses before speaking is one clear strategy to communicate effectively. Another way, much like a speech class, is to practice before the event. Involve other employees in the mock interviews and don't be afraid to ask tough questions. When the day comes to use the training, the questions will be tough, and you will feel better prepared.

Two key strategies for managing effective communication in a crisis situation are to prepare a written statement and to not talk "off the record." A written statement serves you in many ways. It gives you a script to read to the media. It can be copied and distributed, much like a press release, and it can provide important details that may not get recorded or written down. The second suggestion involves the role of the designated spokesperson as the key source for information. Trust is essential in every relationship, and by speaking to one reporter instead of another, you compromise that trust and also cloud the message and impact your credibility. The best advice is to treat everyone equally with respect.

Now that we have examined strategies for effective communication in crisis situations, let's close with five ways to express yourself effectively in both work and emergency environments.

Expressing Yourself Effectively

Whether it is the context of work or an emergency that you are communicating, your skills as an effective communicator will make a significant difference. Recognize your role and responsibility as a communicator and make sure your information is accurate and your message is understood. Here are five guidelines from Beebe, Beebe, and Redmond (2002, p. 272) that we can adapt for our goal of expressing yourself effectively.

1. Describe how you view the situation.   Your interpretation of the information on hand is important and valuable, but recognize that sometimes people get caught up in their own thoughts when handling an issue at work or an emergency. They might not be other-oriented and instead perceive the information or context in one way that may conflict with what you perceive to be accurate. Use "I" statements to assert yourself and state what you know in concrete terms. Use evidence and brief examples to support your view, possibly providing others with information they do not have. Pay attention to nonverbal communication and recognize when the receiver is not ready to receive; choose your strategy to encourage active listening. It is important to promote a supportive climate when being assertive about your view point. If your communication contributes to a defensive climate, it discourages others from listening and becomes personal. Sarcasm and being loud are generally not appropriate and will not encourage effective listening. Focus instead on your listeners' needs and how the information relates to them; make that a part of your introduction or initial communication. Sometimes the information you have may not be recognized for its value right away, but your assertiveness in an appropriate way can help a work project or perhaps even save a life.

2. Identify effects.　　As we discussed in the first point, focus on how the information affects listeners and the situation at hand. Use that awareness to guide your words and actions. By focusing on the facts and the issues, and not personalities, the impact of your information will be more relevant. It may be that you need to discuss how a person's behavior affects a relationship or group project. It is always a good idea to talk to someone in private about an issue involving his or her behavior. As a supervisor, part of your role is to see the overall goal and be a good coach when it comes to individual members of the team. If the communication involves peer-to-peer communication, state clearly how you value others' contributions and your relationship before focusing on an issue. By encouraging a supportive climate, your emphasis on the effects of information or behavior will make a more significant impact.

3. Establish trust and be trustworthy.　　Communication requires trust in order to share information and create understanding. Establishing trust takes time. By providing a supportive climate for communication, you encourage a freer exchange of ideas and information, and people will more readily share their understanding with you. In the work environment, your knowledge and skills combine with others' to form a team as you target a goal. In order to reach your goal, you need all the members to contribute and not perceive themselves as isolated or threatened. There may be a chain of command, or formal channels of communication, that needs to be observed in order to effectively communicate. By displaying respect for everyone, regardless of his or her place in that hierarchy, you promote a positive climate for communication and engender trust.

You also need to build trust by being trustworthy. When you say you will do something, follow through with your statements. It is acceptable to say that you don't know something at this moment, but not researching the answer and failing to get back to the person concerned with the answer does not communicate trust.

Choose to respect people in the workplace, trust in their skills and expertise, and they may exceed your expectations.

4. Paraphrase. A good strategy to communicate active listening is to paraphrase a person's comments. It forms a valuable feedback loop that allows you to clarify your ideas and the other person the opportunity to correct misinformation or misunderstanding. This involves actively listening to a person and then using his or her response to formulate your words and actions. The other person will see and hear that you listened, and the activity will promote clearer communication.

5. Actively listen but don't be silent. Active listening involves attending to the speaker, paraphrasing his or her words, and communicating your respect for those words and the speaker. There may be times when silence is appropriate, but when your understanding of the facts is not in line with what you understand the other person perceives to be the case, you need to clarify your point. There is a common saying, "There is always time to do the job right the second time." This means that you may have rushed through the job the first time, or based the work or activity on a misunderstanding, only to find the work did not meet the understood (or misunderstood) expectations. You then have to redo the work to get it right, wasting time and resources. By clarifying directions at the beginning of the task, you make sure the directions are clear and the outcome or effects are understood. In an emergency context, you may feel reluctant to offer information that challenges the apparent norm or what people think they know, but your contribution could significantly change the outcome.

Summary

In this chapter we have examined the various types of interviews, including the pre-interview phase of information gathering and preparation, and focused on skills to use in interview settings. We have discussed interpersonal communication in the workplace, also discussing sensitivity to the increasingly diverse workplace. Working in teams effectively means recognizing common problems, and we have examined five common barriers to effective meetings. In addition, we have discussed the various types of meetings, including virtual meetings, and how effective communication plays a role in them.

We have also discussed crisis and emergency communication and ways individuals can clearly communicate when people are under stress. This also involves planning ahead and knowing what information is needed to resolve an emergency or issue; emergency communication also involves the formulation of a crisis communication plan.

Finally, we examined five ways to express yourself effectively in both work and emergency environments.

> *There is more than a verbal tie between the words common, community, and communication. . . . Try the experiment of communicating, with fullness and accuracy, some experience to another, especially if it be somewhat complicated, and you will find your own attitude toward your experience changing.*
>
> —John Dewey

For More Information

To learn more about effective job interview skills, the CIBC Company maintains a website entitled "How to Succeed in a Job Interview" at: **http://www.cibc.com/inside/careers/hrr01dir/hrr07.html**

Two additional sites that offer effective job interview tips are: **http://www.jobsearch. about.com/careers/jobsearch/library/weekly/aa061398.htm** and **http://www2.jobtrak. com/help_manuals/jobmanual/**

To learn more about simple body language rules in the work environment, go to *USA Today* by Anita Bruzzese of the Gannett News Service at: **http://www.usatoday.com/careers/news/usa024.htm**

To learn more about online conferences, the Department of Communication Studies at the University of Kansas maintains a website entitled "The Virtual Meeting Assistant" at: **http://www.ukans.edu/cwis/units/coms2/vma/vms.htm**

To learn more about communication in the work environment, Ronald B. Adler and Jeanne M. Elmhorst have a comprehensive text with a wealth of information entitled *Communicating at Work: Principles and Practices for Business and the Professions,* published by McGraw-Hill (ISBN: 0-07-303433-9).

To prepare a generic, basic crisis communication plan or adapt it to your needs, go to: **http://www3.niu.edu/newsplace/crisis.html**

To see an actual crisis communication plan, go to North Carolina State University's website at: **http://www2.ncsu.edu/ncsu/univ_relations/crisis.html**

Or see the crisis communication plan of Meredith College at: **www.meredith.edu/faculty-staff/updated-crisis-plan.doc**

Review Questions

1. Factual Questions
    a. What are three common interview questions?
    b. What are five barriers to effective meetings?
    c. What is one way a person can communicate effectively in an emergency situation?

2. Interpretative Questions
    a. How does the interview process serve both potential employees and potential employers?
    b. What are successful strategies to learn of available positions?

   c. What are examples of interference in a crisis situation and how can you address them before the crisis occurs?

3. Evaluative Questions

   a. Is it possible to completely learn enough about a company to anticipate possible needs? Explain your response.

   b. Is it necessary to understand the company's needs in order to interview effectively? Explain your response.

   c. Can knowledge of effective communication improve crisis response? Provide an example with your response.

4. Application Questions

   a. What do people consider their tasks in a given position or job? Create a survey, identify people who hold similar positions, conduct your survey, and compare the results.

   b. What job-related resources are available on your campus? Investigate the issue and share your findings.

   c. Research one crisis as a case study that involves your area of training. What communication issues were present and how did they impact response? Compare your results with classmates.

References

Adler, R., & Elmhorst, J. (1999). *Communicating at work: Principles and practices for business and the professions.* New York: McGraw-Hill

American Council on Education. (1997). *Spanning the chasm: Corporate and academic cooperation to improve work-force preparation.* Washington, DC: Author.

Auf Der Heide, E. (1989). *Disaster response: Principles of preparation and coordination.* St. Louis, MO: The C.V. Mosby Company.

Beebe, S., Beebe, S., & Redmond, M. (2002). *Interpersonal communication: Relating to others* (3rd ed.). Boston: Allyn and Bacon.

Foster, L. (1983). The Johnson & Johnson credo and the Tylenol crisis. *New Jersey Bell Journal, 6*(1).

Granovetter, M. (1973). The strength of weak ties. *American Journal of Sociology, 78,* 20–21.

Greenwald, J. (2001, May 29). Inside the Ford/Firestone fight. *Time On-line Edition.*

Janis, I. (1983). *Groupthink: Psychological studies of policy decisions and fiascoes* (2nd ed.). Boston: Houghton Mifflin Company.

Kikoski, J., & Kikoski, C. (1996). *Reflexive communication in the culturally diverse workplace* (pp. 2–3). Westport, CT: Quorum.

Laliberte, R. (2003, February). Parents report: Medical mistakes. *Parents,* 92–96.

Maes, J., Weldy, T., & Icenogle, M. (1997). Oral communcation competency in the workplace. *Journal of Business Communication, 34,* 67–80.

Mallet, L., Vaught, C., & Brnich, M. (1999). *The emergency communication triangle.* Centers for Disease Control and Prevention, National Institute for Occupational Safety and Health, U.S. Department of Health and Human Services. Pittsburgh, PA: Pittsburgh Research Laboratory.

Mandell, M. (1993, August). What you don't say can hurt you. *American Journal of Nursing,* 15–16.

McLean, S. (1996). Communication in the clinical setting: The importance of listening. *The Journal of Multicultural Nursing and Health, 2,* 4–7.

Patrick, J., & Alsop, S. (2001). *Net attitude: What it is, How to get it, and why your company can't survive without it.* Cambridge, MA: Perseus Publishing.

Rogers, E. (1983). *Diffusion of innovations* (3rd ed.; p. 297). New York: Free Press.

Sacks, H., Schegloff, E., & Jefferson, G.(1974). A simplest semantics for the organization of turn-taking for conversation. *Language, 50,* 696–735.

Seiler, W., & Beall, M. (2000). *Communication: Making connections* (4th ed.). Boston: Allyn and Bacon.

The Wall Street Journal (1998, December 29), p. A1.

Index